The Daughters of Karl Marx

An example of Laura's handwriting, taken from the first page of her letter to Jenny of 28 February 1869. The transcription is on pages 36–38.

THE
DAUGHTERS
OF
KARL MARX

Family Correspondence 1866–1898

Commentary and notes by Olga Meier

Translated and adapted by Faith Evans

Introduction by Sheila Rowbotham

A HELEN AND KURT WOLFF BOOK

HARCOURT BRACE JOVANOVICH, PUBLISHERS

NEW YORK AND LONDON

Library of Congress Cataloging in Publication Data

Longuet, Jenny Marx, 1844–1883.
The daughters of Karl Marx.

Translation of: Les filles de Karl Marx.
Letters of Jenny Marx Longuet, Laura Marx Lafargue,
and Eleanor Marx Aveling.
"A Helen and Kurt Wolff book."
Includes index.
1. Communists — Correspondence.
I. Lafargue, Laura Marx.
II. Aveling, Eleanor Marx. III. Meier, Olga.
IV. Title.
HX23.L6613   335.4'092'2   81-47302
ISBN   0-15-123971-1   AACR2

PRINTED IN THE UNITED STATES OF AMERICA
FIRST EDITION
B C D E

Contents

Illustrations

Jenny with Karl Marx
Photo Centre de documentation de l'Institut Maurice Thorez

Jenny and Charles Longuet's house in Argenteuil
Photo Centre de documentation de l'Institut Maurice Thorez

Preface

T HE BOTTIGELLI ARCHIVE contains a large collection of documents, among them 339 letters, notes and other material relating to the Marx family. These papers were given to Emile Bottigelli, the distinguished scholar and editor of French editions of the works of Marx and Engels, by Marcel-Charles Longuet, grandson of Marx's eldest daughter Jenny. With customary generosity M. Bottigelli allowed a number of Marx scholars to reproduce extracts from some of the letters contained in his archive, but this is the first time that a full selection has been published in English. For bibliographical reasons and for the interest of readers it is necessary to give something of the background to the publication of this edition.

In the late 1960s M. Bottigelli asked his friend Olga Meier to transcribe the documents (a formidable task, since many of them were in the crossed handwriting common among Victorian letter-writers) with eventual publication in mind. He died in 1975, before this could be achieved, but at the request of his widow, Mme. Marcelle Bottigelli-Tisserand, Olga Meier completed the transcription and prepared a French edition of the correspondence, which was published by Albin Michel in 1979 under the title *Les Filles de Karl Marx: Lettres inédites*. Olga Meier confined her selection to letters to and from members of the Marx family, including husbands, up to Eleanor's death, but scholars may be interested to learn that the Bottigelli Archive also contains letters from Louise Kautsky and others, many of which remain unpublished. This was not intended to be a comprehensive edition and, as with all collections from a particular archive, there are inevitably gaps in the correspondence. Some letters are housed elsewhere, notably in the International Institute of Social History in Amsterdam and the Institute of Marxism-Leninism in Moscow; some were lost and others destroyed. To enable the letters to be read consecutively Olga Meier provided an interlinking commentary and (with Michel Trebitsch) explanatory footnotes.

The Daughters of Karl Marx contains the same letters as those selected for the French volume, with the single addition of a long letter from Jenny (no. 13) on the Irish situation. The commentary and notes have, however, with Olga Meier's permission, been extended for an English-language readership: I have provided more general background for areas with which we are less familiar, such as the Franco-Prussian War and the Paris Commune of 1871, and fuller annotation on topics with which English-language readers can be expected to have some acquaintance, and may wish to explore further. I have written new introductions to each of the six sections into which this edition is divided, and the general introduction by Michelle Perrot has been replaced with one by Sheila Rowbotham.

The majority of the letters were, of course, written in English; those that I have translated, mainly from Paul Lafargue in Part Two, have been marked as such at the top of the letters.

The transcription of the letters is Olga Meier's, as is the placing (in square brackets) of letters of uncertain date and location. Missing, illegible or omitted material, indicated by three centered dots, also follow the French edition.

As for the editing of the letters themselves, spelling has been corrected and punctuation and paragraphing altered when the sense of the original was difficult to follow. However, curious turns of phrase and French or German constructions have been retained (English, French and German were all spoken in the Marx household, and the women slipped easily from one language into another). Foreign words or phrases in English letters are given in italics; translations of all but the simplest of these appear in square brackets or footnotes. English words or phrases in letters originally in French are given in small caps.

Titles of books and pamphlets are in English (e.g., *Capital* rather than *Das Kapital*) unless there was no English translation or unless the reference is to a foreign edition of the work (e.g., Eleanor's translation of Lissagaray's *Histoire de la Commune de 1871*).

To prevent the notes from being too cumbersome and repetitive a list of recurring names has been provided, as well as a list of the many nicknames by which the members of the Marx family were variously known. It has not, however, proved possible to trace all the characters referred to in the correspondence: this applies particularly to Part One, where several of the family friends who were constantly in and out of the Marx household have left no public record of their existence.

In her preface to the French edition of this book Olga Meier acknowledged her indebtedness to Yvonne Kapp's biography *Eleanor Marx* (vol. 1: *Family Life 1855–1883*, 1972; vol. 2: *The Crowded Years 1884–1898*, 1976, Lawrence and Wishart, London; Pantheon Books, New York, 1977), the first volume of which she has translated into French. Meier well describes this biography as "so richly documented and so full of human understanding," and in preparing the English edition I too have found it an essential source. Chushichi Tsuzuki's *The Life of Eleanor Marx, 1855–1898: A Socialist Tragedy* (Clarendon Press, Oxford, 1967) has been another useful guide, particularly for information on Edward Aveling.

Among the most important source-books for the correspondence, all of which are published by Lawrence and Wishart, are *Frederick Engels/Paul and Laura Lafargue: Correspondence* (3 vols., 1959–63), compiled and edited by Emile Bottigelli; the *Collected Works* of Karl Marx and Frederick Engels (9 vols., 1975–77); and *Documents of the First International* (5 vols., 1963–68).

Finally I would like to thank the following people for their help and advice: John Goode, Royden Harrison, Betty Hildwein, Inez Krech, Barbara Leigh Hunt, Françoise Lina, William J. Maher, Paul Martinez, John Radziewicz, Ann Scott, John Stokes, Michel Trebitsch, Helen Wolff and Olga and Paul Meier.

FAITH EVANS

Nicknames

(See pages xiv–xv for family tree.)

KARL MARX: Challey, Charley, Master, Mohr, Moor, Nicky, Old Nick, Steam-Engine

JENNY MARX (née Westphalen): Möhme, Möhmchen, Mützchen

JENNY MARX (later Longuet): Di, Emperor, Empereur de Chine, Janey, Joe, Que-Que

LAURA MARX (later Lafargue): Jane, Kakadou, Lolo, Laurent, Tailor

ELEANOR MARX (later Marx-Aveling): Ellie, Hottentot, Quo-Quo, Tussy, Tussychen

PAUL LAFARGUE: Benedict, Paul-Laurent, Toole, Tooley

Lafargue children

> CHARLES-ETIENNE: Fouchtra, Mimi, Schnaps, Schnappy
>
> JENNY: Jeannie, Maigriotte, Schnapine
>
> MARC-LAURENT: Coco-bel-oeil

Longuet children

> JEAN: Jack, Johnny
>
> HARRY-MICHEL: Harra
>
> EDGAR-MARCEL: Wolf
>
> MARCEL-CHARLES: Par
>
> JENNY: Mémé

Family Tree

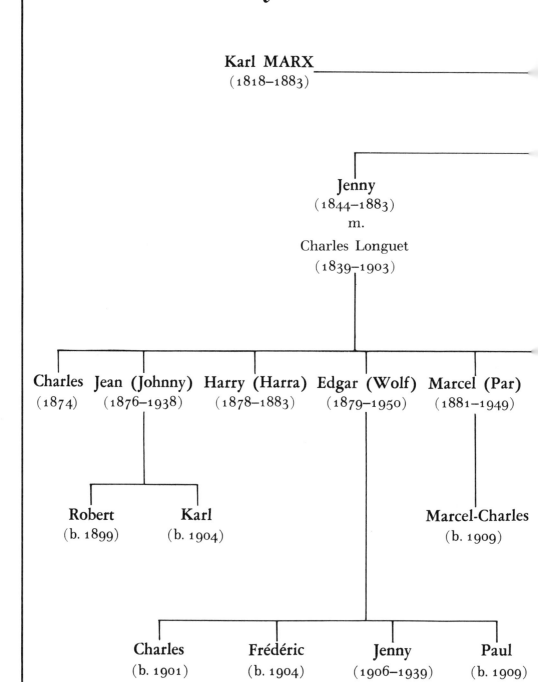

Karl MARX
(1818–1883)

Jenny
(1844–1883)
m.
Charles Longuet
(1839–1903)

Charles   Jean (Johnny)   Harry (Harra)   Edgar (Wolf)   Marcel (Par)
(1874)   (1876–1938)   (1878–1883)   (1879–1950)   (1881–1949)

Robert   Karl   Marcel-Charles
(b. 1899)   (b. 1904)   (b. 1909)

Charles   Frédéric   Jenny   Paul
(b. 1901)   (b. 1904)   (1906–1939)   (b. 1909)

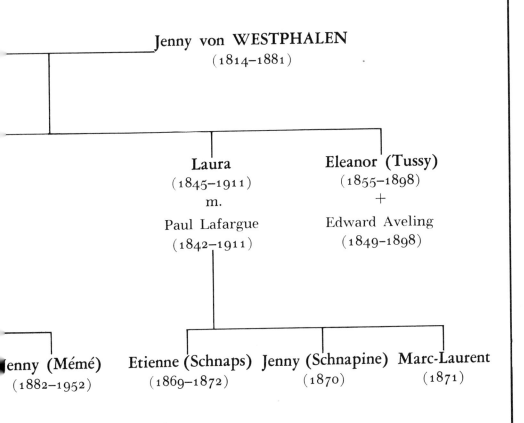

Jenny von **WESTPHALEN**
(1814–1881)

Laura
(1845–1911)
m.
Paul Lafargue
(1842–1911)

Eleanor (Tussy)
(1855–1898)
+
Edward Aveling
(1849–1898)

Jenny (Mémé)
(1882–1952)

Etienne (Schnaps)
(1869–1872)

Jenny (Schnapine)
(1870)

Marc-Laurent
(1871)

Children of Jenny and Karl Marx who died in infancy and are not mentioned in the correspondence have been omitted.

Introduction

by Sheila Rowbotham

E VERYONE KNOWS that bundles of old letters carry mystery. Their discovery transports us to the very brink of someone else's life and then leaves us at the threshold, with only the silhouettes of our own imagination. This is partly because we do not always know the background to the names and places mentioned, partly because within any set of relationships there is much that remains unknown to the living participants themselves. Indeed, if we were to spend our lives attempting to trace exhaustively every shift in the thoughts and feelings of our relatives, friends and acquaintances we should have little time for our own affairs and concerns. After reading a collection of letters, one has a strong sense of having lived among the people who wrote them. And yet this is a half-remembered, shadowy impression, like those recollections of early childhood which become mixed with stories our parents told us when we were older. As our fancy wanders into someone else's past we have to shake ourselves to remember that these people died long ago. We cannot drop in and ask them, "Who was that?", or "What did you feel then?", or even "Did you really say . . . ?"

This intimacy becomes more complex when the people involved are known publicly and their historical reputations are still the subject of controversy. When Marx's correspondence with Engels was first published in 1913, it was seriously abridged by the German socialist leaders Bebel and Bernstein on both moral and propagandist grounds. As a later biographer, Werner Blumenberg, comments, "It was *impermissible* for Marx to be disclosed as himself. Marx, the discoverer of infallible objective laws operating with absolute certainty, must himself be entirely free from subjectivity if he was to serve as a source of certainty."[1]

It was not that the man was to be idolized but that any personal awkwardnesses, vulnerabilities, inconsistencies, follies were to be put on one side. The "Mohr," "Old Nick" and "Steam-Engine" his family knew and loved is not quite the founder of Marxism-Leninism.

Karl Marx's historical influence has obviously meant that biographical attention has focused upon him. However, Chushichi Tsuzuki's and Yvonne Kapp's biographies of Eleanor Marx have opened up fresh perspectives on the Marx family life. This collection of letters brings out another neglected aspect, the relationship between the daughters themselves. Jenny and Laura appear here in their own right along with Eleanor. We also gain a picture of Marx through the eyes of all three of the daughters. In these letters, Marx is the more forceful parent; they alternately cajole, rebuke and adore him. Mrs. Marx (Jenny) comes across only as a vaguely anxious mother; they refer to her with affection, almost as a marginal figure in their lives. We know, however, that in spite of illnesses and the loss of three children, Mrs. Marx attended political meetings, acted as Marx's secretary copying his articles and writing letters, sorted out some of his publishing muddles for him and fended off their creditors. By the time her daughters had grown up and these letters begin, all this had taken its toll on her spirits. For Marx's wife there was no escape into the British Museum from the poverty and insecurity of their family life.

Jenny Marx found the life even harder to bear as her daughters were growing up for, as she told Engels, "the sweet girls, now blooming so lovelily, have to suffer it as well."[2] Early in 1863 she wrote to a friend, Bertha Markheim, when the girls were aged sixteen, fifteen and four:

"Even if the word 'beautiful' is not fitting for them, I must say even at the risk of being laughed at for my maternal pride, that all three of them look very neat and interesting. Jennychen is strikingly dark in hair, eyes and complexion and with her childishly rosy cheeks and deep sweet eyes, has a very attractive appearance. Laura, who is in everything a few degrees lighter and clearer, is in fact prettier than the eldest sister as her features under her dark brown and long lashes shine with a continual fire of joy . . . The third one, the baby, is a true bundle of sweetness, charm and childish frenzy."[3]

Karl Marx the father emerges most passionately through his daughters' letters. It is a complex impression of fatherhood. For us, looking backwards, Karl Marx can never be simply a private father: to consider him in this way would be to display a false and an ahistorical naivety. He is a philosophical and political father, one whose ideas have generated a tradition of thought rich in contradictions. This "dear Dada" was to stimulate millions of men and women to act, sometimes with noble generosity, sometimes with tragic cruelty. Marx's ideas have been taken into circumstances far beyond his own imaginings, sometimes becoming the official face of authorities concerned to cover their tracks with dogmatic certainties. The enormous consequences of his public life are necessarily present in our retrospective consciousness of Marx within his family. Even if we make an effort to experience him within this intimate world, the very need to make such an effort indicates that he is no ordinary parent. In 1866, after struggling with his "damned book" *Capital*, Marx the extraordinary parent wrote to Engels that he had been "naturally delighted to lick the child smooth after so many birthpangs."[4]

Within his own time Marx was a mighty force, fierce and often hasty in his political hatreds, acrimonious in faction fights, yet a stubborn organizer who could gain the respect of dour British trade unionists as well as great opponents like the Anarchist Bakunin. Public political battles were part of his daughters' upbringing. Jenny, Laura and Eleanor assume a knowingness of the kind which stems from being reared in such a political and intellectual atmosphere. Public figures dropped in from revolutionary movements all over the world, and their virtues and frailties were part of everyday talk.

The confidence was not only a precocity common to the children of intellectuals. There was a shared intensity peculiar to the Marx family. By any standards Karl Marx's abundant personality would make him a father to be reckoned with. Moreover, genius at close quarters, breakfast, lunch and tea, must be potent stuff. These three women are inevitably marked by living with such a father; but there is as well that special concentrated certainty. Marx had the strength to draw the energy of other men and women towards him, transform this philosophically, shifting the very openings and reaches of thought in the process. Such a man gulps destiny in giant doses. He left a weighty inheritance for his daughters, infinitely precious but heavy and all-surrounding. It has been hard even for many of Marx's subsequent followers to honour his accomplishments while keeping a sharp eye out for his blind spots. It has not been only because of over-faithful devotion. For he himself heaves us towards a point of such intense dialectical transformation that it is hard to keep our presence of mind and remember that these ideas come along with the human quirks and foibles of Karl Marx, the historical man.

Eleanor, especially, takes on her father's conviction that his political viewpoint transcends any subjective considerations. It is one of the qualities of greatness to defy one's existing historical situation — as Marx himself observed of Aristotle. And yet even genius only momentarily appears to hold off the perils of humdrum life itself. Indeed, very brilliant people can sometimes fail to see what is obvious to those who dwell habitually in the humdrum — subjective insight distributes itself in a democratic manner and seems a little shy of great philosophers. Marx, with his theories of the tension between thought and circumstance, his dismantling of interest and opinion in the scientific laws of others, held an exceptionally unshakeable assumption that his own vision of the world infallibly coincided with reality itself. In many cases his own certainty was vindicated; in others, like any ordinary mortal, he was wildly off the mark.

While these are not, then, the letters of any daughters, but rather of the daughters of an historically famous man, the immediate and personal father was still real enough. He had written passionately to their mother, had loved her, nursed her and been unfaithful to her. He had desperately sought accommodation in the cold and rain in the early days in London; he had fed the family on bread and potatoes when Jenny Marx was ill and had worried about paying the milkman, the baker, grocer, butcher and the man with the tea. And he had been left with heart and mind "deeply shaken"[5] when his young son Edgar had died in 1855 at the age of eight.

When his daughters are grown up Marx the father combines somewhat incongruously with Marx the revolutionary. Writing to Paul when he was courting Laura, he criticizes his "too intimate deportment,"[6] and asks him, like any Victorian father, about his prospects and family. This is, however, more than a mere ritual of fatherly power. Behind the letter lies the experience of those miserable years in Soho and the continuing practical difficulties. The passionate contradition in his own life between his love for his family and his sense of public destiny had not only meant pain for himself, it had consumed his wife Jenny. He writes:

"You know that I have sacrificed my whole fortune to the revolutionary struggle. I do not regret it. On the contrary. Had I my career to start again, I should do the same. But I would not marry. As far as lies in my power I intend to save my daughter from the reefs on which her mother's life has been wrecked."[7]

It has often been observed that although the Marx family were poor when they first came to England, as their daughters grew up the poverty was of a peculiarly middle-class kind. They certainly had social aspirations beyond their means, and Marx clearly felt he had to compensate for what they had been through. Absurdly, they felt they had to keep up appearances in front of Paul Lafargue when he was courting Laura so ardently. Marx was also, ironically, singularly inept at managing money. He considered going bankrupt in this period: instead, on doctor's advice he ended up ordering champagne and gymnastic lessons for Laura! On his fiftieth birthday in 1868 he ruefully recalled his mother's words: "If only Karl had *made Capital* instead of just writing about it."[8]

Despite his reservations about politically active sons-in-law he yielded to Laura and later to Jenny, when she too fell in love with a radical Frenchman. However, he resolutely opposed Eleanor's relationship with the dashing Lissagaray, who was seventeen years her senior. He might admire Lissagaray's *History of the Commune*, but he did not want him for a son-in-law.

Marx's daughters certainly did not see their father as a tyrant. As Yvonne Kapp has shown in her painstaking reconstruction of the family's life, there was a great deal of warmth, fun and affection, despite their topsy-turvy impecunity. Laura writes fondly in this collection of letters of Marx's "roguish twinkle,'"[9] and this "twinkle," though not often commented on, is in fact present in much of his writing. Even when Eleanor was so distressed by his attitude to Lissagaray, her love for her father remained unshaken. She told her friend Olive Schreiner: "For long miserable years there was a shadow between myself and my father . . . yet our love was always the same and despite everything, our faith and trust in one another."[10]

The difficulty was not that he was a domineering external authority. It was rather that the enormous force of his personality marked his daughters' very beings. This was particularly true for Eleanor. She told Olive Schreiner that he had said, "Jenny is most like me, but Tussy is me."[11]

Health problems preoccupy them all, and are ever present in the letters. There are Marx's dreadful carbuncles, his bronchitis, laryngitis and tumour of the lung. There are Mrs. Marx's frequent illnesses, Laura's eternal colds, Eleanor's nervous complaints. The chronicling of death makes this in many ways a sombre family record. In the course of the correspondence three of Laura's children die and two of Jenny's. We read of the death of Mrs. Marx, of Jenny at only thirty-eight and of Marx himself, all within the space of a few years. The sadness of loss pervades the later letters rather like the atmosphere evoked by an old photograph album.

To a modern reader, the deaths of the babies and children are the most shocking of all. It is one thing to note the high infant mortality of the nineteenth century, or even to read in history books or in a biography that Laura Marx lost all her children and that two of Jenny's died. It is quite another to read in intimate letters of the pregnancies, the parents' delight in the babies, the debate about whether to get a wet-nurse or to breast-feed or bottle-feed — and later to hear of the children's illness and death.

Paul Lafargue writes to Marx from Bordeaux in 1871 reporting on political events in France. He adds:

"Marc-Laurent, still the Silent One, drinks, sleeps and pisses in an enviable manner. Laura is well, she would be quite recovered if she hadn't got it into her head that she should feed him; luckily *Coco-bel-oeil* (he has magnificent eyes) also sucks cow's milk, otherwise she wouldn't be able to stand it, for he's a *guzzler*. The illustrious Schnaps is full of beans and fat enough for four."[12]

We know now that Laura was wise to insist on breast-feeding, for cow's milk, even if it was being boiled, was not the right food for such a young baby. But Marc-Laurent (Coco-bel-oeil) fell ill in April, when Paul was away involved in the Commune, and in July he died, only five months old. In July the following year Schnaps also died, aged three and a half. The effect of these tragedies on Laura and Paul is not recorded in the letters, but we can infer Laura's distress from her earlier account of carrying her baby all day and rocking him all night when he was ill, and Paul's from his abandonment of his medical career. Reading their letters I longed to be able to parcel a few babycare books, antibiotics and baby clinics back into the past to defy time and avert all these tiny acute tragedies.

As young wives living in France both Laura and Jenny (who married Charles Longuet in 1872) had the special problems of women living apart from their own families. The sisters did travel to see one another, but contact and support was necessarily restricted by distance. Though they could not afford the normal trappings of the middle classes, Laura and Jenny perpetuated the jumbled social aspirations of their parents and were similarly dependent upon accoutrements which were beyond their means.

There were added complications inherited from their unusual upbringing. All three daughters had been encouraged to think about politics and to involve themselves actively in political events. Their letters in the early days refer to the Fenians in Ireland, to the Commune, to faction fights with the followers of the French socialist Proudhon and with the Anarchists in the First International. Later in life Laura, like Eleanor, was to be involved in the Second International. However, in the days when Laura, and later Jenny, had small children, it was exceedingly difficult for them to keep up with any reading, let alone with any practical political work, and the clash between their upbringing and their domestic life as married women was obviously painful. This shared experience was an important bond between Jenny and Laura, which has been overshadowed by the focus on the affection between Jenny and Eleanor. Jenny can pour out her heart to Laura knowing that she will easily identify with the despair of the childbound.

In April 1881 Jenny tells her sister that she fears she will become an idiot. "I feel wretchedly hopelessly nervous — ill at ease mentally and physically."[13] It was hardly surprising, for one of her three children generally kept her awake every night, and one had been ill with gastric fever. About a year later she complains from Argenteuil: "I hear and see nothing but the baker and butcher and cheesemonger and greengrocer. I do believe that even the dull routine of factory work is not more killing than are the endless duties of the *ménage*. . . . Some women I know . . . glory in this home drudgery — but we are not all made of the same stuff."[14]

Her husband, Charles Longuet, was away from home a good deal and she was isolated just as Laura had been a decade earlier. Her mother had been prophetically uneasy when Jenny and Charles had first become engaged. "I can't help being afraid that Jenny's fate as a political wife is exposed to all the cares and troubles that are inseparable from it."[15]

The dichotomy between their own domestic circumstances and the socialist politics which they support emerges in many of the letters between Jenny and Laura. Observations about the social and material circumstances which shaped their lives remain always personal. Both women, brought up to be intensely thinking people, describe how they can hardly snatch a moment to write letters: they have to manoeuvre fragments of time while babies sleep or children are taken for walks. Such conditions of life make intellectual development as impossible as the alienating effect of machinery Marx described in *Capital*, reducing the workers to "hands." But, paradoxically, Jenny's and Laura's situation was still perceived by everyone in the family as personal misfortune rather than as the oppressive outcome of a male-dominated society. These family difficulties have simply to be borne with private fortitude: they have no wider social meaning.

This was not, of course, an attitude that was peculiar to the Marx family. There did not exist at that time a political language in either European socialism or in the feminism of the day which could properly express these conflicts and sufferings. "The Woman question" was persistently discussed, but in the broad sweep of debate the dilemma of educated mothers tended to be passed over.

In France, the adoptive country of both Jenny and Laura, there was actually a greater awareness of motherhood as a political issue than in the socialist movements elsewhere. In the 1860s there had been considerable debate about women's social and political rights, arguments about work, marriage, divorce. Some of the women participants were later active in the Paris Commune of 1871. Briefly, during the Commune, visionary plans appeared for nurseries with aviaries, bright toys and medical care for all children.[16] Even after the Commune collapsed, discussion of women's liberation continued in the anarchist and socialist movement in France in the 1870s and 80s.

There were problems with this recognition of motherhood in the French socialist tradition. It was often presented as a backward-looking romantic ideal and opposed to women's right to work; it also tended to be expressed in terms of utopian schemes rather than practical needs. When Léonie Rouzade, a feminist influenced by Fourier and utopian socialism, argued in 1880 that children should be brought up collectively, her long-term visions did not solve the immediate problems of political wives like Laura Lafargue and Jenny Longuet.[17]

After the loss of their children and their return to France in 1882, Paul Lafargue wrote articles and helped to draft socialist statements about women. (He may have discussed these with Laura, who herself wrote for the Viennese socialist women's paper *Arbeiterinnenzeitung* in the early 90s.) He was also instrumental in introducing Bebel's and Engels's ideas to the French socialists. In 1878 Bebel published *Woman and Socialism*, and six years later Engels's *Origin of the Family, Private Property and the State* appeared. Engels emphasized the need to involve women in production. It was assumed under socialism that housework and childcare would be taken over by public agencies; although the work would still be done by women, their economic independence would enable them to be equal to men in the family. However, in 1886 Lafargue gave Engels's ideas a rather different meaning by stressing the supposed matriarchy of primitive communism. In the early twentieth century he developed his interest in an early Golden Age to argue that the maternal role gave women an innate superiority which would be recovered in a communist society. This elevation of motherhood was a continuous theme in the feminist and social thought of the period. It had both radical and conservative aspects. It could be used to argue for better conditions for real mothers, but it also carried eugenic assumptions about breeding a "superior" stock and implied that motherhood was women's main role.[18]

Lafargue was intellectually aware of the importance of "the Woman question" in the socialist movement. He had also been much more involved with his own children than many men of his era. Nonetheless, these later paeans to motherhood contrast with Laura's earlier tragic experiences as a mother. In the early years of their marriage Paul Lafargue does not appear to have been sensitive to his wife's real vulnerability.

When domesticity enclosed her in 1870 Laura tended to make rather arch comments on Paul's approach to "the Woman question." There is a hint that a cigar-smoking emancipated woman was rather threatening to Laura, the young wife and mother: "Formerly, you know, Tooley [Paul] would hear nothing of women out of the kitchen and the ballroom: at present he prefers seeing them in the readingroom."[19]

On another occasion she was irritated by Paul's liking for Paule Mink, founder of the "Société Fraternelle de l'Ouvrière" and editor of a paper called *Les Mouches et les Araignées*. Madame Mink's emphasis upon "*'les devoirs' des femmes*"[20] annoyed Laura, presumably because she had too many *devoirs* herself at the time. She is scathing at the expense of a male visitor who is described as "busy as usual making all sorts of propaganda, from Atheism and woman's emancipation down to gymnastics."[21] For Laura, clinging desperately to a fragile sense of herself as an independent person, emancipated women were disturbing and men talking of women's rights just hot air.

There was, however, more to it than the rather abstract terms in which women's rights were being discussed and her own domestic circumstances. As well as their innate political confidence Marx's daughters had inherited a special pride. Their political heritage kept them aloof from the "fine lady" suffrage movement, with its class limitations. It also made them a little dismissive of women's rights' enthusiasts in the socialist movement. As thoughtful revolutionary women they were necessarily at odds with many aspects of conventional middle-class assumptions about women's destiny. The significant point is that, in their different ways, they tackled it as a purely private matter.

It is Eleanor's life which reveals this most strikingly of all, because she was the most active politically. Yvonne Kapp says of her: "She went her own way without fuss, feminism or false constraint."[22] It was then, as now, possible for a gifted woman to make her way in radical circles as an organizer and speaker and to be accepted as an equal by men — because she can be seen as the exception, as being quite unlike their own wives or girl friends.

Eleanor, a thoroughly political person, carried her father's philosophy and politics with all the Marx confidence. She simply assumed she was an equal human being and that was that. She scrupulously deciphered his manuscripts and edited his writings. She took on his opponents manfully, the Anarchists in the Socialist League as well as the leader of the Social Democratic Federation H. M. Hyndman. Yet for herself she took no delight in the internal wranglings and was obviously at her happiest when she could be of service to the unskilled and semi-skilled workers who had been swept into new unionism in the late 1880s.

The discovery that she had the gift to move people when she spoke allowed her to integrate her powers as an actress with her public work as a socialist. She would speak regardless of the weather, her own health or exhaustion. Towards the end of her life she wrote to *Justice*, the S.D.F. paper, saying that she had given forty-one lectures and spoken or taken the chair at ten meetings in the last eight months, not counting a week's lecturing in Holland.

. . . "in order to save time and trouble *and* postage stamps, will you let me tell the many S.D.F. branches that are so kindly asking me to lecture for them that I am obliged to decline for the present at any rate, all open-air work. My throat unfortunately will not stand the strain. Those who know me will not suspect me of shirking work."[23]

Eleanor Marx was by no means the only prominent woman speaker in the socialist and anarchist movement of this period. Although there were many more men speakers, there was a small significant minority of women who were very popular with the various socialist branches. However, the freedom these women enjoyed had certain boundaries. The nationally known figures tended to be middle-class educated women, and they were also invariably single or, most significantly, childless.

Eleanor avoided the domestic predicament of Jenny and Laura because she did not have children. And as she scraped a living from literary work, learning the new machine-based skill of typewriting, she was never economically dependent on the man with whom she lived, Edward Aveling. It was a difficult and arduous life — "I'd rather be a kitten and cry mew than a woman trying to earn a living"[24] — and despite her unconventional relationship with Aveling it is still Eleanor who is in the midst of "whitewashing and cleaning"[25] when Edward goes away. She was neither mother nor spinster, and this unusual status singled her out from other women of her class.

Yet many of the traditional responsibilities of the single woman in a family gravitated towards her; care for the sick, for Marx's illegitimate son, Freddy, and for other people's children, especially little Johnny Longuet, Jenny's son. Like Engels, she loved children. Again there is a strong connection here between her personal and public worlds. She helped to organize socialist treats for children, and on one occasion ran a Christmas party for two hundred children from Socialist League branches — a hair-raising feat as she was not told in advance how many they were bringing. After moving to Sydenham in 1896 she helped in the Battersea Socialist Sunday School. But it was not the same as having a family of her own. The new house made her aware of its emptiness. She wrote to Laura after her second Christmas there: "I sometimes wonder if it is worse to have had and lost little ones or never to have had them."[26]

The public and private demands which were made on Eleanor were significantly different from those made upon the men who were active in the socialist movement, and the combination added a positive and enriching element to her socialism. It was a two-way process, for she derived great warmth and strength from her socialist and trade union work as well as from her family. Her politics involved a living connection to other people. She knew she was needed and was useful, and for most of her life she responded with exuberance and ingenuity. Nonetheless, there were times when the private and public pressures appear relentless and threaten to overwhelm her.

Amidst the exuberance there were shadows. Her love for her father was darkened by the painful conflict of loyalty to him and to Lissagaray. There is also an unreconciled difficulty in her relation to her mother. She suffered from anorexia nervosa during her mother's terminal illness in 1881, and after her death she wrote to Jenny saying impatiently that she wanted to be "doing something." She criticized the doctors and her father for advising rest: "What neither Papa nor the doctors nor anyone will understand is that it is chiefly *mental worry* that affects me."[27]

The growth of the socialist movement and Eleanor's role within it meant that she did indeed "do something" in the years to come. In the 1880s and 1890s the socialist milieu was beginning to develop a culture in which "reformed dress," bicycling and the personal aspirations of the New Woman were playing an important part. Eleanor herself did much to popularize Ibsenism among socialists. She was ready to put up a fight for women's right to sexual knowledge on discovering that the *Kama Sutra* was banned to women in the British Museum,[28] and in her review of Bebel's *Woman and Socialism*, which she wrote with Aveling, the sexual oppression of women, both as prostitutes and through enforced celibacy, is criticized.[29]

These discussions of the New Woman's claims to freedom nevertheless skirted many of the most important questions. What should the New Woman do about her own dependence and about those who depend upon her? How could she find a new balance between public activity, personal freedom and loving relationships with other people? The truth is that Eleanor found it exceedingly difficult to develop such a balance. This problem, which she never resolved, explains why there appears to be a disjuncture between the public Eleanor, the brilliant and hard-headed socialist writer, speaker and organizer, and the private Eleanor, writing intimately to her sister with gentle enquiries about family pets and the children's health.

There is a long socialist tradition, in which Eleanor had some making, whereby the personal frailties of the great socialists, especially the women, are protected from hostile bourgeois scrutiny. In one sense this is a sound instinct, for opponents of socialism and anarchism take a particularly salacious delight in discovering any vulnerability in radical women, as if contradictory emotions somehow reduce the significance of their political work. However, like all chivalry, this protection in fact restricts the growth of our understanding. Nor, in its assumption that the expression of emotional frailty is a failing, does it strike at the root of the matter. The points at which women who possess great strength express fear are indications of the deeply contradictory tensions affecting all women who strain against the confines of the prevailing social ideas of femininity. Vulnerabilities reveal the restraints upon women's full development as human beings, while the cultural and social understanding of this humanity are still defined by men, in their own image.

The individual expression of these tensions obviously varies. In Eleanor's case the balance of public engagement with personal love and freedom was made the more precarious by the weight of her political heritage and the callousness of the man she loved. Her friend Olive Schreiner, who was primarily a writer rather than an activist, did not face quite the same dilemma. Olive Schreiner pursued love and freedom far into the recesses of her soul. She reached painfully towards some glimpse of how women might be able to achieve autonomy without subordinating themselves or cutting themselves off from their feelings. Eleanor loved her, and in the mid-1880s Havelock Ellis describes Eleanor as Olive's "chief friend."[30]

Perhaps there was jealousy in Olive's dread of Edward Aveling. Or perhaps she did fear for her friend. A year after Eleanor began living with Edward she wrote desperately to Olive expressing her yearning for love, for the unquestioning love of her parents, especially her father. If only Olive could have "known what he was to me."[31] Already at the beginning of her life with Aveling she understood the clash in their natures, could see the delight he took in attracting women for its own sake. There is no hint of such frivolity in Eleanor. Her agony must have been a source of irritation to Aveling. He could not respond to her enormous desire to be needed; her constancy merely nurtured his self-esteem, and over the years a great inequality of emotional powers developed between them. We can guess that Aveling was adroit at emotional manipulation. He possessed a brilliance and sexual energy which must have reminded Eleanor of some of her father's powers. But there was not the same depth and integrity in her lover. Eleanor was aware of Aveling's hollowness but it did not diminish the power he had over her. This *poseur* dressing to attract other women could still drain her of that tremendous Marx confidence, leaving her suddenly vulnerable and wretched. It is significant that when she acknowledges this she should turn to a woman's love to heal her. She writes to Olive in utter depression: "There is so little in me to like or interest people. That *you* care for me is one of those mysteries that remain for ever inexplicable."[32]

Externally it is Eleanor's self-deprecation which is inexplicable. She was so clearly a vital and fascinating person. Yet her sense of inner worthlessness remained buried within her being through all those busy years. Olive, a woman who knew something of the same painful struggles, could touch this pain as an equal. They were equally vulnerable.

Edward Aveling remains an enigmatic figure whose letters and postscripts reveal nothing but his capacity for elaborate self-disguise. Many socialists held him responsible for Eleanor's suicide. Kapp has argued that this is to over-emphasize Eleanor's dependence upon him and simplify the motives behind her suicide. She stresses Eleanor's isolation from the workers' movement in Britain as it moved away from Marxism, leaving Eleanor ineffectual and unable to justify the faith which her father and Engels had both had in her as a political human being.

But to be content with this interpretation is only to endorse the paradox within which Eleanor was caught. It extracts her deep involvement in public life from those aspects of her inner life which disturb her biographer: her less conscious and possibly uneasy feelings for her mother, her desire for a close friendship with Olive Schreiner, with whom she could probe a new emotional world as well as discuss ideas, and of course the destructive aspects of her love for Aveling. Aaron Rosebury's memory of Eleanor is illuminating. She told him: "My father used to say that I was more like a boy than a girl. It was Edward who really brought out the feminine in me. I was irresistibly drawn to him."[33]

The attraction was not just sexual; there was also a cultural and political affinity between them. They both delighted in the theatre, both were moving speakers. Certainly in the early days there was an exciting energy in their relationship. Yet this man continually betrayed her, emotionally as well as sexually; he humiliated her and used her coldly. Despite her exuberant strength, "the feminine" in her remained fixed in suffering. Eleanor's womanhood was first denied and then assailed without mercy. This must have surely been a part of her culminating despair. She was, after all, a woman.

Freddy Demuth appears to have been the only person in whom Eleanor could confide after Edward's final desertion. There is no hint in her letters to Laura of the depth of her unhappiness. Edward had borrowed money even from Freddy, and it seemed to Eleanor that she and Freddy were two victims bound together in suffering. In fact Freddy had been wronged not only by her lover, but much more fundamentally by her father, who disowned his natural son and allowed Engels to assume responsibility for his paternity. (Eleanor had only learned of this as Engels lay dying, and distressingly partly through Louise Kautsky, Engels's companion in his later years. Eleanor felt an intense, almost obsessive, resentment towards Louise who, she believed, was responsible for her estrangement from Engels.) Yet if Marx had acknowledged Freddy he would have wounded her mother even more than by his infidelity. Eleanor's passionate loyalty to her family was torn open. If she had failed her father, he had failed Freddy. But how could she be loyal to her mother and to Freddy? Her memory of her parents could not contain these conflicts.

E. P. Thompson observes of Eleanor's suicide:

"The greatest tragedy, as it seems to me, is that when she came to her end — and she had a right to choose that end — she did not realize how much she had come to be loved and honoured in the movement, and how clearly her many friends dissociated Aveling from her."[34]

As he says, it was her work in the New Unionism of the late '80s and early '90s and in the broader socialist and radical movement which had gained her this love, not the part she took in the faction fights within the London socialist groups.

The early socialist movement now has a substantial history. Eleanor's political role is traced by her biographers Chushichi Tsuzuki and Yvonne Kapp. Yet there are gaps in this historiography which make a full assessment of Eleanor Marx rather difficult. This is particularly noticeable in relation to the participation of less prominent women, whose names remain unremembered, in New Unionism, in the early socialist movement in Britain, and in the rest of Europe. Eleanor Marx's biographers can show how it was possible for her to play a leading role but tell us little about the women with whom she worked in the trades unions or the composition of the audiences who heard her speak, and the circumstances and consciousness which have enabled women to participate in some popular movements and not in others remain unclear. It would be interesting in this connection to investigate further the stress on democracy and the social demands of New Unionism and search for repercussions of that militancy in the community and social life. It would be equally illuminating to enquire how women were recruited into particular union branches and socialist meetings.

It is not just a problem of further study and wider questions. Historians in the Marxist tradition have sometimes been content to vindicate the political ideas and choices of famous Marxists of the past, scoffing rather complacently at the underdevelopment of rival radical theories and the objections of political opponents. They have been inclined to berate those who have deviated from orthodox positions without pausing to examine whether their paragons might have erred in determining "correctness." This over-possessive and defensive reaction to right-wing interpretations of the socialist past, whilst polemically understandable, nonetheless fatally inhibits the deeper and more flexible historical approach necessary to sustain an opposing culture.

In the case of Eleanor Marx, E. P. Thompson warns against an uncritical acceptance of her political infallibility. She was not an "all-wise Marxist homing pigeon."[35] He suggests we take a cooler and closer view. He asks whether the secession from the Social Democratic Federation and the formation of the Socialist League in 1884 was *really* the best tactic. Later Eleanor Marx, Edward Aveling and Engels withdrew support from the Socialist League and then condemned it. This is a time-honoured sectarian device which tends to be self-fulfilling. Thompson argues that in this instance it drove their former ally William Morris closer to the Anarchist-Communists who were opposed to involvement with parliament.

It is easier to be broad-minded about the faction fights of a hundred years ago than one's own. With hindsight I believe Eleanor's opponents in this quarrel deserve a fairer hearing than she gives them in her letters. Indeed, the Eleanor Marx-Aveling-Engels perspective is not only dismissive of the original power of William Morris's creative vision but also fails to recognize the validity of the Anarchists' concern about authoritarianism within the socialist movement and their suspicion of the use of state legislature to effect change.[36] Unfortunately, this wariness hardened in Anarchism into an abstract moral principle with little sense of how alternative strategies might develop in practice. It is often the case in political quarrels that the combatants retire with partial and divided understandings. These pathetic and tattered spoils are then jealously guarded in the cafés, pubs and backrooms where the sectarian spirit is seedily nurtured, to be raised aloft as sacred standards for new battles. So it was in the conflicts between Anarchists and socialists in the First and Second International.

If we shift our perspective somewhat, looking into the gifted family circle and Engels's household from the outside, the aura of absolute correctness must have become wearing. It was not a sectarian rigidity but a cliquish rectitude, even harder to oppose politically. Eleanor Marx was better informed about the international socialist movement than many British socialists, and she was familiar with the London working-class movement. But her knowledge of the north of England was limited. Nor did she ever understand the importance of a libertarian strand in British working-class politics which was present in the Socialist League and the Independent Labour Party. Eleanor had been trained by a father who would simply move the organizational centre of the First International if he lost a faction fight and close sections down if they persistently disagreed with him, regardless of the local support they might have. When Keir Hardie and Tom Mann supported the admission of the Anarchists to the Socialist Congress of the International in 1896, she was simply exasperated. Tom Mann said that he was willing to learn from others "as good and better than I."*[37] Fighting for the right of people whom you did not support was politically incomprehensible to her.

Eleanor's disagreement with Hardie and Mann pinpointed

---

* The issue was whether or not to participate in Parliament. The background to Mann's and Hardie's defence of the Anarchists was the renewed campaign to release the Anarchists imprisoned in the Walsall bomb conspiracy, which involved socialists as well as Anarchists. Greater dialogue was developing between the Anarchists and the Independent Labour Party [ILP] in this context. However, the Anarchist movement itself was in real difficulties by 1896. Their papers were collapsing for lack of support and they were squabbling among themselves.

fundamentally different approaches to how socialists should act
and how ideas were to be developed. There was greater clarity
in Eleanor's approach, yet she was capable of missing connections which developed in a less coherent way among the Anarchist-Communists or non-Marxist socialists in the ILP. Nor
could she comprehend the importance of the principle which
Tom Mann and Keir Hardie were struggling to defend, which
assumed a basic comradeship between different sections of the
Left, Anarchists as well as socialists.

Marx and Engels had developed a style of politics in which,
having decided on a line, they would attempt to make sure it
was universally imposed. Though it would be a mistake to
equate this with the discipline imposed upon the Communist
Parties from the Soviet Union later, in an informal way it
nonetheless assumed the right to intervene regardless of the
views of the socialists on the spot. Eleanor does not appear to
have been uneasy about this. In the early 1890s Engels encouraged Eleanor, Laura and Louise Kautsky to write in the new
Austrian socialist women's paper in order to "straighten out"
the women's movement there. By this he meant detaching
socialist and working-class women from the dreaded bogey of
"bourgeois feminism."[38]

The limits of liberal feminism had been noted in a friendly
but critical way by Eleanor in the mid-1880s. She had known
personally some of the British women struggling for political
rights and education in the 1870s. But when the women's socialist organizations begin to develop in Germany and Austria
in the early 1890s her tone becomes much more severe. The
background to this shift in Eleanor's attitude is not clear. It is
possible that the sharp class conflict which emerged in the
battles of the new unionists made her more generally suspicious
of cross-class alliances. However, the immediate evidence used
by Louise Kautsky to attack "bourgeois feminism" was an article in a Boston feminist paper, *The Woman's Journal*, arguing
against the reduction of hours by law on the grounds that it
would also reduce women's jobs. This was an old argument in
the European and American Left and trade union movement.
It was a complicated issue, for while employers would try and
exploit workers to the limits, ignoring the predicament of
pregnant or breast-feeding women, the extra work women did
at home or the differences in strength between workers, within

the competitive labour market male trade unionists could use the protective legislation for women workers to exclude them from skilled work. Women workers themselves disagreed on the question; there were differences between the needs of married and single women and between skilled and unskilled. The Boston article had simply demanded that the working women should decide themselves. Engels polarizes the issue as a clear fight between the "drivel of the swell-mob ladies"[39] in Boston and the women workers and socialists in Germany and Austria.

This article sparked off a general attack on any alliance between socialist women and bourgeois feminists which tended to become official orthodoxy in the German and Austrian movements, though it proved impossible to apply it in Britain, France and the United States, where "bourgeois feminism" had a vigorous life and there were many shades of socialist women involved in the feminist movements.[40] There was an assumption that the "bourgeois feminists" would always take control unless they were rigorously excluded from any contact with working women. Class tensions are certainly present when working-class women combine with middle-class ones. But there is no universal historical law which decrees that the interests of the working-class women will always be subordinated. This depends on the political balance of forces in any given Alliance.

In both Britain and the United States there were also many examples of middle-class women genuinely helping working-class women. In Chicago in the late 1880s and early '90s the Illinois Women's Alliance successfully campaigned to improve the conditions of women and children. It included feminist organizations, religious groups, socialists, anarchists, spiritualists, dress reformers, trade unionists. Florence Kelly, a friend of Engels's, was involved in the Alliance and corresponded with him about it.[41] His Boston informant was the German Marxist Sorge, who had clashed with native American feminism earlier in the First International.

Whatever the rights and wrongs of Engels's opinion, it had an unfortunate outcome in the German and Austrian context. There is little doubt that he oversimplified the relationship of American feminists, socialists and trade unionists for his own reasons, and then transported his irritation into the discussions in Europe. The mustering of Laura, Eleanor and Louise, none of whom had any real base in the Austrian movement, reveals the continuing assumption that the perspectives of the international socialist movement were to be fixed from an informal headquarters of Engels's household and the Marx family. This must have been most galling for people who disagreed with Engels's position — neither was it exactly a democratic procedure.

There were also real problems with Engels's approach to women's emancipation, which tended to be concealed when they came to be accepted as orthodoxy in the Second International. The Marxist insistence that women's sexual equality would follow from economic independence was inclined to stress the class struggle at the expense of the struggle involved in the power relationships between men and women. The assumption that housework and childcare would be taken over by public agencies did not question women as a sex being responsible for these activities. Engels did not explain who would be left with domestic work which could not be conveniently socialized or take into account the possibility that both parents might wish to spend more time with their children. Bebel and Engels developed a socialist theory of women's oppression which was much more coherent than that·expressed by other contemporary socialists; the problem was that their work came to be seen as the final socialist statement, as primary sources of the correct line. This meant that the scattered insights which persisted from utopian socialism and were appearing among Anarchists, feminists and non-Marxist socialists, tended to be overlooked by Marxist socialists, even those which might usefully have been incorporated into the orthodoxy.

Engels presented the liberation of women as the outcome of objective changes in society. He does not stress the importance of women's own activity as part of the process of liberation. The assertion of consciousness and will to change became detached from the attempt to assess the historical possibilities for action. The Anarchists were left expecting women to change simply by an effort of will, while the Marxists relied mainly on the unfolding of capitalist society to free women. The denial of subjectivity and consciousness made it difficult, especially for middle-class women, to draw on their personal experience to inform the theory within the prevailing Marxist approach. On the other hand, when working-class women write about women's emancipation they relate what they have experienced in their own lives. For example Adelheid Popp, who was to become the leader of the Austrian women's movement, describes in her autobiography the difficulty she encountered when she spoke at a meeting for the first time. The kind of personal description is acceptable as confirmation of theory. But subjective accounts were not acknowledged if they contradicted the approach worked out in the early 1890s.

If Engels had been more interested in assimilating the personal experiences of the middle-class women he knew, the Marx daughters' own lives might have served as a warning that there were a few snags in his theories. Eleanor was economically independent yet still sexually dependent on Edward. And it would be difficult to socialize the lack of sleep which made Jenny so distraught when her three children were waking in the night. Engels recognizes the significance of procreation and the upbringing of children as part of the continuation of life, but he reduces them to an economic activity rather than a relationship between people. If he had remembered the passion and excitement which surrounded the Lafargue and Longuet babies in these letters perhaps he would not have made this mistake.

If histories of women and of the international socialist movement are to be written in the future they will need to probe the theory and the public platforms at the congresses, behind programmes and pamphlets, to reveal the gap between what was said and what was done. This will mean recognizing that the unequal power between men and women in capitalist society does not miraculously vanish within the organizations for revolutionary change. Eleanor writes indignantly about the hidden assumptions of male authority in the German Social-Democratic Party. After Helen Demuth's death the German leaders decided that Louise Kautsky, who was separated from her husband, should be sent to look after Engels. Without realizing that Louise was able to look after her own interests with wiles quite alien to Eleanor's frank nature, Eleanor observes:

"I am sorry for Louise. Bebel and all the others have told her it is her *duty* to the Party to stop. It hardly seems fair to her. She was getting on so well at Vienna, and to sacrifice her whole career is no trivial matter — no one would ask a *man* to do that."[42]

This is a good example of a personal comment in a letter

being of more than biographical interest, illuminating as it does the interior life of a political organization. While the socialists certainly believed in equality and while women could indeed gain respect for their political work there were nonetheless unacknowledged limits. The terms in which the Marxist approach to women's emancipation were set made it very difficult to challenge these theoretically. Many aspects of women's subjective experience were simply dismissed or passed over as inadmissible evidence and relegated to letters or novels.

The private predicament which emerges from reading these letters means we begin to feel that we almost know the three sisters and their families and friends. But the letters are clearly about more than private lives. All three women had a certain influence upon their own times and must be counted as making history. Although, as their father wisely observed, this was not in circumstances of their own choosing.

1. Werner Blumenberg, *Karl Marx*, 1972, p. 2.
2. Mrs. Marx to F. Engels, quoted in David McLellan, *Karl Marx: His Life and Thought*, 1973, p. 332.
3. Mrs. Marx to Bertha Markheim, quoted in *ibid*, pp. 332–333.
4. Marx to F. Engels, quoted in *ibid*, p. 339.
5. Marx to F. Lassalle, quoted in *ibid*, p. 275.
6. Marx to P. Lafargue, quoted in Yvonne Kapp, *Eleanor Marx*, vol. 1, *Family Life 1855–1883*, 1972, pp. 298–299.
7. *ibid*.
8. Marx to F. Engels, quoted in McLellan, p. 356.
9. Laura to Marx, 8 May 1867. Letter 9, p. 29.
10. Eleanor to O. Schreiner, quoted in McLellan, p. 417.
11. *ibid*.
12. P. Lafargue to Marx, 4 February 1871. Letter 28, pp. 91–92.
13. Jenny to Laura, 22 April 1881. Letter 42, p. 131.
14. Jenny to Laura, end March 1882. Letter 51, p. 152.
15. Mrs. Marx to Liebknecht, quoted in McLellan, p. 414.
16. See Edith Thomas, *The Women Incendiaries*, 1967, pp. x–xv, 1–27, 97.
17. On these debates see Charles Sowerine, *Les Femmes et le Socialisme*, Paris, 1978, pp. 9–42.
18. *ibid*, pp. 51–53.
19. Laura to Jenny, 9 June 1870. Letter 22, p. 70.
20. Laura to Jenny, 9 February 1870. Letter 20, p. 63.
21. *ibid*.
22. Kapp, vol. 2. *The Crowded Years, 1884–1898*, 1976, p. 89.
23. quoted in *ibid*. p. 650.
24. Eleanor to Laura, 11 April 1889. Letter 70, p. 210.
25. Eleanor to Laura, 12 April 1885. Letter 62, p. 186.
26. Eleanor to Laura, quoted in Kapp, *The Crowded Years*, p. 642.
27. Eleanor to Jenny, 8 January 1882. Letter 48, p. 145.

28. See Ruth First and Ann Scott, *Olive Schreiner*, 1980, fn., p. 136.
29. Eleanor reviewed the English translation in the August 1885 Supplement to *Commonweal*. This was later developed into an article in the *Westminster Review*, 9 May 1886. It appeared also as a pamphlet. Edward and Eleanor Marx Aveling, *The Woman Question*, Swan Sonnenschein, Lowrey and Co., 1886.
30. Quoted in First and Scott, p. 124.
31. Eleanor to O. Schreiner, quoted in *ibid*, p. 134.
32. *ibid.*
33. quoted in *ibid*, p. 204.
34. E. P. Thompson, "English Daughter," review of Kapp, *The Crowded Years*, *New Society*, 3 March 1977, p. 457.
35. *ibid.*
36. See E. P. Thompson, *William Morris, Romantic to Revolutionary*, 1955, 1977. For the Anarchists' point of view, see John Quail, *The Slow-Burning Fuse: the Lost History of the British Anarchists*, pp. 200–208.
37. See Kapp, *The Crowded Years*, pp. 659–660.
38. Hal Draper and Anne G. Lipow, *Marxist Women versus Bourgeois Feminism* in *The Socialist Register*, ed. Ralph Miliband and John Saville, 1976, p. 217.
39. Quoted in *ibid*, p. 218.
40. See Richard J. Evans, *The Feminists*, 1977, pp. 170–177.
41. Meredith Tax, *The Rising of the Women, Feminist Solidarity and Class Conflict 1880–1917*, 1980, pp. 65–89.
42. Eleanor to Laura, 19 December 1890. Letter 74, p. 224.

PART ONE

March 1866 – July 1869

The Family Circle

T HIS FIRST PART contains a representative selection of letters, mainly from the three girls to each other and to their father, written in the late 1860s. At this time they were living in Modena Villas, Maitland Park, between Hampstead and Kentish Town. There are also some letters from both Paul and Laura Lafargue in Paris, after their marriage. The selection begins, appropriately, with a childish, flirtatious letter from Eleanor to her father in Margate, where, in common with other Victorians, he confidently expected that the sea air would cure his carbuncles, and ends in the libertarian household of Marx's friend and collaborator Frederick Engels.

The worst period of hardship, when the Marxes had been living in cramped lodgings in Soho after Marx's exile from Europe and three children had died in infancy, was now over, though they were still chronically short of money and dependent on Engels for constant injections of funds. However, various small legacies had meant that at least a semblance of a middle-class way of life had become possible.

The main concerns of the correspondence are already evident in this selection. From an early age — Jenny was twenty-one when the letters begin, Laura twenty and Eleanor eleven — the girls were, in their different ways, involved in the socialist movement and their father's work. They write about the political issues of the day: Ireland, Poland, the Reform League, the trade unions and the International Working Men's Association. They write about literature, and scatter their letters with puns, literary allusions and theatrical gossip; Shakespeare was a special passion, and was frequently recited and performed in the household. They write of Engels, who had no legitimate children of his own and willingly acted as a second father, both spiritually and materially; of their mother, a Prussian who had devoted her life to her family, to politics, and to the transcription of Marx's work; and of Helen Demuth, their servant and faithful friend, upon whom they all depended. The pattern emerges of a very closely-knit family to whom the publication of *Capital* and the work of the IWMA are of central importance. Marx's daughters are literate, they are witty, they are multi-lingual and they are, to a degree, exclusive.

On 14 March 1866 Marx had gone to Margate to re-cuperate from a severe attack of carbuncles. At first he stayed in a hotel, the King's Arms, where he was struck by the odd behaviour of one of his fellow-guests; he assumed that the man was blind, but later discovered him to be deaf. Marx moved to a boarding-house run by a Mrs. Grach, took bracing walks and bathed in the March sea, which he declared to be "de-licious." He returned to London briefly for a party given by his daughters on 22 March.

Ellie was one of Eleanor's many nicknames; the one that stuck, and with which she signed her letters, was Tussy, pronounced as in "pussy."

1. Eleanor to Karl Marx

1, Modena Villas
19 March 1866

My dear Dada,
As Jenny is going to write to you I may as well enclose a short letter. Your first adventure is very amusing. That you took a *deaf* man for *blind* is capital. I wonder the "ears of the deaf" were not unstopped at your arrival. I can quite understand your having felt *shy* at being left alone with a deaf man, who was blind.

Now — Dr. Karl Marx of bad philosophy I hope you will keep your promise and come on Thursday. So with love good-bye and believe me.

Your affectionate
ELLIE

After the party Marx returned to Margate where Eleanor and Jenny joined him. Laura stayed in London with Mrs. Marx (Möhme).

2. Laura to Jenny

[*London, after 22 March 1866*]

My dear Jane,

I should have written to you all before this had I been able. But the only time I had for doing so was taken from me by our very good friend Mr. Faraday, with whom I had a long *tête-à-tête* conversation on Thursday evening, in which by the way we both made ourselves as agreeable as we could and I was as much delighted with him as I dare say he was with me. After our stock of observations (not flirtatious) was exhausted and being not like that of Mrs. Marks *née* Hubbard — inexhaustible — we were joined by Möhme, who entered minus her boots — with just so much of drapery as to relieve her from the charge of trusting entirely to nature for effects, and that drapery just so disposed as to show more than it concealed. You know the delicate sensibilities of our friend and how easily he is put to the blush. He certainly had good reason to be so now. For my part I shut my eyes and so escaped the sight of what I could not look upon and retain my natural colour.

On Friday morning I was busy at "Easter-work" which you will become acquainted with by and by. After noon I dressed, dined and had seen Möhme off on her pilgrimage to King Street (National Reformers)[1] when who should come in upon my solitude but — Peter Fox[2] of all men in the world. Goodness gracious me! how frightened I was! The man who had recognized at first sight that I was wanting in that spark for which nothing can atone and who had never yet spoken half a dozen words with me — how should I make shift to get on alone with him! He had a weight of grievances on his heart and head which were so overpowering as to be impossible to hide. Out came his skeletons — Poland — Ireland — Reform League — "Feudal aristocracy" — "British Ministry" — not one by one but all in a lump, till the room actually darkened with what I suppose were living incarnations of dead things invoked by his wild words and till his stammering and stuttering increased to that extent which rendered further *exposition* impossible.

All this time (one hour and a half) I sat listening to him, scarcely able to suppress my laughter at the newness of my situation being harangued to upon subjects I know nothing about — and with perfect faith on the part of the haranguer that I was "up" to everything he said or might say.

I was not sorry when Möhme's arrival at length relieved me from confidences which however flattering to my intelligence were very alarming to my ignorance and nervousness.

Evelina came a little later.[3] I walked out with her and took her home to her house where I was made to stay all night. Forced to listen for an indefinite length of time to the musical impromptus of Mr. Hirsch, to witness Azelia's rather unconscionable behaviour, Mr. Strong's discomfort and finally to partake of rabbit-pie — which felt considerably the worse for Charles was there. The fool has bought himself a pin-brooch cameo for eight guineas and has put my likeness into the back of it and Möhme is surprised that I am annoyed at this. He sends you his love.

It is very injustifiable [*sic*] in you to be abroad on a Good Friday. They are miserable bunglers here at bun-eating and the whole burden of the play has fallen upon me—unsupported I have had to sustain a reputation of twenty years standing for a character which you know none is better suited for. However, a hero must have his heroine and it is dry work playing to empty boards. Thus although I have been as reckless as ever where such matters are concerned of consequences, although I have for the "credit of the family" eaten way through a mountain of buns, the exertions of one solitary performer will not save a play from being damned — and Möhme and Helen[4] walking through their parts without zeal or spirit — it was a sorry farce. I assure you I have almost succumbed beneath the burden of the *crosses* that I bore.

I have not yet written a line to Challey[5] who is angry and with whom I have yet my peace to make. Moreover why should I write to you. For although had I not written you would call me worse than lazy, you will attribute this scribble to nothing better than a desire to hear myself talk. Therefore goodbye until that desire may be justified in me by my having something to say.

Yours affectionately

LAURA MARX

It is not unlikely that an erratic box may find its way to you at Margate. Should it do so you will find in [it] a book *Delphine*[6] (which Möhme insists upon sending as she declares you will make occasion for reading it, but which I think will not give you much pleasure as the story breaks off where you will most wish it to go on), a letter from Nelly Cunningham.[7] Verily I say mind you I have not looked into it, having opened it merely to look for some scrap for myself from Alice. But like a certain widow whom you sing about (in music which is rather confused in my remembrance), it seems "*I am forgotten.*"[8]

Delphine is from the library and must be carefully looked after by you. I have not read it, of course.

Goodbye.

I am very sorry your cold is still bad. My own is reducing me to the condition of those that are deaf and dumb and without vision.

When you look upon this handwriting you will think too that it has deprived my "right hand of her cunning."[9] *Benedicite*.

I have written like a whirlwind mistakes and all!

1. Possibly a reference to the National Reform League, which had its headquarters in King Street, off the Strand.
2. One of the founders of the First International.
3. Charles, Azelia and Evelina Manning were family friends with whom Jenny later took up a post as a governess. Charles Manning had proposed to Laura, and had been rejected, in May 1865.
4. Helen Demuth, sometimes spelled Helene and also known as Nim, Nym, Nimmie, Nymmy or Lenchen.
5. Challey was one of Marx's many nicknames: others were Charley, Mohr (the Moor), Master, Old Nick or Nicky (the devil).
6. Probably the novel by Mme. de Staël (1802).
7. Alice and Nelly Cunningham were friends of Jenny's and Laura's.
8. Probably "Widow Machree" by Samuel Lover, a favourite writer of Eleanor's, who wrote popular ballads about Irish peasant life.
9. A reference to *Psalms* 137:5: "Let my right hand forget her cunning."

At the end of August 1866 Laura and Eleanor went to Hastings, where they stayed in a boarding-house run by a Miss Davies; Jenny joined them there later. When Laura wrote the following letter, she had been unofficially engaged to Paul Lafargue, a twenty-four-year-old French medical student, for a month. Her charged romantic memories of "scenes of former pleasure," with their distinct Wordsworthian overtones, refer to holidays spent in Hastings in 1862 and 1863, when Mrs. Marx and her children had been accompanied by Henry Banner, a music teacher.

3. Laura to Jenny

6, Havelock Road
Hastings
1 September 1866 Oh dear!

My dear Jenny,

Miss Davies tells me that I must post my letter before half-past eleven if I wish it to reach London before Monday. I therefore sit down to write as much as I can in five minutes.

Yesterday was the first really fine day — warm and bright. We went to Ecclesbourne Valley and the Dripping Well and saw again all the rocks and hills and valleys seen years ago with you — I missed you, as you may think.

I wish that natural scenes had something of Paul's mania of "transformation," that they might not mock, in their unaltered loveliness and repose, men and women that return to places, abandoned for brief time, *too* changed. The well drips on as ever and the trees as ever overarch the broken and damp ground: but where are those with whom we walked here and talked here and drank milk here (out of one cup)?

I hope I am not sentimental, but to forget is an art I have not learned and with me memory of that which is no more, is regret.

I had intended at once to write to Challey to send you over here. But somehow my mind is changed. For our own sakes I want you here of course — as for your health's sake — but many things here would, I think, interfere with your enjoyment. You do not like to revisit scenes of former pleasure, and you are right where the scene remains the same and the delight is lost.

A thousand recollections haunt *me* (so unchanged is the place) of the dead time: *you* therefore would not be free from many uncomfortable sensations.

Still, the bathing is so jolly and the waves and winds and weather! Tussy says we can sleep three in a bed: can we?

Miss Davies is really very amiable: a little constitutional "crabbedness" she cannot help, but she is anxious to please us and makes many additions to the table and concessions on our account. She and the "pigeon-livered" lady spar constantly at each other: surreptitiously of course — they stab, smiling. They dose me with their twaddle — but I take what amusement I can out of it and have lost the sense of annoyance it first caused.

Their peculiarities and "little winning ways" are a source of great fun to Tussy and myself, and we spend hours abroad laughing over and mimicking the scenes we witness at home.

The bands still play here from morning till night and the shouts of bathers, niggers, strollers and sailors, fill the air with all manner of pleasant noises.

A melancholy man haunts the beach who plays dolorous airs upon a sorry instrument and who, if he is not the identical man Kaub,[1] must be Kaub's brother.

This morning it rained again (I will not say "cats and dogs" because I am not a poet's daughter) heavily and fast.

Hastings never looks two days alike but "Hastings with all thy faults I love thee still"![2]

No more time. Love to Mohr and Helen from

Yours ever

LAURA

P.S. I write to you but am nevertheless very much aggrieved. I have no letter from you yet. Your conscience is an odd one.

---

1. Karl Kaub, a German worker who had emigrated to London the previous year.
2. "England, with all thy faults, I love thee still" (William Cowper, "The Time-piece").

Jenny's postscript below contains the first reference in these letters to the International Working Men's Association (IWMA), or the First International, as it came to be called, which had been inaugurated at St. Martin's Hall, London, in September 1864. Founded with the help of other European refugees and some British trade unions leaders, the First International had as its chief aim the advancement and emancipation of the working classes, and the provision of a central means of communication between working men's societies in different countries. For the eight years of its existence, Marx worked unceasingly for the First International, adhering rigidly to its principles and fighting bitter battles with those who construed them differently.

On 3 to 8 September the first Congress of the International was held in Geneva. Marx was too busy working on Capital to attend, but Paul Lafargue was present as a translator. The Congress confirmed that the seat of the General Council should remain in London, and elections were held later in the month. Marx declined to be put forward as President, declaring that as a "head worker" rather than a "hand worker" he was an unsuitable candidate. He proposed instead the incumbent George Odger, a shoe-maker and founder member of the London Trades Council, and Odger was duly re-elected, with Johann Eccarius, a German tailor, as vice-president. Marx was re-elected corresponding secretary for Germany.

4. Jenny to Laura and Eleanor

[*London, September 1866*]
Thursday afternoon

Noble Successor, low-born Hottentot,
Zwei auf einem Strich![1] I haven't time to write to each of you — it is past three o'clock and I have promised to see to the dinner. Woe to Lafargue if he expects a nice pie today — he will be

11

doomed to disappointment! How to mix the flour and butter before me I haven't the slightest notion. Yesterday I baked a tart and it turned out as hard as a stone. Helen thinks I rolled it too much — had you seen me at work you would have imagined Trojans had risen up from the dead. I fear my instalment as cook won't improve Challey's health — but Helen is so busy with other things — she is scouring the boards with such energy that I sometimes fancy they will give way and that she will come down on my head (I am in the kitchen).

The House is a very Pandemonium — all is disorder, hurry, dirt, noise. Carpets, chairs, brooms, blankets are flying about in all directions. Doors are being banged, water splashed right and left. Parker's continual cackling is almost drowned by all the other noises.

H[elen] is delighted to hear that her artistic efforts have been appreciated and thanks the Hottentot for his letter, the contents of which she has however been unable to master, having been deprived of the services of secretary Tommy, who has had other things to attend to. He has been blessing us with an additional lot of kittens — there are I believe two tabbies and one marked like Tibi. They have not yet been sent into a better world. With the exception of the advent of these three strangers, nothing has taken place during your absence. One day is so much like his neighbour that it is no easy matter to say which is which. The butcher, baker, greengrocer and paper-boy make their daily calls. I take myself and Challey out for a constitutional, go through the four meals (I have not practised since your departure), have a chat with Paul or some other stray visitor and go to bed. *Voilà tout.* The smitten youth is growing more and more fidgety. His eyes are with his heart at Hastings. Last Sunday he worked away like a nigger at the swing. All the iron is covered over with pretty cream-coloured leather — even Lessner[2] expressed his admiration of the workmanship (he has had to sew the leather on to the handle).

The Mannings[3] have been alarmingly affectionate to me. Every day I have seen one of them. Little Eva has just left me and "sends her love and ever so many kisses to you." She is rather offended you have not written to her as you had promised to do so. If you have a little time to spare — do so yet. It will give her so much pleasure, the poor child is so unhappy. Last week I went with the "Grand" and Helena to see their new house. It is very pretty. The drawing room is as large as ours, Charles' bedroom is immense and the breakfast room is light and airy. It is the nicest room in the house and is at the back, leading out into a pretty garden which the fair Azelia has converted into a lawn for croquet. Goodness gracious me! a pianoforte, guitar, singing and croquet. Who will be able to stand such a battery! What will become of the susceptible-hearted!

Of the Faradays I have seen nothing since their return, so I cannot inform you how far the old guy has been driving matters. To gather some information as to the actual state of affairs I called at the College, but unfortunately only found Mrs. Boydell[4] at home. She gave me the following piece of news, which you must promise me, you Hottentot, by the respect you have for your superiors, the Emperors, and your Successor by the marks you have received, not to let out to anyone. It is a great secret known only to myself, Mrs. Fletcher and Hove. Mrs. Cs. has resigned and is going to leave the throne she has for so many years occupied to Marion [?]. Poor Marion [?]! I don't envy her these honours. What anxiety and troubles she will have. They have not as yet been able to find a partner or to sell out the whole concern — so that Mrs. Cs. will lose a great deal of money by it.[5] I pity the poor old thing. "If Marion could but find a husband and were comfortably settled I should not mind my own losses so much," she said. "Oh *men, men*, if there were only more men in the world!" she moaned. A truce of this gabble — if Paul had heard me, he would exclaim, "*Ah que vous êtes bavarde, pire qu'une vieille commère.*"[6] I enclose a letter from Möhme and also a Scotch poem, written by Burns . . . Hoping to see you both on Monday, fat, fair and not forty,[7]

Believe me,
Affectionately yours
THE EMPEROR

The Congress, it appears, is a great success. The deputations were received very enthusiastically. Drums and trumpets did their best to give *éclat* to the entrance of the great men, they were fêted and flattered. I fear Eccarius has been entirely forgotten by George.[8] Jung[9] has not written so we don't know who has been elected president of the Congress.

How frightful the weather is! I am afraid you are spending

very dull hours under the eye of Miss D[avies] and her charming spinster-friends.

1. "Two at a stroke."
2. Friedrich Lessner, a member of the IWMA, tailor and family friend.
3. See page 8, note 3.
4. Mrs. Elizabeth Boydell was a principal of South Hampstead College for Ladies, 18 Haverstock Hill, which both Jenny and Laura had attended.
5. Although it has not been possible to trace this crisis facing South Hampstead College, we can fairly assume that the "Marion" referred to is Miss Marion Susan Rentzsch who, together with Mrs. Boydell, is listed in the ratebooks for the period as occupier of the property.
6. "How talkative you are, worse than an old crone."
7. "Fat, fair and forty/Were all the toast of the young men" (John O'Keefe, "Irish Minnie").
8. Odger.
9. Hermann Jung, a German watchmaker, member of the IWMA.

On 26 September 1866 Laura Marx and Paul Lafargue became officially engaged. Paul now spent most of his time at Modena Villas, and the Marxes were concerned to keep up appearances in his presence despite the expense of the wedding and their continuing financial problems. Some creditors threatened Marx with legal proceedings, and he wrote for help to his uncle Lion Philips in Holland (one of his mother's legal executors), to Dr. Kugelmann, a well-to-do member of the International in Hanover, and to Engels, who sent money twice during this period.

Son of a wealthy Bordeaux wine-merchant, Paul Lafargue was a Proudhonist of Creole descent who had been involved in the explosive Students' International Congress in Liège in 1865. Earlier that year he had met the Marx family when he had visited London to present a report on the French situation to the General Council of the International, and had become accepted as a member of the "inner circle." Marx was unhappy, however, about Paul's courtship of Laura. Though Mrs. Marx claimed to be delighted by the engagement, Marx was troubled by the prospect of another revolutionary in the family and the life it would mean for Laura.

In mid-November, Marx sent the first chapters of Capital to Meissner, his German publisher. By April 1867 the first volume was complete, and he set off for Hamburg to deliver it to Meissner in person. He stayed there for six weeks so as to be able to correct the proofs. Marx was very impressed by Meissner, who put the book in hand immediately and published the first edition, of a thousand copies, on 14 September.

From 17 April Marx stayed with the Kugelmanns in Hanover. During his absence his family bombarded him with letters.

5. Jenny to Karl Marx

[London, end April 1867]

My dear Challey,

The last letter you had from Modena V[illas] was such a weighty one, containing epistles from Möhme, Fox and Tussy, that I did not like to try your patience still more by adding a scrawl from myself. But I don't mean to spare you any longer. My tongue itches — I must have a chat with you. First and foremost then, let me tell you, how *delighted* I am to hear such a good account of your publisher. What a blessing it is, he does not resemble that confounded slow-coach Duncker,[1] and what a still greater blessing that this book will not make its appearance under the auspices of your very good friend Lassalle.[2] Heaven preserves us from our friends! This morning, Möhme had a letter from Engels (enclosed 10£). The good old boy is frantic with joy. He says he has never experienced more pleasure than on receiving your last letter. To *Ida*[3] I fear the news of the speedy publication of your book will give no such unqualified delight.

Many thanks, my dear Mohr, for the birthday present contained in your letter. How much I shall miss you on the 1st of May. It will be the first birthday without you. Shall you be back before the 5th of that month?[4] It is very kind indeed of you to think of preparing a pleasant stay for me in Germany. However, I must protest against one thing. You seem to think I am much in need of a change, whereas, on the contrary, I can assure you, I am very comfortable where I am. Indeed you are wrong, dear Challey, in supposing that I am in any way "pining away." Really there isn't the slightest demand for fantastic smiles of pity (I don't know why or wherefore), although there is a plentiful supply of them. I have not yet come to the strait of requiring all kinds of amusements and excitements. I always find plenty of things to amuse myself with. At present I am thoroughly enjoying Carlyle's *Chartism*. I much admire his original style, noble aspirations, good instincts and above all his supreme contempt for the present "perfect state of society," the "model English constitution" and the palaver of its Parliaments reformed and unreformed. But for a' that and a' that, when compared with Engels' book,[5] Carlyle's appears to me "stale and unprofitable";[6] I have never before so clearly seen what a difference there is between a scientific and a literary man.

A few days ago we had a very agreeable surprise. A parcel reached us, containing an iron cross, a silver medal, and a little ring — I don't know whether of brass or gold. Things we have won at the Polish lottery. Isn't it jolly? The cross was struck in commemoration of the massacres of '61,[7] and has been worn by a Polish woman, until torn from her by the Moscovites. It has a palm branch and crown of thorns, and the word Warsaw engraved on it. The silver medal was made of the spoons, etc., offered by the nation, and was struck in memory of the gifts of land to the peasants. You can imagine how delighted Tussy is with these things and with what pleasure "Joe"[8] will sport them. At home matters are going on smoothly. Quicksands have been carefully avoided and up to this moment we have steered clear of rocks and shallows, and are tranquilly floating along on the glassy ocean. The friends we have seen are Jung, who called on us with his wife, Fox calls every Sunday and is eloquent on the de Staël, Polish, Irish questions and his beloved Feuillants.[9] When he pulls the currency question out of his bag, I can no longer stand it, and take to my heels and run. We see much of the Secretary of Spain.[10] If you fall in with a likeness of Hegel's you will greatly oblige *him* by bringing one with you. A propos, speaking of likenesses, reminds me of your promise to have yours taken — a large *vignette*, you know. I *should so much* like to have one. Laura is much better. Today she is taking a riding-lesson. She sits her horse capitally and looks particularly nice on it. Paul is a "leetle" shaky and sometimes makes free of the horse's mane instead of the reins. These equestrian performances are of course creating quite a sensation at Haverstock Hill — all the neighbours are in a hubbub.

With love and many kisses, I am, my dearest Challey, yours,

JENNY

Laura would like to read Hegel's *Philosophy of History*. Perhaps you could pick it up in Germany.

---

1. Franz Duncker (1822–88), Marx's previous publisher, who had published *A Contribution to the Critique of Political Economy*.

2. Ferdinand Lassalle, a passionate Hegelian and opportunist who had created the new German Social-Democratic movement after the 1848 revolution, had been involved in the German publication of Marx's works. Though Marx was strongly critical of Lassalle he was deeply shaken by his death in a duel in 1864.
3. Wife of the poet Freiligrath, one of Marx's oldest friends. Marx broke off their relationship in 1870 because of Freiligrath's "patriotic odes." (Isaiah Berlin, *Karl Marx*, p. 198)
4. Marx's birthday.
5. *The Condition of the Working Class in England in 1844.*
6. "How weary, stale, flat, and unprofitable" (*Hamlet*, Act I, scene ii).
7. In February 1861 Russian police in Warsaw had charged a Polish Nationalist march, killing and wounding some of the participants. The whole population of Warsaw went into mourning, and sent a petition to the Tsar. The movement for Polish independence, which had many supporters in England, including the IWMA, culminated in a general uprising against Russian rule in 1863. The insurrection was brutally suppressed.
8. Nickname for Jenny, from Louisa May Alcott's *Little Women*.
9. The Feuillants were a club consisting of moderate members of the Jacobins, who met at the Feuillant convent in Paris. They were constitutionalists and moderates. The name as a party designation survived the death of the club (August 1792). The term "beloved" is presumably ironical.
10. Paul Lafargue.

6. Eleanor to Karl Marx

1, Modena Villas
26 April 1867

My dear Dada,

Just as your letter came I was declaring that I thought you never could stay away a whole fortnight without writing, and that I never would forgive you, but my rage began to evaporate amazingly quickly, as soon as your letter was read, and now I am actually writing to you. I have not as I used to do looked in the beds for you, but I constantly sing, "Oh! would I were a bird that I might fly to thee and breathe a loving word to one so dear to me."[1] Paul [Lafargue] has been keeping me in books, he got me Cooper's *Deerslayer, Homeward Bound, Eve Effingham*, and I am going to read the *Watermate* and *Two Admirals*.[2] You see I'm quite "going the hog." We had £5 sent us from the Cape[3] which was a very agreeable surprise. I have not arranged your books yet, but I'm going to tomorrow. "The Knight of the Rueful Countenance"[4] is looking more rueful than ever because his holidays are up next week. On Good Friday I eat [*sic*] 16 hot cross buns, Laura and Jenny eat [*sic*] 8. Louisa and Percy Freiligrath came here the other day and Percy jumped out of the window on the first landing, because I said he could not, and he wrote me that he would jump out again if I asked him to. Tommy, Blackie, and Whisky[5] send their compliments. Paul and Laura have had three riding lessons. Laura looks very nice in her riding habit, and Paul looks a little shakey [*sic*]. The days after the lessons however both were rather *stiff* and I had to make Paul a cushion to rest his bruised behind upon. I was much surprised to receive a letter from Franziska.[6]

Now dear Daddy, goodbye.

Believe me

Your UNdutyful daughter,

ELEANOR

1. From a German seventeenth-century folksong.
2. All novels by James Fenimore Cooper: *The Deerslayer* (1841); *Homeward Bound* (1838); *Eve Effingham* or *Home* (1838, published in the U.S. as *Home as Found*); *The Water Witch* (1831); *The Two Admirals* (1842).
3. One of Marx's sisters, Louise, had married Jan-Carel Juta, a Cape bookseller.
4. Lafargue: a reference to Cervantes's *Don Quixote*, Part 1, ch. 19.
5. Marx family pets.
6. Daughter of Dr. Kugelmann.

After Marx's departure for Germany Paul sent him the following account of developments within the IWMA Council and of the struggles between the various trade unions and the Conservative Government. In 1867, after the so-called Sheffield outrages had sent a shiver down the spine of the middle classes, the Government appointed a Royal Commission of Inquiry to conduct a thorough survey of the whole question of unionism in Britain. The evidence of the union leaders was fully reported by The Times, *whose correspondent wrote scathingly of their "tyrannical spirit" (16 April 1867). In France, too, there was increasing confrontation between the workers and the Government.*

7. Paul Lafargue to Karl Marx

(in French)

[*London, end April 1867*]

My dear Mr. Marx,

So, you were afraid that the house would fall in on you the day you left; that's surely what made you leave so soon rather than waiting for me until the agreed time, for I arrived punctually at our rendezvous; but the cage was empty, you had taken Jenny and Tussy with you. Laura was in the kitchen waiting for me. Not finding you there I wanted at least to shake your hand on the boat: we took a cab and left; when we got to the Thames we realized, though rather late, that your impatience would have prevented you from remaining on the quay. Laura and I consoled ourselves in our disappointment by going for a very long walk.

I have delivered your message to the General Council.[1] The first time I put up your request to the Council they postponed discussion of it until Odger was present; he was written to, but he did not come, did not even condescend to apologize for his absence. At my suggestion we went ahead immediately; Carter[2] assaulted us with three or four long speeches, which had only one drawback, that they were full of endless repetitions, each weaker and feebler than the last. He stood up for Odger as an

Englishman and not as President of the International; I tried desperately, but to no avail, to convey to him that we have to deal not only with Mr. Odger the Englishman but also with Mr. Odger the President of the General Council; but I had about as much chance of getting such a simple fact across to that pompous windbag as of changing lead into gold. When Carter's soporific speeches were finally over, the following resolution was passed, proposed by me and seconded by Lessner. Here is the gist of it: that the General Council firmly repudiates the eulogy of Bismarck expressed by its President. You should feel pleased.

Afterwards we took up another very important matter, the salary of the Secretary. It was Young[3] who raised the matter. It was agreed that we should give him 10s. per week, and that this sum would be provided voluntarily by the members of the Council; we drew up a list on the spot and found that we could raise 14s. When the matter of the money was settled once and for all, there remained the question of finding a Secretary. Shaw[4] offered his resignation, he didn't want to be paid; Fox refused, and Eccarius; very noble of Eccarius, for he is on strike at the moment; and Fox claimed that he should accept because that would enable him to endure the strike more easily. But he refused point blank, adding that in such a matter *humanitarian considerations* should never come into it.

This meant that Shaw was obliged to keep his position as Secretary and to be paid against his will. He wouldn't even take the money when it was thrown down on the table, so I said to him: "Take it and chuck it through the window if you want to."

You must have heard talk of the strikes; it's magnificent. The *Journal des Débats* launched an explosive article against *entente* between workers of different countries.[5] Veuillot, in that journal of his which has recently started up again,[6] thundered against the strike, claiming it to be the *roarings of the socialist lion* and that all decent people should unite under the same flag to charge the monster. The priests would bless the combatants and, like crows, go to drink their blood after the battle; as for M. Veuillot, he'd make a lot of cash repeating the story and singing the praises of this army of God. The modesty of *The Times*, these last few days, has been severely put to the test; may God preserve it from similar trials, they are more than human nature can stand, especially that of the bourgeoisie.

The inquiry into the TRADES UNIONS continues with a great

deal of activity: the LEADERS of the working class are being called in, and are having to undergo an extremely rigorous examination. One of them, Colonny,[7] STONEMASON, claimed that the working class had nothing in common with the interests of capital, and that on the contrary they should fight against it with all their might. Imagine the grousing from *The Times*; but that's not all. Colonny, with a splendid cynicism worthy of the great days, then said that a workman (STONE-MASON) considered it his duty to put one faulty brick into a building or not to do his job properly. I know that conventional morality would find fault with this, he said, but we don't give a fig for morality (WE DON'T CARE). That was going too far, *The Times* devoted an entire article to this remark.[8]

I don't need to give you news of your family, all the world has written to you, but I don't know if anyone has told you that we make a great hue and cry about you, especially Tussy, who seems to need your presence in order to survive at all. I'm glad to hear that your news is good; I wish you every success, both intellectual and financial; but, for God's sake, come back as soon as possible. You'll find enclosed a letter for Moilin;[9] I'm also going to write to him, but I am very grateful to you for having found my friend a patient.

Cordially,

PAUL LAFARGUE

1. At the meeting of the General Council of 16 April Lafargue, acting on Marx's instructions, demanded that a vote of censure be passed against Odger, the President, for his behaviour at a Reform League Council meeting, when he had moved a resolution congratulating Bismarck for achieving full representation in the elections to the North German Reichstag. As Lafargue relates, the General Council repudiated Odger's attitude. However, on 14 May Odger was exonerated after explaining that he had meant simply to thank Bismarck for giving the vote to the people of Germany rather than to approve of his policies in general. See *Documents of the First International*, 1866–68, pages 110–123. Odger resigned from the IWMA in 1871.
2. James Carter, a member of the General Council.
3. Lafargue has translated the name into English: he is referring to Hermann Jung.
4. Robert Shaw, a member of the General Council.
5. *Journal des Débats politiques et littéraires*, 22–23 April 1867. One of the most significant of the French strikes was that of the Barbedienne bronze-workers, whose employers had forbidden them to affiliate with the *Société de Solidarité*. The men called for sympathy strikes by other workers and the General Council sent money raised in England and declared international solidarity. On 24 March the employers were forced to give into the workers' demands.

6. *L'Univers Religieux.*
7. Lafargue means Thomas Connolly, leader of the stonemasons' union.
8. A paragraph in *The Times* of 18 April 1867.
9. Jules-Antoine Moilin, one of Lafargue's professors of medicine, later shot by the Versaillists.

Electoral reform was one of the most contentious po-
litical issues of the 1860s. The following letters from
Jenny and Laura to their father, still in Hanover, re-
fer to the activities of the Reform League, which had
been founded in 1865 with the support of the IWMA.
Its aim was to unite working-class radicals to agitate
for manhood suffrage and the ballot. In 1866–67 the
League held a number of meetings in Hyde Park at
which Edmond Beales, its middle-class President, and
Charles Bradlaugh, a fiery secularist, gave impas-
sioned speeches denouncing the government's inade-
quate proposals.

Jenny and Laura relate the extraordinary cir-
cumstances surrounding one of these Hyde Park meet-
ings. It took place on 6 May, just before the passing
of the Second Reform Act, which nearly doubled the
electorate but still denied two thirds of the population,
including all women, the right to vote. Walpole, the
Conservative Home Secretary, attempted to deny the
League the use of the Park for their meeting but at the
last minute, apparently realizing that he was on un-
certain legal ground, withdrew his opposition. In the
event the meeting passed off peacefully.

8. Jenny to Karl Marx

[London, early May 1867]

My dear Challey,

I am delighted with the photograph. I don't remember ever
having been more agreeably surprised. It is a splendid one —
lifelike. No painter could have put more expression into it. I
am beginning to think the man is no mean artist. I have already framed it, and in doing so, you will be glad to hear, have
"brought out the tone of my mind" — I have surpassed myself.
So, *at last*, dear Mohr, there is some chance of having you here
again. We were *so glad* to hear from you this morning. Your
prolonged silence gave rise to the most unpleasant imaginings.
I feared you might be unwell, or that you had gone to Berlin,

and that Bismarck had paid you more attention than is pleasant, or that you had taken root in Holland. We all thought you had left Hanover long ago, and that was the reason Laura has not written to you.

Here the people are up and stirring. The heat, which is excessive — more than 80 deg. in the shade — has warmed the blood of Beales & Co. For the last fortnight there have been continual skirmishes between the Government and the Reformers, in which the former have been most disgracefully routed. The success of the League is due to Bradlaugh who has behaved throughout with great pluck: at the last sitting of the League,[1] most of the Reformers, believing discretion to be the better part of valour, had thought it wisest to give in. But Bradlaugh, in a warlike speech, declared that if no one else would lead the people to the pack, he alone was ready to do so. While he was speaking, officers arrived from Walpole, with a proclamation to the effect that as the park is kept for the recreation of the people, it is illegal to put it to other uses, in short, that any attempt at holding a meeting would be stopped, the leaders imprisoned and the lookers-on fined. At this old Beales winced ever so little, sneak Connolly was downrightly cowed, Thomas Hughes[2] held forth on moderation — but Bradlaugh overruled them all. This resolution to go in spite of Queen and Government was carried, amidst enthusiastic cheers and throwing up of caps. From that moment a regular panic ran through the "Upper Classes." Fear turned them into perfect low-comedians. Formidable detachments of mounted police, guards, the artillery of Woolwich, special constables (15,000) were put into readiness. *The Times* by turns exhorted, entreated, and called down vengeance on the rioters. The *Standard* grew rabid, the gentle *Star*, ever meek and mild, wept over the danger threatening property.[3] Jeremiahs and Cassandras filled the air with lamentations and dark prophecies. "Woe to Life and Property," "Woe to Property and Life!" was the cry.

Parliament was in the greatest hubbub, Benjamin[4] didn't know whether to laugh or to cry. Walpole tried to do the heroic, Gladstone shilly-shallied — John Bright[5] was the only man and frightened the hysterical women round him into fits.

In the Courts of Westminster there was an incessant waggling of wigs; dry hands untied old parchments, to find out legal quibbles to prove the illegality of political demonstrations

in a park. The patriotic Sergeant Knox[6] declared himself willing to sit on Monday, from eight in the morning until ten in
the evening, to bring the disturbers of Peace to justice. This
devotion to his country was however not put to the test. Before
the ominous 6th of May had arrived, the high-strung nerves
of Walpole gave way, he became lachrymose and gave in;
Beales had his say, all went off merrily as a wedding-feast —
the battle ended in a picnic. King Mab did not play with heads
but with ginger-nuts.[7] And what else could the people do? How
are they to *break* a Government which *bends* like india-rubber.

There were no accidents, one solitary special constable was
roughly handled, and had to take away himself, and his osten-
tatiously displayed staffs, with all possible speed.

The tailors' strike continues.[8] The masters are wild. *The
Times* sings dirges on Free Trade and Free Competition. But I
am running on at an unconscionable length. I had intended
just only to write a few lines to thank you for the very pleasant
surprise of this morning.

In the hope soon to see you,
Believe me, dear Challey,

Your affectionate "JOE"

1. At Sussex Hall, Bouverie Street, on 1 May 1867.
2. Radical MP, Christian Socialist, member of the Commission of Inquiry into
   the Trade Unions.
3. *The Times* reported the row over the meeting very fully, supporting the government's attempts to prevent it and advising its readers (4 May) not to go
   near Hyde Park. The *Standard* (7 May) claimed that the Reform League had
   not much following, whereas the anti-Tory *Star*, in its leader of the same day,
   described the meeting as "great in every respect." All three newspapers accused the government of vacillation.
4. Disraeli, then Chancellor of the Exchequer.
5. Liberal MP and supporter of the Reform League.
6. Alexander Andrew Knox, journalist and police magistrate at Marlborough
   Street from 1862–78.
7. Presumably a reference to Shelley's long poem *Queen Mab* (1813), acclaimed
   by Marx as an inspiration to the Chartist Movement, though the connection
   here remains elusive.
8. The London tailors' strike, affecting about 3,000 people, lasted from April to
   October 1867. The tailors' union was affiliated to the IWMA, and received
   financial support from various branches, including Germany.

9. Laura to Karl Marx

[London] 8 May 1867

My dear Master,

I was much disappointed on the arrival of your letters to my two natural superiors as I had, somehow, expected some lines directed to myself; which expectation, being altogether unjustifiable, please set down to the natural presumption of tailors in general and of a certain tailor in particular. I was also greatly mortified to hear that you supposed my equestrian or any other exercise had kept me from writing to you: the truth is that since the departure of Jenny's letter — of which had I known anything I should have sent some lines with her own — we have been daily in expectation of news from you or of your return, and that whenever I was on the point of writing to you I was dissuaded from my purpose . . .

I am delighted to hear that you have some thoughts of coming home, for at one time I really began to think that you had taken French leave and stolen out of our company for good and all: do you know that you have been away full four weeks now and that you have hardly in all that time given a sign of your existence? But I will not be hard upon you: this is a nice time of the year for flitting, and I am sure there must be something delightful in the mere temporary "riddance" of that conventional "rubbish" one's "family," "Quo-quo's" and tailors[1] and all; to say nothing of the relief you must feel since that incubus, your book, weighs no longer on your shoulders or, at all events, only with such a pressure as is pleasant; to say nothing of the society you are in. There is a certain lady, I have noticed, occupies a large portion of your letters:[2] is she young? is she witty? is she pretty? Do you flirt with her or suffer her to flirt with you? You seem to admire her very much and it would be *trop bête* to suppose all the admiration was on your side. If I were Möhme I should be jealous.

We are having the delightfullest weather: the day of the Reformers' last expedition was a lovely one. This last, by the by, was a great success, or as *The Times* says with a sneer, "a famous victory." The Tories, all along aiming at keeping the people out of the Park, charged them with illegality in their proceedings and only at the last moment discovered that the men who insisted on walking Parkwards were all right and they themselves all wrong. So the people were allowed to walk there, after all due precaution, however, on the part of the Tories, for 5,000 mounted policemen were drawn up and 15,000 special constables (*Mr. Waldeck included*) sworn in for the occasion. So Beales had it all his own way, coming out strong both in his outward man and in that more mysterious Beales within Beales, and Bradlaugh too, as well as all the rest of the Luminaries of the Reform League, shone, it appears, with peculiar brightness, with his own or borrowed light. The mob was as orderly as could be, much to the chagrin of the *special constables* who with their newly-made truncheons "marched up the Park and then marched back again," rather the worse for marching. These particulars I have from hearsay, not from the papers, which Möhme and Joe (who has not it appears given up all ideas of her propagandizing "provincial tour") exclusively monopolize, but I learn enough from the rumours in the air; and from these I gather that the wind sits Bradlaugh-ward: that the *idol-breaker* is the god of the hour.

> *Who of heroes is the last?*
> *'Tis the famed Iconoclast!*
> *In whose favour blows the blast?*
> *His — the bold Iconoclast!*
> *Beales within Beales dwindling fast,*
> *Who remains? Iconoclast!*[3]

News you will not expect from me, for what I have is old news. For my own part, having since your departure nothing to do in "my own peculiar line" and tailordom being on strike, my attention has of late been turned to Cookery, at which I assure you I am now a very respectable hand — being able to turn out a pudding to the public satisfaction — a pudding very palatable and not *very* indigestible.

What with walking and riding this is about all that I have been idling away time with.

Old Morality[4] favoured us last night: as usual he put in his appearance at half-past ten: as usual *"il venait de souper"* but as he was more than *usually* sombre I conclude his better spirits were with his heart and that was — with Sarah.

Madame Lormier[5] has eight cigarettes in keeping for you. We had a gymnastic lesson shortly ago in which the fair Azelia[6] took part, distinguishing herself by feats of great daring and of great dexterity in the lower limits, although as ever a perfect anarchy reigns among the different members of her body. These it seems are unable to come to any kind of understanding: forever unable to adapt themselves each to the other and yet forever bound to keep together.

Your photograph pleased us immensely. I admire especially the eyes and forehead and expression: the first have the true "roguish twinkle" I am so fond of in the original, and this is the only one of your shadows which unites the two expressions of a sarcasm and good nature of the substance: a stranger, I think, would consider only the last but I, who look upon it with a peculiar "bird's-eye" of my own, spy a little maliciousness in the likeness, very pleasant no doubt to your friends but calculated to play the deuce with your enemies. Paul and I fell out on the subject of your picture, for he declared he had never seen you so well arranged and got up — but always (only with one exception) in your frock-coat and with ruffled hair, while I told him that I had seen you *often* in precisely such trim, and that I know you better than he does.

I have said nothing of the Chinese tyrants — the Quo-quos and the Que-ques,[7] for they have spoken for themselves: I have simply wished to recall a certain tailor to your recollection whom in your absence there may be some chance of your forgetting. I hope you will not quarrel with me on the score of the length of this scrawl, but if you are so disposed I am content to forfeit a week's wages to propitiate you.

Goodbye my dearest master,

I am always your affectionate

KAKADOU[8]

I invite you to a "Hampstead tea" on your return — tea and sugar you will of course bring with you, but everything else you shall have in plenty and of the best. If this will not tempt you to come back soon — what will? Wheeler[9] sent back the "I owe you" some days ago thanking for the note received from Engels.

1. Nicknames for Eleanor and Laura respectively. Laura as "tailor" is probably an oblique reference to the tailors' strike.
2. Frau Tenge, wife of a Westphalian landowner and friend of Frau Kugelmann.

3. Laura is alluding to the rift between Beales and Bradlaugh, who sometimes wrote under the name of "Iconoclast." The Reform League was disbanded in the late 1860s.
4. Possibly a reference to Scott's *Old Mortality* (1816), whose hero was a religious fanatic who devoted his life to erecting gravestones for persecuted Covenanters; the identity of the lugubrious friend has not been traced.
5. The Lormiers were family friends of the Marxes.
6. Manning.
7. Jenny.
8. *Kakadu* is German for cockatoo.
9. George Wheeler, member of the executive of the Reform League and of the General Council of the IWMA.

Marx returned to London on 19 May 1867, after spending two more days in Hamburg with his publisher. He left home again almost immediately to stay with Engels in Manchester.

Meanwhile Paul Lafargue's parents had invited the three sisters to spend the summer with them, first in Bordeaux, then in Royan. The clothes and other possessions required for the journey had to be retrieved from pawn, and their tickets were bought with the rent money. They stayed in France from 21 July to 10 September, but we have no letters from them for this period.

In September, while the Second Congress of the International was being held in Lausanne, Volume I of Capital *was published.*

On 2 April 1868 Laura and Paul Lafargue were married, in a civil ceremony. The following letter from Laura was written the next day, on their journey to France, where they were to set up house. They returned to London to celebrate Marx's birthday on 5 May, and Lafargue took his final medical examinations in July. In August they were back again, this time with Paul's parents, for a holiday in Margate, accompanied by Mrs. Marx, Jenny and Eleanor (Marx made a brief appearance late in the month). The Lafargues did not leave London until mid-October.

10. Laura Lafargue to Karl Marx

[Dieppe] Friday 3 April [1868]

My dear Challey,

You will see from this sheet that we did not, as we originally intended, stay at Newhaven but are already installed at Dieppe. The fact is that when we arrived at the former place we could discover in it nothing worth while our passing a day and a half there, which was the period between the arrival of one boat and departure of another. I therefore proposed starting at once for Dieppe, and Paul having no objection, we did so.

We had the loveliest weather for our journey, but although the sea was as smooth as a glass our fellow travellers indulged in the most disgusting fits of sickness, not much to my edification. This part of our adventures is, however, too long to be told you now, so I put it up together with a lot of other anecdotes for my next letter. We fell in with a splendid specimen of a big "adipose" merchant who was taking a day or two for himself, but who could not speak a word of any language but his own (though travelling to and fro from London to Paris for the last twenty years) and was terribly afraid of being imposed upon on the way. The only word he had picked up on his manifold journeys was the word "damp-skipper" which he informed me with much unction was the German for "steam-boat." He thought I was French.

We are at present stopping in an hotel at Dieppe where we have found all we want and rather more than we absolutely want. The weather is beautiful and the place exceedingly pretty.

We shall start for Paris on Saturday morning at 11 o'clock and as soon as we arrive, Paul or I will write to you. I hope you are better, my dear Papa; I am very much afraid the black-coat ceremony you went through on Thursday may have hurt you.

I can't fancy that I have left you all, for good, etc., etc. If I were to speak to you on that subject I should keep you too long.

I am your affectionate tailor

                                        KAKADOU

My love to all: Mama, Jenny, Tussy, Helen and not to forget Engels. Also to Master Whisky, little Santo and Joco, and Blackie and Martha [illegible].

My dear Janey,

I have really too much to tell you for this letter, and as Paul is rather fidgety already, I leave the rest of this sheet for him to fill up.

                    I am your affectionate sister

                                        LAURA LAFARGUE

(in French)

My dear Jenny,
I often think of you, and of the idiotic things we did on our famous journey. I would love to see you and your papa. One day I'll see you again. My wife has already told you all the most interesting things that happened on our journey. Whisper in Engels's ear that we didn't miss the train.

Cordially,
PAUL LAFARGUE

11. Laura Lafargue to Karl Marx

25, rue des Saints-Pères
Paris
26 October 1868

My dear Challey,
As I had a good many letters to write since our arrival at Paris, I put off writing to you the first few days, thinking that my old master would be, of all my correspondents, the most likely to take my silence in good part, and not to grieve overmuch at it. But by this time I am quite ready to have a little epistolary chat with him and hope he will keep one of his ears open for me, but not the deaf one.

Enclosed is the letter you desired. Schily is against taking possession of the copies of your book before having fuller information as to the contract existing between Frank and his successor.[1]

The old gentleman was as usual very amiable, but seems a little nettled at the interruption of your correspondence with him. He is not much brighter than he was six months ago: I rather fancy he has been indulging more than was good for him in domino-playing.

As regards the sending over of our boxes, I am much obliged to Mama for inquiring about the best mode of doing so, but for the present they must remain in London. The fact is, that we may have to stop in our present apartment much longer than we expected, for Paul's prospects with regard to getting his diploma here are as yet quite problematical. In the first place he must have an interview with Duruy[2] and his "sub," to state his desire to work for his diploma in Paris. The permission to do so depends not on the decision of the minister alone but on that of the *Conseil académique*, which does not meet before December. Should this permission be withheld, Paul would have to pass his examinations in some other town of France. Thus, you see, whatever turn things may take, we shall be in the dark respecting them for some time to come. It would therefore, as Paul's father wishes, be absurd to furnish a set of rooms when we might perhaps have to sell our furniture a few months after having bought it.

What news at home? How about the English elections?[3] The French newspapers give no news from abroad except from Spain.[4] The *Univers* is highly amusing in its outbreaks against the revolution there. It denies that it is a popular one, says that Spain is being victimized by ten thieves, and styles Prim[5] *son domestique endimanché*. In its opinion, the most shameful fact of this glorious nineteenth century is the calling of Prim upon Girardin to new-model the country of the Cid, of Ferdinand and Charles the Vth.

And so the shouts of Le Lubez[6] and consorts have ended in the customary *whisper*. I was expecting news to that effect and was very glad that you had allowed them to "let off" their pop-guns unnoticed.

How is everybody at home? I hope the little Sprat[?][7] is quite well again and quite equal to her physiology and the rest of her arduous studies. I wish some good wind would take it into its head to blow you over here: up to the present it has only succeeded in giving me a cold, which, Paul says, is making me very stupid.

And now goodbye, my dear little Mr. Marx (as Evelina[8] says) for today.

I am your affectionate
KAKADOU

1. A reference to Marx's *The Poverty of Philosophy*, published by A. Frank in Brussels and Paris, as a rejoinder to Proudhon's *The Philosophy of Poverty*. In 1865 Frank had sold his business to the publisher F. Vieweg. Marx, anxious to retrieve the ninety-two remaining copies and to sell them with the help of Lafargue and his friends, gave Schily, a German lawyer, power of attorney to deal with the matter.

2. Victor Duruy, historian and minister under the Second Empire, important educational reformer who created the "Ecole des Hautes Etudes."
3. The elections which took place after the passing of the Reform Act, bringing the Liberals to power.
4. Spanish revolution against the reactionary monarchy of Isabella II, which broke out on 18 September 1868.
5. Prim y Prats, Spanish general, Minister of War in the provisional government of 1868, who helped depose Isabella and then suppressed republican uprisings. He was murdered in 1870, just before his own chosen candidate, the Italian Amadeo, Duke of Aosta, was crowned King of Spain. *L'Univers* ran a series of articles, from 20 to 26 October 1868, condemning the revolution.
6. Le Lubez, founder member of the IWMA who had been excluded from the Geneva Congress, accused of conspiracy against other members of the General Council.
7. Eleanor.
8. Manning.

In the autumn of 1868, without telling her parents, Jenny took a job as governess to a Scottish family, the Monroes. She was determined to earn her own keep, though the Monroes turned out to be dilatory in paying her and dubious about her political heritage.

At the end of December the Lafargues moved to an apartment in the rue du Cherche-Midi in Paris, where on 1 January 1869 Laura gave birth to a son, Charles-Etienne, variously known as Schnaps, Schnappy, Fouchtra and Mimi.

For a young radical like Paul Lafargue, the final years of Napoleon III's Empire were an exciting period. As the 1869 elections approached, there was a marked increase in republican activity, one manifestation of which was the rapid development of the International in France. Lafargue, who had intended to retake his medical examinations in Strasbourg to obtain the equivalent of his British degree, now threw himself into political journalism instead. La Renaissance, *referred to in this letter and in Laura's to Jenny of 9 May, was to have been a weekly magazine with both moderate and radical contributors but, like many other similar ventures, it never materialized.*

12. Laura to Jenny

[Paris] 28 February 1869

My dear Jenny,

Your last letter containing all the Hampstead latest intelligence amused me very much and I take the earliest opportunity of replying to it. The Browning's affair is really a very dramatic one and would make a book and sensational drama, containing as it does all the elements of the tragic and the comic. I had already intended writing either to Azelia[1] or to Helena and will do so as soon as possible. But what amused me most was your account of Annette's[2] love-course, which I suppose does not run more smoothly than most people's. Mrs. Walter Hunt that is to be, appears to be in a very despondent state of mind and no wonder, if she intends leading her married life at London. Why doesn't [illeg.] *la bella* come over to Paris *avec son éditeur responsable?* Here there would be some chance of her enjoying herself and of successfully carrying on the pretty mode of existence begun at Hampstead. The French are not like the English, the women here don't think with Annette that their husbands alone have the *right to "pay them attention"*: on the contrary their husbands are sometimes the only men in their world who pay them none. A Frenchman is often enough ashamed of confessing that he loves his wife, a Frenchwoman is never afraid of confessing that she is loved by a host of men, excepting indeed her husband. Mr. Walter Hunt must be an impossible individual if owning only one fourth of the qualities with which his future better half endows him.

Leigh Hunt,[3] his grandfather who made himself a name and got himself locked up in a prison for attacking the Georges early in his life, turned into a most respectable Bourgeois afterwards and I have no doubt that Mr. Walter Hunt will imitate the latter half of his grandfather's existence.

La Renaissance, the new paper which its projectors expect so much from, has not a little trouble in starting itself. The money, about £250 required for the *cautionnement*[4] is nowhere to be had. Moilin, who could give it if he chose and who had gone so far as to positively promising it to Paul, refused at the last moment finding that he couldn't get quite what he wanted for his money. Paul was much exasperated against him, but I am not sorry that he has learnt to know his friend a little better. Tooley[5] had written to Prudhomme[6] too to ask his help in looking for subscribers to the paper, but that little man, whose spirits are as usual *noir sur noir*, replied at once by a definite refusal to do anything for a journal which advocated principles quite opposed to his own and which left *la morale* quite out of the question, the very thing on which he wished to found the new organization of society.

So, up to the present, you see Tooley has not had much chance with his friends. But he has not said "Die" yet and yesterday wrote to Delvoi to ask his assistance. There will be an answer next week, I suppose.

Marion[7] wrote to me some time ago to announce her intended visit to me on the 3rd of March; I sent her word to say I should be very glad to see her, although I was rather amazed at the idea of her coming. I get up for but a very short time every day and as I have been in bed for very nearly three months our rooms are not exactly in apple-pie order. But it can't be helped.

I am very sorry to hear of your catching cold so often. I don't quite understand your being so well and yet ill at the same time. Paul's fellow-students would declare you were a "bird," for according to them, birds are the only creatures who can feel two things and be in two places at one and the same time.

I am greatly disappointed to learn that Papa's *Brumaire*[8] is not to be translated into French. De Paepe's[9] letters seem to have produced a slight revolution in your feelings; I agree with you in admiring his perseverance and his activity, but don't like him the better for not having a chin, but on the contrary, rather the worse.

You appear to be a great favourite with the Monroes,[10] but I shouldn't allow the wife of a lunatic to be so lofty on the subject of education but should take her down a peg or two whenever she declaims on that subject. On the whole you appear to have been pretty fortunate, for the lunatics don't seem to be worse than the common run of people.

I am delighted to hear that you don't stay over your time with them.

Goodbye my dear Jenny, my little Drunkard sends you his love. Give mine to everybody and believe me

Your affectionate sister

LAURA

It is a nuisance that the Mannings bother you so much about the christening of Schnaps, but you know that you can tell them anything you please, that he is going to be a good Protestant and that some one or other of you are his godparents.

By the by, we shall in future address all our letters to Miss H. Demuth and you must direct yours Madame *Santi*.[11]

You will find a brochure of Moilin's, *La Liquidation Sociale*, among the papers sent you. Have a look at it. It wouldn't take you long and requires no great effort of attention or of thought.

Goodbye

L.L.

1. Manning.
2. Annette Baumer, who was later to marry Walter Hunt, grandson of James Henry Leigh Hunt (1784–1859), essayist and poet, editor of the *Examiner*, friend and champion of Shelley, Keats, Byron and others. Annette bore Walter Hunt nine children.
3. In 1813 Leigh Hunt and his brother had been sentenced to two years' imprisonment for their attacks on the Prince Regent.
4. "guarantee."
5. Toole or Tooley were nicknames for Lafargue.
6. Prudhomme was a member of the Bordeaux section of the IWMA.
7. Possibly Marion Rentzsch of South Hampstead College (see p. 14, n. 5).
8. *The Eighteenth Brumaire of Louis-Napoleon*, first published in New York in 1852 in the German journal *Die Revolution*. It appeared in French in *Le Socialiste* in 1891.
9. De Paepe was one of the founders of the Belgian Workers' Party who sought to bring about a reconciliation between the Marxists and the Bakuninists.
10. Variously spelled Monroe, Monro or Munro; standardized to Monroe.
11. A cousin of Paul's mother's who helped Laura run her household.

In the following letter Jenny reports to Paul on the troubled situation in Ireland.

The Fenians, a revolutionary organization dedicated to the overthrow of British rule in Ireland, had staged a brave but unsuccessful uprising in March 1867, with the aid of a militant group of Irish-Americans who had emigrated after the Famine of 1845–50. Marx was sympathetic to the Fenians' objectives but could not wholly approve of their conspiratorial, often violent, tactics. Both Jenny and Eleanor, however, were fervent supporters of the Irish Nationalist movement.

After the Liberal Party's triumphant success in the 1868 elections, Gladstone came to office declaring that his mission was to "pacify Ireland." This he attempted to achieve by severing the connection between the Protestant Church and the State—a major source of discontent given that the overwhelming majority of the population were Catholic peasants — and by securing a fairer relationship between landlord and tenant. The disestablishment and disendowment bill, formally known as the Irish Church Act, had been passed in the House of Commons soon before Jenny's letter; the Land Act, which on paper offered the tenant increased security but still failed to protect him against eviction, was passed the following year.

13. Jenny to Paul Lafargue

[*London, end March 1869*]

My dear Paul,

As you have of your own accord interrupted your *tête-à-tête* by visits right and left, you will pardon me, if for a few moments I draw your attention from private to public affairs: in our little family circle nothing happens worth speaking of (today Papa proposed a fresh leg of mutton for dinner, by way of an excitement, as he said). We live on in the normal way, indifferent to the march of time, even unaffected by the change of seasons

— but fortunately there is a great busy world out of Modena Villas, a world all astir. The Irish question has given a new lease of life to demagogues great and small, to penny-a-liners of all descriptions! Tongues and pens are running a desperate race. *Mais ne craignez rien.* It is not my intention to inflict on you a report of the "words, words, words" of English political costermongers, it is of the conduct of the Irish at this critical moment that I am anxious to give you an account, for no doubt at Paris you have the strangest information respecting it. Of course you have seen from the French papers that the vote for the disendowment of the Irish church was carried in the House of Commons by a majority of sixty,[1] but no doubt those papers have given you a very incorrect notion of the impression made by that event on the Irish, that is, if they have taken their information from the London press. To judge from the articles in *The Times, Star, Standard* all is *couleur de rose* in Ireland, throughout the length and breadth of that happy land there is a feeling of tumultuous joy, the mere vote has proved a sop for the hungry monster discontent, who *now* has nothing to do but to crawl about on all fours in order to catch a ray of sunshine from the luminous body of Royalty.[2]

Irishmen, we are told by special correspondents, are decorating their wretched hovels so that things may look pleasing to royal eyes, are furnishing their rusty harps with strings to prepare a proper accompaniment to the performances on royal light fantastic toes — they are prepared, it is said, ever after the glorious advent of the Queen's son, you know gratitude is one of their chief characteristics, to starve themselves, their wives and children, and fatten sheep and oxen and pigs for their English masters.

This is the English translation and now listen to the Irish original. The following are the words of the Irish leader John Martin:[3] "If, he says, the Prince of Wales is authorized to bear to Ireland any reassuring message from her Majesty or the English Cabinet, with an intention to restore our national rights, then let the Irish people receive him not with cold and silent politeness only . . . If the Prince comes authorized to open the prison doors for every Irishman convicted and suspected of political offence, then let the people cheer him heartily . . ."

Yes, their nationality, an amnesty for their imprisoned countrymen,[4] the Irish are willing to receive at the hands of a

Royal or any other "Jolly Nash" — and that is about the whole extent of their loyalty. Of course I do not mean to deny that great preparations *are* being made for the royal reception. The question is by *whom* are they made? By official corporations, by the Lord Mayor, by worthies elected to their lucrative offices by the English, by householders who have houses to let, by shopkeepers who have goods to sell, by the servile scum that floats on all societies?

On the church question the Irish also have opinions of their own, opinions that do not find their way into English journals. In a capital article, the *Irishman*[5] declares that there are in Ireland other and greater grievances than the endowment of Protestant parsons, and in reply to the phrase now much *en vogue*, that the church is a "badge of conquest" and ought therefore to be removed, it wittily observes: "If it is intended to remove the badge of conquest, what are we to say to the great and grand evil of the conquest itself. Until our independent legislature is restored, we are not only *wearing* the *badge* but *enduring* the *reality* of conquest." Even the *Universal News*, the particular organ of the Catholic party, does not go into ecstasies at this defeat of Protestantism, but simply observes that the removal of the Church will do little for Ireland if the great and overshadowing evil of the land question be allowed to remain as it is.[6] This is an unmistakable sign of the times, a proof that religious fanaticism is dying out — that even in priest-ridden Ireland Gods are shelved when there is serious work to be done. Men are growing out of their childhood, toys no longer attract them, no longer have the power to divert them from the great objects they are determined to attain. (As you are a *Méridional*[7] and rather addicted to the vice of enthusiasm, whatever you may profess to the contrary, I do not mind confessing to you that I have been sufficiently stupid twice to walk to the Red Cap[8] for the sole purpose there to feast my eyes on a placard bearing the inscription "The destruction of the Church is at hand!" You see I have yet much to learn even of imaginative Paddy.)

Gladstone, the *Irishman* treats sarcastically and is rather surprised at the fact that that patriotic statesman should now rush about in frenzied haste to redress in the twinkling of an eye a wrong which has existed for three centuries and against which he never before opened his lips. The case is suspicious and therefore he advises his countrymen to be on their guard and to have no confidence in the Liberal leader, to trust neither Whigs nor Tories, Gladstone nor Disraeli, and to avoid above all things the position of partisans in parliamentary contests of English factions. If the *Irishman* proceeds to say, "we owe a debt of gratitude"—it is not to Gladstone but to Stephens the head centre.[9] Fenians have effected in a few months, that which moral force, agitation, constitutional means, had for years, nay centuries, striven ineffectually to bring about. (A lesson for the Working Classes of England! a proof that Greek fire and a few shots are very useful when applied at the right moment!) Yes, the *Fenians* have forced the most respectable Englishman to tear from that venerable institution the Church, the mystical covering that has protected it for years. Nay they have done more, for the disendowment question leads to the question of vested interests to the desecration of that Holy of Holies — *private property!* Is there to be *no* compensation for those who are losers by the disestablishment of the Church? are vested interests not to be respected? is the shriek ringing out high and clear above all other sounds? Bradlaugh last Sunday at Cleveland Hall gave the best and most popular answer to it I have yet heard. "What," cried he, "when you take from a thief goods, which he has unlawfully acquired, do you give him compensation for the loss he has sustained! The parsons on the contrary should be grateful to us for taking the weight of riches off their shoulders; unencumbered by worldly goods they will slip like eels through the narrow lock which leads to Heaven! . . . [several lines illegible]

But stop. I fear I am taxing your patience — the deciphering of so many pages of my *pattes de mouche*[10] will give you an incurable headache, Worthy Benedict.[11] I pity you and now leave you to pleasanter occupations — and beg you to believe me.

Always affectionately yours

JENNY MARX

Not free yet!

Challey wants me to copy for you the description given in the *Irishman* of Disraeli and Gladstone or others [illegible] to the House of Commons. It is most amusing. I think your "better half" will appreciate it. It is entitled — "The Rivals."

I was as near to Gladstone as the paper on which this is being written. His face was unmistakably the colour of nacre. A black dress coat, and a white tie lent a greater ghostliness to the stolid pallor of his countenance. His head as he left the carriage drooped forwards, as if the weight of the destinies of his party had been superimposed on his shoulders. He went in and Dizzy came. He, Disraeli, had taken a friend's arm. Who that friend was I have not yet discovered. The Premier was cheered but he was also hissed, and I could find in his look or manner none of the trepidation which make his great rival so painfully remarkable. For Benjamin held his head high and walked on to his goal with something like the confidence of Alexander Selkirk,[12] who, as everybody knows, was "monarch of all he surveyed." If none of your readers have seen the man in the flesh, then they have lost a sight. Fancy a placid-faced Jew, with broad nostrils and full luminous eye, a mouth as flexible as india rubber and a great rice-coloured forehead, over which a dyed ringlet hangs carelessly dependent. Then he dresses well, wearing by way of contrast to the remainder of his . . . [letter incomplete]

1. In fact the bill was carried, at its second reading, by 118 votes (368 for, 250 against) at 2.30 A.M. on 24 March 1869, after lengthy and heated debate in the House of Commons.

2. Prince Arthur was to tour Ireland from 5 April to 4 May 1869. He received a mixed welcome and there were violent riots during his visit to Derry in early May.

3. A former Young Irelander who, twenty years earlier, had been briefly deported to Tasmania for seditious activities. Martin was outspoken in his denunciation of the inadequacy of the disestablishment bill.

4. A reference to Fenian prisoners serving terms of penal servitude in English prisons.

5. *The Irishman* was an Irish Nationalist weekly paper. It has proved impossible to trace the extracts referred to in this letter.

6. Probably a reference to the leader of 27 March, though this opinion was frequently expressed by the *Universal News*.

7. "from the Midi."

8. The Mother Red Cap Tavern, situated at a busy crossroads in Camden Town, was well known in Victorian London as an omnibus station and meeting-place.

9. James Stephens, one of the founders of the Fenian movement. The Irish Republican Brotherhood (IRB) was organized on highly ritualistic lines, with "Head Centre" the code for "Chief Executive." Stephens was arrested in 1865 but escaped to America, where he energetically rallied support for a Fenian rising.

10. "scrawl."

11. A reference to *Much Ado About Nothing*.

12. "I am monarch of all I survey": William Cowper, *Verses Supposed to be Written by Alexander Selkirk*. Selkirk was the prototype of Defoe's Robinson Crusoe.

In March Jenny and Eleanor visited the Lafargues in Paris, and in the following letter Eleanor, now fourteen, reports to Mrs. Marx on Laura's first child. Mrs. Marx joined them later; she and Eleanor stayed until mid-May, but Jenny returned to her job on 14 April.

14. Eleanor to Mrs. Marx

47, rue du Cherche-Midi
31 March 1869

My dear Mama,

I would have written yesterday or the day before but that little Turk of a Fouchtra won't let one do anything but nurse him, or if he be asleep in his cradle admire his good looks. No, but really, I've never seen such a lovely child. He has a sweet little face, most beautiful eyes and mouth, the nose too is not so bad as they made it, and his forehead is immense! Just like Papa's.

He is also wonderfully good-tempered, and if he begins to cry, one need only let him suck your finger, or thump his little belly, and he quits in a minute. As to his teeth he really is cutting them; for you can see them quite plainly. I took him into bed with me for two hours this morning, and he behaved beautifully.

We have had very bad weather, but today I think there's a prospect of its clearing up. On Sunday evening we went to the fair of the *pain d'épis* [*sic*].[1] It was very amusing at first, but when we came out of a little theatre, it was snowing dreadfully hard, and the worst of it was we had to walk an immensely long way before we got a cab. On Monday we went to the Gymnase and saw a piece of Sardou entitled *Séraphine*.[2] It is really a very nice piece and was beautifully acted. Yesterday Sassonov came to see Paul. He's wonderfully improved in looks, and is now very handsom [*sic*]. Paul, Jenny, and I also walked about Paris and looked at the shops. But talking about Fouchtra and what we've been doing here I've quite forgotten to tell you about a very queer adventure that happened to us when coming from a station where we changed carriages. It is an adventure worthy of only three persons, "Harry Lorrequer," "Handy Andy,"[3] and "Jenny Marx." We had, as I've already told you, to change carriages, and Jenny, instead of getting into a "Ladies," got into a "smoking" carriage. Presently, of course several gentlemen got in, principally French. They had spectacles for the prevention of sea-sickness! Did you ever hear of such a think [sic]. Our boxes were not opened at all, Jenny was only asked if they were for her own use. Paul and Laura met us at the station. Both look very well. As to Paul I shouldn't have known him again. He has grown a great thick beard, and looks so queer with it, I liked him much better without beard than with. Madame Santi their servant is very amiable though very confused, and rather cracked. Laura was so pleased with the little frocks for Fouchtra, she thought they were beautifully made. Their rooms are very small after ours, but still they are very nice. Their furniture is splendid, though they haven't got the furniture for Paul's room. I hope Helen hasn't forgotten about the *Irishman*.

Now, dear Mama, goodbye. I'm going to nurse Fouchtra, so must finish at once. With thousands of kisses for yourself, Papa, and Helen, and also my other friends.

Believe me to be

Your
ELEANOR

They all send their love to you.

1. *pain d'épice* = gingerbread.
2. *Séraphine* had opened at the Théâtre du Gymnase on 29 December 1868.
3. Heroes of two novels by Irish writers: Charles Lever (*Harry Lorrequer*) and Samuel Lover (*Handy Andy*). See page 8, note 8.

15. Laura to Jenny

47, rue du Cherche-Midi
9 May 1869

My dear Jenny,

I owe you many thanks for your letter: it is really very good of you, having so little time for yourself, to write to us so often.

You will not be angry with me for having been rather slow in replying: I don't know how the time manages to kill itself, but at any rate, I never find much left even for filling a sheet or two with gossip. My poor little Mimi has not been out of doors of late; the vaccinating gave him a little fever, but unfortunately, nothing resulted from the pricking of his little arm and I fear he will have to "undergo a second operation" as Tussy calls it. The little hat that Mama brought him we were all enchanted with: it is just what we wanted, especially for the country where we still hope to spend some weeks. We put it on him, the hat, I mean, the other day and he looks lovely in it, with his queer pantomime stare. I find that he is getting much nicer — I mean in temper not in beauty — since your departure; you know that he was very good while you were here, but now he laughs much more and quite loudly, which is the funniest thing to listen to in the world. He has a sound pair of lungs too, but he doesn't cry more than is good for them.

So much for Mimi: now for Mama. I am very sorry that Möhme should be so much bothered with her hearing during her stay here: it prevents her from enjoying herself. I thought at first that it was simply the effect of a cold, but I begin to fancy now that it is really rather serious. Of course going to the theatre would not give her much pleasure: Paul proposed taking us to the Opéra Comique but Mama says she would prefer a play — something truly Parisian. But you know that what constitutes the "truly Parisian" are the expressions having double meaning, and to catch these you require very acute hearing. I hope, however, that in a day or two, her ear will be better: in the meantime I shall try and get her to see *Vert-Vert*,[1] the new comic opera which has turned half Paris (the feminine half) stark mad. Papoul the "tenorino" sings there, [of] whom you have heard mention here.

I am utterly disgusted at the family-tyrant, Mrs. Monroe's behaviour as regards payment of the services you have rendered her (as Proudhon would say). It is forgetfulness, of course, and nothing more, but it is curious how the owing of debts weakens the best of memories. As for the exploitation practised upon you by the chips of that majestic female block, I hope you will put a stop to it. Why don't they get their august mother to draw up their commercial scrawls for them. Hint to her that by so doing she would keep them eternally under her thumb — even under her little finger. They seem to be a set of blockheads and the

Queen Monroe must not find it an extraordinary task to reign over such a people.

By the bye the *Renaissance* — the late announcement of whose appearance on the 12th was a false alarm — will not be printed until after the elections.

Moilin wrote a letter a day or two ago to invite Paul to call upon him. Paul did so and learned that the great Doctor was holding meetings at his own house; that he had formed a body of adherents to his theories and principles, whom he styles his "partisans," and to crown all, that he was meditating the publication of a journal (an economical one). He had the impudence to ask Paul to contribute to it and also begged of him to procure him editors for his future paper. After his late behaviour to Tooley, I call this rather cool.

He also invited Paul to take part . . . [letter incomplete].

Love to Nicky from all the world and his wife.

1. *Vert-Vert*, with words by Meilhac and Nuitter and music by Offenbach, opened at the Opéra Comique on 10 March 1869.

Almost as soon as she returned from Paris, Eleanor
left for Manchester with her father to stay with
Engels. She was there from 25 May to 14 October
1869, and accompanied Engels and Lizzie Burns,
Engels's lover and housekeeper, on a short visit to
Ireland. Public indignation at the harsh treatment of
Fenian prisoners in English gaols was at its peak, and
Eleanor's sympathies for the Irish Nationalists were
strongly aroused by the demonstrations and the sight
of government troops in the streets.

16. Eleanor and Karl Marx to Jenny

86, Mornington Street
Stockport Rd. [Manchester]
2 June 1869

My dearest Jenny,

We have this minute received your letter, and as you seem
anxious about Papa, I answer you at once. I am happy to tell
you that dear Papa *is* much better, and that I think his arm
will soon be quite well. On Friday, Engels, Papa, Moore,[1] Jollymeier,[2] Mrs. Burns, Mary Ellen[3] and I are going to Yorkshire
to see a friend of Moore's and we're going to stay there from the
Friday to either Sunday evening or Monday morning. Won't it
be jolly?

This evening we're going to Belle Vue to see the fireworks.
Yesterday Mrs. Burns and I went to see the Market, and Mrs.
Burns showed me the stall where Kelly sold pots and the house
where he lived. It was really very amusing and Mrs. B. has been
telling me a great many amusing things about "Kelly and
Daisy",[4] whom Mrs. B. knew quite well, having been to their
house and seen them three or four times a week.

Papa is going home on Tuesday or Wednesday, at least I
think so, but I believe he's going to leave me here a little longer.
Papa's corn had been rather bad so he put a salve on last night
which Mrs. B. made and which both Engels and she declare will
cure any corn. Next time I write I will give you the receipt for
Helen, but I can't today as I want to finish this letter as soon as

possible, so that you get [it] tomorrow morning. I have finished the antimacassar I was making and I've only to put on the fringe now. Poor Lessner! I was so sorry to hear that the poor fellow is going to leave for Brazil. Will he take Nelly with him or leave her with her grandmother? Now dearest Jenny good-bye, for I think Papa wishes to add a few lines. I embrace you all and send you my best love,

So, dear Jenny
Believe me to be
YOUR AFFECTIONATE SISTER

I am glad you like "Willy Reilly." You must read "Rory O'More" too.[5]

My dear Emperor,

The thing under the arm was no carbuncle, but another sort of abscess, which bothered me much but, since yesterday, is quickly healing. It was a fortune I was at Manchester. Otherwise it might have turned out a troublesome affair. I am now quite in good health.

I hope to be with you in the course of next week. Tussy will probably somewhat prolong her stay at Manchester. After the restraint at Paris, she feels here quite at her ease, like a new-fledged bird.

I hope Lessner's departure to Brazil is not yet definitively decided upon. I regret very much being not able to do something for him. With your usual kindness you seem to have sacrificed yourself in the interminable *tête-à-tête* of Sunday last.

As to Lafargue's paper, I feel rather uneasy.[6] On the one hand, I should like to oblige Blanqui. On the other hand, my other occupations will not allow me to do much for them, but, above all things, I fear lest *old* Lafargue should suspect me to push his son to premature political action and making him neglect his professional duties. As it is, he has not much reason to delight in his connection with the Marx family.

And now dear, bye-bye, goodbye, and my compliments to all.

Your retainer
OLD NICK

1. Sam Moore, lawyer, executor and close friend of Engels.
2. "Jollymeier" was the nickname of Carl Schorlemmer, a professor of Chemistry at Manchester University and intimate of Engels.
3. Mary Ellen Burns, Lizzie's niece, nicknamed Pumps.
4. Thomas J. Kelly, a Glaswegian in command of the Fenian troops in Britain and Ireland, and Captain Timothy Deasy (Mrs. Burns pronounced it "Daisy") had been arrested for suspicious behaviour in Manchester in September 1867. The van taking them to Belle Vue Gaol was sprung by a group of Fenians and a police sergeant accidentally killed. The incident led to widespread police persecution of the Irish in Manchester and three men—Allen, Larkin and O'Brien— were executed for their alleged part in the attack. They became known as the Manchester Martyrs.
5. Irish ballads.
6. Marx had been asked to contribute to *La Renaissance*. Blanqui was a revolutionary who believed in violent insurrection by minority groups.

17. Eleanor to Jenny

[*Manchester*] 20 *July* 1869

My dearest little Jenny,

I have just received your nice letter, and though I've been upbraiding myself all the week for not writing to you, I never could summon up courage to sit down and write letters, till now, for I really felt thoroughly ashamed of myself when I saw that you had been so good to write to me, and I was so lazy. One excuse there is for me and that's the confounded heat. On Saturday it was so warm that we, that is Auntie and myself and Sarah,[1] laid down on the floor the whole day drinking beer, claret, etc. Engels, poor fellow, was at a picnic where there were about thirty people, "Periodical ladies" (as Moore says) were there in great quantities and the unfortunate "Lords of the Creation" had to dance attendance on their "inferiors" all day. In the evening when Uncle came home he found Auntie, me, and [Mary] Ellen, who was telling us Irish tales, all lying our full length on the floor, with no stays, no boots, and one petticoat and a cotton dress on, and that was all.

Jollymeier will, we think, be coming home next Saturday. You know he's been in Germany for a month. He came to our house the evening before he went away, and he got so "screwed" that we had to make a bed for him, and he slept there too, for he couldn't get home. Uncle two or three weeks ago treated some of his friends at the wharehouse [*sic*], and came home "as drunk as jelly." Now, my dearest Jenny, I'm sure you'll be astonished to hear me speaking of "Auntie, and Uncle" but you must know that till about a month ago Mrs. Burns, more to tease me than anything else, persisted in calling me "Miss Marx." At last however I would stand it no longer, so we came to an agreement that if I would call her "Auntie" like Mary Ellen, she would call me Tussy. We also made a rule that if anyone did not call me Tussy they were to stand on a chair [and] say Tussy six times, and if I said "Mrs. Burns" I had to say "Auntie." The evening they had all called me "Miss Marx," so I made Auntie, and Moore, and Jollymeier and Sarah all stand in a row and say Tussy twenty-four times. As to calling Engels "Uncle," I've got into the habit of doing that through hearing Mary Ellen call him so.

You say, my darling Jenny, that I've forgotten you. You may be sure, *acushla machree*,[2] that I won't do this. In fact I talk about you so much that they all want to have you over here. Now dear, goodbye. Enjoy yourself as much as you can at Eastbourne.

Believe me to be

Your loving sister

TUSSY

How well you manage with the Monroes. Auntie sends you her best love, and so does Uncle.

The Prince and Princess of Wales go through Manchester tomorrow. We're going to see them. What fun if a lot of children sing "The Prince of Wales in Belle Vue jail/For robbing a man of a pint of ale." Its a song that's sung very much here so perhaps they will. Belle Vue is the large jail here.

1. Sarah Parker, Engels's maid.
2. "dearest heart" (Gaelic).

PART TWO

October 1869 – May 1871

Death of an Empire

ALMOST ALL THE LETTERS in this part are concerned with the political upheaval which took place in France in the early 1870s: the Franco-Prussian War, the collapse of the Second Empire, and the Paris Commune. Most of the letters are from Paul and Laura Lafargue, who were living in France throughout the period, and they provide a useful commentary on these historic events. Domestically, they document the early days of Laura's marriage, the pleasure she took in her children countered by the unfamiliar and unwelcome burden of household responsibilities; and in spite of her very real commitment to radical republicanism, they reveal some interestingly bourgeois characteristics, such as her disapproval of singing as a profession. We hear little of either Eleanor or of Jenny, who was still working as a governess.

In July 1870 Engels left the Manchester textile firm of Ermen and Engels, and moved to London, not far from the Marxes. From now on he was able to devote himself to his own work and to assure the financial stability of the Marx family. He and the Lafargues kept up a continuous correspondence until his death, and he sent them money almost whenever they asked for it.

During this period Paul Lafargue was working as a political journalist; with Guesde, he was to become one of the leaders of the French Workers' Movement. He had moved away from Proudhonism and was now aligned with Marx in opposing the threat to the internal coherence of the International posed by Bakunin's influence.

After a holiday in London in October 1869, the La-
fargues returned home to find Paris in a state of great
unrest. Public disenchantment with Napoleon III's in-
effective government had been reflected in the over-
whelming successes of the opposition in the May elec-
tions, when about thirty Republicans were elected.
Many workers were on strike, and the opening meet-
ing of the new legislature, originally scheduled for 26
October, was postponed until 29 November.

18. Laura to Jenny

[*Paris*] *Monday*
25 October [*1869*]

My dear Jenny,

You must not grumble at my laziness: I should have written at
once to you had I found time to do so. But what with Schnappy
and the things to set to rights in our apartment which we had
left behind us not exactly in apple-pie order, I have been very
busy during the last week.

I had intended giving you some account of our new acquaintance, M. Keller,[1] and had told Paul to choose other subjects for his letter: he said he would do so but on looking through
his epistle I find that he has said all that is possible after a
single visit and I shall spare you therefore a repetition of what
you know.

Since our return to Paris I have scarcely been out of doors,
so I have nothing to tell you about Paris seen in the streets: as
regards the newspapers you have them in London and must
have seen all about the fuss made with the manifestation intended to be got up on the 26th and then given over again at the
last minute.[2] You have seen I suppose Raspail's letter:[3] it is
rather long, isn't it? Poor fellow, he has got himself into a dirty
place and must feel ill-at-ease in the chambers in the midst of
des honorables and *des irréconciliables*.[4] There have been some
réunions privées of late in which the Favres and Pelletans and
Bancels* have been putting their foot pretty deeply into it: they

* For brief descriptions of these and other political figures, particularly in this
section, the List of Names on pages 313–328 should be consulted.

57

are becoming more and more *maladroits*, these members of the *Gauche*. Jules Simon[5] appears to smell a rat and shows himself *un peu moins doux que d'habitude*.

You have heard about the STRIKE of the employés.[6] It is greatly talked about here.

My little Schnaps is getting on famously: Hampstead appears to have done him an immense deal of good. He has never been better or merrier. He is becoming so lively and restless that Paul is obliged to tie him down in his cradle to prevent some "horrible" accident, and the little chair he sits on will have to be screwed down into the floor if he is to go on using it. He is becoming really amusing. At present he lets himself be played with and tossed about for hours.

I am looking forward for news from you — about your doings at the Monroes. Let me know whether you have made any fresh conquests either of old maiden ladies or of young Irishmen. Thank Mama from me for her letter.

My love to everybody, great and small, and I hope to see some one or other of you in the spring.

I am, dear Jenny,

Your affectionate sister

LAURA

Tell Helen that I don't see much prospect just yet for her gold brooch — but don't let her fancy that we have given up trying for it. Good gracious, it would be throwing one's fortune to the winds.

Will you please send me Caroline Schmalhausen's[7] — Smith's I mean — address. She announced her marriage to us. I must write to her.

1. Charles Keller was the French translator of the first volume of *Capital,* but never completed it. A translation by Joseph Roy was eventually published by Lachâtre in 1872.
2. The Deputies of the Left appealed to the workers to join them in a mass demonstration on the 26th; however, they abstained overwhelmingly and the demonstration was a failure.
3. François Raspail, a naturalist and popular advocate of self-medication, who had taken part in the 1848 revolution, was the only Deputy among the bourgeois republican opposition to protest at the illegal deferral of the opening of the new legislature.
4. "Honorables": derisive name for the Deputies. "Irréconciliables": Republicans who refused any compromise with the Empire.

5. Jules Simon was a moderate republican member of the Legislature Assembly who later became the first Minister of Education in the Third Republic.
6. Strike of the Paris clerical workers. The IWMA strongly supported the strikers of 1869 and gained many recruits during this period.
7. Marx's niece, daughter of his sister Sophie.

Early in January Laura gave birth to a daughter, Jenny, known as Schnapine or Maigriotte, who survived less than two months.

19. Paul Lafargue to Jenny
(in French)

[*Paris*] *9 January 1870*

My dear Jenny,

I see that you have found the use of your fingers again; that's good, but I'm annoyed that it's taken Schnapine's arrival to inspire this fondness for letters — though not for writing them. However, I shouldn't really make an issue of it as I too have a bad conscience.

Reassure Helen and all the other members of the family about Schnapine; although she's thin, her body has a devil of a lot of life in it. This reveals itself in piercing cries whenever her stomach is seized by hunger that isn't satisfied immediately: since she was born she's done only two things — drink and sleep — she drinks in order to sleep and sleeps in order to drink. Which is not to say that she doesn't fulfil her other functions: and one extraordinary thing is that ever since her birth she has had absolutely no sign of colic. This drives the midwife into a fury — like all midwives she has nurses to place, and wanted to foist one on us. I told her that if the child didn't take to cow's milk I would bring over a nurse from London; that shut her up; at which point she started to niggle at me about her food — you must give her this and that; give her gruel, make her a little pomade, it acts as a lining for the stomach. I put cotton in my ears and steel in my determination, I am firmer than a rock: and since the child is doing excellently and is *picking up again*, I can congratulate myself on my firm resolve. Laura is much better this time than last; I think that in a few days she will be able to leave her room, an event that I await very impatiently.

You can see how busy we are, I have an invalid and two helpless creatures to care for; and I must say, to Schnaps' disgrace, that it's he who gives me the most trouble of the three. However, for some time now he has been as nice and as well-behaved as can be; and he's getting disgustingly fat, he'll soon be a good little pig for market. I tell you all this so that you can make my excuses to Mme. Lormier, if I haven't written to give her the good news. How pleased she will be, she who dreams of daughters and is so disdainful of sons. Tell her too that we enormously appreciate her offer, which was all the more attractive because of the easy terms of payment; but I don't want to go into this area — I do intend to write to her about it.

Thank Helen for the five francs, tell her that at the moment we are rich, but that we will call on her if we need to in a few months, when we move house. We are expecting to leave our rue du Cherche-Midi some time in April. I'm going to start looking for a little house with a garden; I think I should be able to find one . . .

My love to all; cordially,

P. L.

Though often ill, and clearly oppressed by her domestic duties, Laura kept up her reports to Jenny on the political situation in Paris. Paul was now involved with La Marseillaise, *a weekly journal founded by Blanquists which was violently opposed to the Second Empire and opened its columns to the members of the International. In April 1870* La Marseillaise *published a series of articles by Jenny, signing herself Williams, on Ireland. According to Laura's letter of 20 March Jenny appears to have had more success with the journal than Paul.*

20. Laura to Jenny

[*Paris*] *9 February 1870*

My dear Jenny,

I was delighted to hear that poor Challey was better and I thank you for your letter announcing his recovery.[1] Since I heard from you last I have been a good deal occupied by the babies, etc., or you would have received a letter from me before this. I have been catching cold, have had a swollen throat, have been shut up anew indoors which imprisonment I am beginning to get a little tired of. However, I hope to be set free one of these days . . .

M. Schnaps et Mdlle. Schnapine have just struck up their last new duet: I fancy it might be somewhat more harmonious; it is true that if their music were all that is pretty and melodious I should probably pay less attention to it than as it is, and the confounded little brats seem to think so.

I have sent Schnaps out for a walk with Madame Santi and have given my little Maigriotte a bottleful of milk which she is falling asleep over. So I can go on with my letter.

Paris is in a state of more than usual excitement today: Rochefort having been shut up at Ste. Pélagie[2] yesterday. All the editors of the *Marseillaise* have been seized or will be: the paper, in consequence, has not appeared today. Last night there was a good deal of commotion in the workingmen's quarters: barricades or something of the kind were erected in a number of streets. I don't know how far the riots will go this time, but what surprises me is that none really serious have broken out before this. Since June last, the people have been kept in a continual state of excitement; the government, represented for the moment by the spectacled Judas Ollivier,[3] commits blunder upon blunder and provokes mutiny; you have read Paul de Cassagnac's *Excitations à la révolte*.[4] Victor Noir's assassination and the partial treatment of his murderer gave a fresh impulse to the agitation and resentment of the *charognes*,[5] as they now call themselves. The *réunions publics* held in all quarters of Paris entertain and stimulate the movement.

The *gamins de Paris* last night, as they generally are, I believe, were the first to set to work at forming *barricades:* the women since Noir's death and Ollivier's success are enraged against the emperor: if you read the list of subscriptions for Noir's monument you will see how *exaltées* they are and what part they take in the affair. Some of the signatures are curious and some of course ridiculous. Enough.

You will receive the papers together with these lines: from them you will learn all that we know up to the present.

How are you all? So Challey [is] quite well again and is Helen all right by this time?

Paul assisted at Diafo[i]rus's[6] meeting on Monday last: the learned Dr. seems to do with his thirty men pretty much as he likes by this time. He imposes upon his audience, it appears, by his vast learning and by his huge bell which he agitates at the slightest tumult.

I don't know whether I have told you that Madame Paule Mink, the lady orator at many of the popular meetings here, has called upon us once or twice. She is a very simple and amiable and I believe, intelligent person but very tiresome when she happens to stumble upon *"les devoirs" des femmes*. I suppose you saw her *mouches et araignées*[7] which for my part I *don't* much admire, apart [from] the *intention* of the paper which is excellent. Paul has called upon her once or twice and likes her very much.

We see Sassonov now and then: he is a good deal indebted and about to draw for the conscription.

Keller we have heard nothing of lately: Paul not having been to see him since some time. Probably he is busy as usual in making all sorts of propaganda, from Atheism and woman's emancipation down to gymnastics, in favour of which exercise he battles bravely.

I should be glad to know how he gets on with Challey's book. He is enthusiastic in praise of the *Brumaire*. Unfortunately I have had to sacrifice my copy and my ex-master seems not to intend sending me another.

The other night Paul and I cracked a bottle of champagne — my Christmas bottle — and we drank to Challey's speedy recovery and to all your healths. I hope you all felt the good effects of our health-drinking.

My little Maigriotte is getting on very well, she is not quite so good and quiet since two or three days as formerly but is getting fatter. Schnaps is growing into a charming little fellow, it is impossible to give you an idea of his thousand pretty tricks and ways: nothing is funnier than to see him lay hold of Maigriotte's head, he strokes and caresses her face, takes hold of her nose and plays with her hands and feet. He is a little afraid of her and is half-inclined to cry when she cries: he looks at us to see what he must do and when he catches us laughing he bursts out into laughter himself and shouts and crows. He is an amusing and good little chap.

We shall move in July; before, if we find an apartment or house empty. Paul wishes to go to Neuilly as we should find a garden easily and as we should economize in all sorts of ways there. Neuilly is outside Paris, which prevents my being altogether delighted at the idea. However, we shall see.

I have no more room and so bid you goodbye in the hope of speedy news from home.

I am, dear Jenny,

Your very affectionate

LAURA

Paul sends you *L'Homme sauvage*,[8] he *said* in order to confirm [you] in your theory on the power of the will.

1. Marx had been suffering from an abscess and glandular inflammation.
2. One of the editors of the *Marseillaise*, Paschal Grousset, had challenged Prince Pierre-Napoleon Bonaparte, the Emperor's cousin, to a duel after being slandered by the Prince. Victor Noir, a colleague, was chosen as Grousset's second, but was killed by the Prince on a visit to his house. After this incident Henri de Rochefort, famous for his radical paper *La Lanterne* and now editor-in-chief of

the *Marseillaise*, was sentenced to six months' imprisonment for an article on the assassination. On 8 February 1870 he was arrested and sent to Sainte-Pélagie prison.
3. Emile Ollivier, a former opponent of the Empire, described as Judas because of his acceptance of Napoleon III's request that he lead a new Ministry which would answer to both parliament and the Empire.
4. Cassagnac, leader-writer on *Le Pays*, who accused Rochefort and his friends of provocative behaviour, especially at the demonstration at Noir's funeral.
5. lit., "decaying carcasses or corpses," also used figuratively to mean "scoundrels."
6. Dr. Moilin.
7. Paule Mink edited a newspaper called *Les Mouches et les Araignées*.
8. Possibly a reference to *L'Homme sauvage et l'homme civilisé* by Cleri Malège (1864); many works on this theme appeared in the 1860s.

21. Laura to Jenny

47, rue du Cherche-Midi
20 March 1870

My dear Jenny,

I hope you are not angry with me for my past silence, for I have no excuse to give you except that I was too much knocked up by the death of my poor little Jeannie to think of writing or reading.

I must congratulate you upon your letters to the *Marseillaise*. You may flatter yourself on your success, for I assure you that not everybody is so favoured as yourself in his communications with that paper. In case you should discover something of hyper-criticism in Tooley's note to you, attribute it to nothing else than an *amour-propre d'auteur qui a été un peu froissé*[1] by a series of disasters. During the incarceration of the editors of the *Marseillaise*, Paul, you must know, made several attempts at getting hold of that journal; but never to any purpose. Dubosc, the individual who was regent of the *Marseillaise* for a time, received Tooley, every time that he called at the office with an article, with open arms and the usual dose of French enthusiasm. Paul was his best friend; after having seen him for a couple of minutes Dubosc was his sworn friend and brother — ready to give his life for him, or if that was unnecessary ready at any rate to wash as much of his *linge sale*[2] as he wished in his company. He pronounced Paul's productions to be first-rate and promised that whatever article he might bring would be inserted.

No single line, as you may imagine, ever made its appearance: Paul ran to and from the office of the paper to no other purpose than the destruction of his boots. Jaclard, Regnard and other friends of Paul's met with the same treatment at this gentleman's hands. On the return of some of the editors it turned out that M. Dubosc was a very suspicious *personnage*, having been in the pay of the *Gauche* and installed in the enemy's camp with a view to turn the paper of the *sainte canaille*[3] into a publication *honnête et modérée*. Since the restoration of the *Marseillaise* into the hands of its rightful editors, Tooley, I am sorry to say, has fared no better: and the attempts of several of his friends to write in it have been unsuccessful.

You see from what I have said that you are favoured by the staff of the *Marseillaise*. The question treated in your letters is really of the greatest importance: not a paper gives the least attention to English affairs, or if they do so, it is to represent England like an Eldorado and English laws and customs *comme tout ce qu'il y a de mieux dans le meilleur des mondes possibles*.[4] The *Marseillaise* itself, for a time, used England as a foil to show off the deformity of France. It is a good thing — especially as the Gladstonians seem to fear the opinion of their French neighbours — to show the Parisians that there is no more difference between the two governments than twixt Tweedle-dum and Tweedle-dee.[5] The letters from Mod[ena] Vil[las] are first-rate in every respect.

Paul is very busy since some weeks. He is writing a series of articles on Victor Hugo[6] and as he is obliged to re-read the greater part of his works as well as to consult a number of books in order to get into the secret of the political career *de cet homme immense*, it will take some time to get through with his biography.

Paul begs of you to send him Hugo's pamphlet on *Napoléon le Petit*[7] under cover of some paper or other. No doubt it is easily to be found at London; here it cannot be had.

The weather continues to be atrocious. I caught such a cold by changing my linsey[8] for my black silk dress that I completely lost my voice for two or three days. At present, I am all right again. Schnappy, who has spent a great part of the winter indoors, takes his "constitutionals" again and is as gay as ever.

It is no use trying to give you an idea of his numberless tricks; he is a regular little monkey and mimes every sound one utters, and every movement one makes. We bought him a "chariot" the other day, which enchants him, for as he is very fond of being his own Cromwell he does not like to be in leading-strings but prefers fancying that he leads while he is being led. His chariot encourages this *douce illusion*, which he shares with a good many persons.

*   *   *

I must ask you to give my best thanks to Challey and Mama for their letters, which it was very kind of them to send me. Schnappy will write to Tussy shortly. He has not quite forgiven her yet for leaving his letter so long unanswered.

I am, dear Jenny, with love to all,

Your very affectionate sister

LAURA

1. "self-esteem of an author who has been a little ruffled."
2. "dirty linen."
3. "riff-raff."
4. "as all that is best in the best of all possible worlds"; a reference to Voltaire's *Candide*.
5. i.e., between the Conservatives and the Liberals. The Liberal Party, led by Gladstone, remained in power until 1874.
6. Hugo was violently opposed to Napoleon III and had been in exile in Jersey since 1852; it was there that he wrote his epic satire against Napoleon, *Les Châtiments*. Paul later revised his opinion of Hugo and attacked him in print.
7. *Napoléon le Petit* (1852) was written in Brussels after Hugo's escape from Paris.
8. woollen-mixture dress.

As the number of strikes multiplied and the atmosphere in Paris became increasingly militant, the French federation of the International began to be identified with the revolutionary opposition to the Second Empire. Because of its support for some of the large strikes, thousands of working men throughout the country joined the organization, and the authorities came to believe that it posed a serious political threat.

On 8 May the Government, concerned at the upsurge of opposition, held a cleverly worded referendum. The electorate was asked to support the few measures of political reform which suggested that the Empire was moving in a more liberal direction, and a negative vote or abstention was tantamount to a rejection of this tendency. The referendum was a triumph for Napoleon III; only in the cities were there any real signs of opposition. With new confidence the Government engaged in a fresh wave of repression against the International.

22. Laura to Jenny

[Paris] Thursday 9 June 1870

My dear Jenny,

I have not been able to find time to write to you for the last few weeks. Schnaps takes up the whole morning and during the daytime we have of late been doing the wandering Jew's business. I don't know how many times we have been down to Levallois — the place we are about to move to — looking for a house. We have had some half-dozen apartments and cottages in view but up to the present had been always prevented by some reason or other from fixing upon one. At last we are going to settle down in a little house — very pretty but unfortunately very nearly garden-less. There is a small plot before the house — big enough for Schnaps — but that is all. Luckily the house is very well situated — there is an open space planted with trees just in front. The little man will be able to make as good use of it as if it were our private property.

We had discovered many other cottages with large and

most beautiful gardens — some of them containing trees covered with apricots and cherries that made one's mouth water, but these cottages were so lonely — in such out-of-the-way places — that we could not think of taking them. Thieves and house-breakers are driving a terrible trade just now in the *faubourgs* of Paris and as Paul very frequently comes home late at night we might have had to pay very dearly for our fruits and flowers. We have therefore given up the idea of having a large garden — not without some regret, as you may suppose.

I was exceedingly surprised at the news you gave us in your last letter. Furtardo is not at all the man I took him for.[1] It is a thousand pities that you cannot profit by his lessons. But the profession of singer — even of the Pattis and the Nilssons[2] — seems to me a very disagreable one. The actor's is far preferable, when it is not precisely money that one works for, although in both cases the boards are equally sure to make one acquainted with rather nasty company. Did you receive the papers we sent you? What did you think of the *Figaro* hoax?[3] Hundreds of persons throughout the whole of France were made fools of, and were dumbfounded on discovery of the sham. The writers of the *Marseillaise* were furious; Paul says *"qu'ils riaient jaune."* *Hugo, lui, a dû rire vert, tellement on a ri de ses vers.*[4]

Talking of the *Marseillaise*, as you are one of its correspondents, I suppose you take some interest in its existence behind the scenes. An immense split is about to take place between the different editors. Most of these are friends of Rochefort's and patronized by him, but Rochefort himself — although *rédacteur en chef* — is completely under the thumb — lantern and all[5] — of Millière.[6] This latter *est l'homme sérieux du journal* — Rochefort's schoolmaster, who deals out good or bad marks to his pupil. *Le petit Henri*, like a lazy scholar, is a good deal afraid of the rod and dreads being put into the stocks. But when Millière's back is once turned, the schoolboy cuts grimaces and makes fun of his master. He asks everybody he sees, *"Dites-donc, est-ce que vous lisez Millière, vous? Moi, je ne le peux pas, cela m'est impossible. Mais c'est dans les campagnes qu'il est aimé; si vous saviez combien il est lu et apprécié dans les campagnes!"*[7] Now, this same Millière has a grudge against one half of the writers of the *Marseillaise* and is going to turn them out — and not in the most delicate manner of the world. As all these poor fellows write for their living, you can imagine the state they are in. Millière is of course hated: Rochefort is liked but not being king in his own kingdom, his friendship is little worth. At any rate the paper will undergo considerable changes on its reappearance.

The *Libre Pensée* will most probably be converted into a political paper, appearing three times a week and calling itself *L'Egalitaire*.[8] Paul is, as you may believe, delighted; he and Jaclard have been dreaming of nothing else for months past. *Il est si bon de pouvoir placer sa prose quelque part*[9] — especially when one happens to be as voluminous a writer as Tooley! I am very glad of the fact, for the paper will be a fresh trumpeter of the International and one can't trumpet too much in so good a cause.

I think I spoke to you about Jaclard's Russian Lady. At present they are M. and Mme. Jaclard.[10] She is an authoress and is well known, it appears, in Russia. Paul has met her frequently at the library and takes great interest in her. Formerly, you know, Tooley would hear nothing of women out of the kitchen and the ballroom: at present he prefers seeing them in the readingroom. He is a little changeable in his tastes and his opinions, but as he generally only changes for the better *il n'y a rien à dire*.

I have not seen Mme. Jaclard, and am less curious to see her since I have heard that she smokes. I don't like women who like cigars. Have you received the visit of M. Rothschild?[11] Fancy my surprise some days ago, to see a great, bearded fellow stalk into our room, asking for Mme. Lafargue! I thought who the devil can this illustrious stranger be. He was dressed out very smartly, while Paul and I were as usual considerably more shabby than genteel. My astonishment increased every moment, when he addressed me in German and as if he had known me some twenty years. I told him that I really hadn't the pleasure to remember who he was. He gave his name, Rothschild, and at once a vision of the grand ball of the International dawned upon me, where I remembered having seen a similar pair of long legs. He is a very friendly fellow and rather handsome, *mais par trop Juif*.[12]

Schnaps is growing into the most affectionate child I ever saw. He kisses us all day long. He will be a great favourite of yours, for you have a predilection for boys who are a little *gnognotte*.[13]

Many thanks for Challey's and Mama's letters. I am glad

to have the list of books Challey sent us as I should like to know something about the French peasants, etc., etc. I cannot go on, having filled up my paper and supposing into the bargain that you have had enough.

We move on Monday or Tuesday — so we shall be up to the eyes in dust and work for some time.

I am, dear Jenny, very affectionately yours

LAURA LAFARGUE

Do write soon. I look forward to nothing with so much pleasure as letters from Mod[ena] Villas.

Notre adresse — 7 Place de la Reine Hortense, à Levallois-Perret — près Paris.

1. Furtardo was presumably a singer from whom Jenny had been expecting to receive coaching.
2. Two famous singers: Adelina Patti (1843–1919) and Christine Nilsson (1843–1921).
3. On 8 June the reactionary daily *Le Figaro* announced that it had been sold, for a huge sum, to the Republican party. The whole edition was a spoof, with fake letters from leading Republicans and even a verse signed "Victor Hugo."
4. "that they laughed on the other sides of their faces. Hugo must have laughed hardest, given how much people laughed at 'his' verse."
5. A reference to Rochefort's satirical paper *La Lanterne*.
6. Jean-Baptiste Millière, radical lawyer and journalist.
7. "Tell me, are *you* reading Millière? *I* can't read it, I just can't get through it. But he's much loved in the provinces; if you knew how much they read and appreciate him in the provinces!"
8. This never happened.
9. "It is so good to be able to place one's work somewhere."
10. Mme. Jaclard = Anna Korvin-Krukovskaya (1844–87), a general's daughter who, after refusing an offer of marriage from Dostoevsky, travelled to Paris where she met and married Jaclard, a member of the IWMA.
11. Probably Baron Alphonse de Rothschild (1827–1905), an art patron and head of the Parisian branch of the banking family, who was to play a major part in raising the indemnity to Bismarck after the Franco-Prussian War.
12. "but altogether too Jewish."
13. "soft."

23. Paul Lafargue to Karl Marx
(in French)

[*July*] *1870*

My dear Mr. Marx,

Your philosophical mind must have made it easy for you to discover the reason why I have not yet replied to your letter, so full of useful information for which Paul and Laurent offer their sincere thanks.

For the past week we have been deep in dust, in boxes, in linen, and in God knows what else besides! — but we are beginning to emerge from the midst of this hubbub and one of the first *altruistic* tasks in which I'm indulging myself is to write to you. (The word *altruistic* will show you that I am involved with positivism at the moment.)[1] We have been very appreciative of the altruistic concern that you have for us with regard to the smallpox. If we haven't had a more intimate acquaintance with this delightful malady it's through no fault of circumstance, for we were living in a very hotbed of infection. The rue de Sèvres, which is parallel to ours and only a few metres away, was full of people who'd died from smallpox, who were ill with smallpox, who were in the process of catching smallpox, or who were living in hopes of its appearance. Now we have got out, and we are in a little road which opens out on to the fortifications, near the Boulevard de Neuilly, with a beautiful garden 110 metres square. We leave M. Schnaps in the garden all day long, as if he were a little horse. You cannot imagine the change that's come about in the little chap these last few days: he's tubby, fat, he bustles about like a sliced worm, he rushes into the water, flounders around in the dust, licks the earth, squashes the cherries, grinds them into the dust and then eats the whole lot afterwards. Throughout all these more or less unsavoury exercises, which he enjoys enormously, he accompanies himself with chants and cries, each one more delightful than the last. Ta ta, mama, baba, gragra — kaka, gaga, maniloula, *à r'voir, à boire, nanan!* etc.

Toole and Madame Toole, dressed in very simple, unaffected clothing, smile beatifically at Schnaps's prodigious behaviour (collecting pebbles and washing them with his saliva). If this admiration for their offspring continues I believe that Paul and Laurent's partnership will become stronger every day, for the silliness which acts as the connecting link in their union will become so great that all corrosives, social or otherwise, will be powerless to dissolve it.

The other day Keller,[2] the young man with the red beard, came to the house accompanied by a young man with a fair beard, of Russian origin and by the name of Lopatin; like most Russians he had a great admiration for you and was exceedingly anxious to see you, to reassure himself that you didn't have some abnormal appendage, like those sylvan ancestors of mine to whom Considérant[3] wanted to make us return. Moreover, it seems that the youth of Russia had charged him with conveying their admiration for you if ever he happened to meet you. I had no alternative but to give him your address and a word of introduction. I know that you don't like being on show, so my letter is of minimal length. You should lay the blame on your great admirer Keller, who would be quite capable of cutting you up into small pieces in order to give a little bit of you to everyone. That's more or less what he did in *Le Socialiste*, the journal of the Paris federation [of the International] — you must have seen it — in which he has translated an extract of your book in the clumsiest possible manner.

Thank Jenny for her charming letter, and Mrs. Marx too. All good wishes. Affectionately,

P. LAFARGUE

P.S. from Laura (in English):
Kisses from Schnaps and myself, hoping you are all right again.

KAKADOU 1ST

1. Positivism was a "Religion of Humanity," extremely influential during this period through the work of Auguste Comte and others, which was based on the application to politics of "scientific" methods derived from the study of history and human behaviour. Lafargue is referring to its belief in the supremacy of altruism over egotism as the logical outcome of man's intellectual progress.
2. See page 58, note 1.
3. Victor Considérant was a follower of Rousseau who took over from Charles Fourier as leader of the "phalanstery," a group of industrial-agricultural "communes." Considérant's *Principe du socialisme* (1847), which dealt with the exploitation of the industrial working classes, may have influenced Marx.

*On 19 July 1870 the Second Empire, increasingly
humiliated by Bismarck's high-handed attitude to
France and goaded by public opinion, declared war
on Prussia. France was without allies or a properly
organized military force and had little chance of victory from the outset. Prussia quickly took the offensive
and after a series of defeats Napoleon III, trapped at
Sedan, surrendered on 1 September.*

*Three days later the Republic was proclaimed.
The Paris Deputies formed a provisional government
known as the Government of National Defence, with
General Trochu as its President and including both
moderate Republicans such as Jules Simon and young
radicals like Léon Gambetta.*

*Much to the relief of the Marx parents, who had
been trying to persuade them for some time of the
dangers of remaining in the capital, the Lafargues
left Paris for Paul's parents' house in Bordeaux just
two weeks before Paris was surrounded by Prussian
troops on 18 September. The following letter, written
before the fall of the Empire, reveals the Lafargues'
disappointment at the apathy of the Parisian workers
and at the superficial* ambiance *of imperial Paris.*

24. Laura and Paul Lafargue to Marx

[Paris, between 23 and 27 August 1870]

My dear Challey,
We were delighted to hear that you are rather better and hope
that the sea air may completely set you up again.[1]

Paul has just started in search of lodgings: we are obliged
at last to turn out. The houses surrounding the fortifications are
about to be pulled down and people here are beginning to look
out for the Prussians. We shall stay a few days longer at Paris
in order to put our furniture into security and to make ready
for our journey to Bordeaux. We cannot of course think of letting
[*sic*] Schnappy in Paris while in a state of siege. Even had we
ever intended stopping here, we should have had to change our

74

minds in the end, as all the *bouches inutiles*[2] are going to be expulsed from Paris. Schnaps and myself come under this category; Paul is supposed to be *une bouche utile*. It is certain that were Fritz's[3] future subjects to bring cakes with them, he would make a terrible havoc amongst them.

Paris continues to offer the most ludicrous and the most shameful spectacle. The cafés are crowded nightly; refreshments are consumed at a fearful rate to the sounds of music anything but military. Bands of soldiers pass along the streets while the *moblots*[4] — ridiculous in their warlike *accoutrements* — swagger to make themselves conspicuous, promising to make mincemeat of the enemy so soon as he shall show himself. They still however declare that he dares not; Paris [is] preparing him a *tombeau* outside her walls. And the crowd gives a shout or two and moves on.

These brave *moblots* refuse however to come to blows anywhere but within Paris and insisted on being transported from Châlons to St. Maur where at present they make merry, attracting flocks of sightseers.

At the same time the walls were placarded last night with notices that all the *bouches inutiles* would be turned out on the first occasion that might offer. This announcement left the Parisians in much the same state as before; they are getting used to excitement and rather like it.

Not a few of them are looking forward as a treat to the coming visit: the director of a theatre declared the other day that he was waiting to bring out his new piece for the arrival of the Prussians; that they liked plays and that he hoped to reap a famous harvest on the occasion. The beauties of the Boulevards are impatiently awaiting the invaders; a certain part of the population, as Johannard[5] said to Paul, will certainly make themselves a pleasure of promenading the Prussians about Paris, to show them all that is worth seeing in the city. And yet there was a moment when the bourgeois all took to the cholera, so panic-struck and terrified were they. There was but one cry: arms and munition and Paris made able to defend itself. They offered themselves up body and soul for their country and yet when invited to put a shoulder to the wheel and to work at the trenches, not a man appeared.

As for the workmen, strange to say, they seem to be in a state of lethargy; several to whom Paul spoke, declared that the great mass look upon the whole business as something which does not concern them. And in the meanwhile they are being butchered and by and by will be starved. How they allowed the first few days following upon the defeats of the French army to slip by without making a move, is a miracle, for everything was in their favour. The *Gauche* itself had demanded arms, telling the people to take them if they were not given them. A body of sailors commanded by the government to fire upon the crowd, refused positively to obey. The soldiers on guard at the gates of the *Corps Législatif*, pointing to their arms and address-ing the workmen, said: *"Nous ne pouvons pourtant pas vous les donner"*;[6] a very cordial invitation to the men to come and *take* them. And nobody stirred. At a meeting held at the house of Jules Simon, the *Gauche* accused the workingmen of their in-difference and their calm demeanour; Combault[7] answered that if the *Gauche* wanted to do something, they must begin by giving their demission in a body, and in that case they might count upon a movement among the workmen. You can imagine the indescribable indignation called forth by this proposition. Do you suppose, roared all the great and the little Gambettas, that we want to be shut up at Ste. Pélagie? *Allons donc!* And really that was an absurd supposition, considering those gentle-men's avowed love of *liberty*.

This meeting, like all the rest, passed off without results. At present, everything seems smooth enough at the surface, and people look quietly on while the unfortunate men of the Villette affair are being shot down.[8]

The Press is making furious onslaughts of late against *The Times*, accusing that paper of being sold to Bismarck and of being as usual in the service of the highest bidder. "Times is money," they say. Lowe being a member of the English cabinet and at the same time an editor of *The Times*,[9] Paul fancies this might be an occasion for attacking the whole Gladstone party. If you think so, would you send him some particulars useful for the purpose. However, as France is not in a position just now for provoking any government capable of mediating in its favour, I don't suppose the Press would be likely to publish anything of the kind.

But you will judge and let Tooley know. That gentleman is wild at the idea of giving up his house and garden, in which latter he has done wonders, pruning, planting and spoiling trees and vegetables and flowers. Our walls are covered with grapes which we are obliged to leave behind us. Tooley feels inclined to kill the old Guillaume.[10] I should like to bake him and the old Emperor[11] in a pie with Fritz on the crust in the shape of an ornament. Unfortunately, the royal mess would be uneatable.

Goodbye, my dear Challey, I hope my talk has not given you a fresh attack of rheumatism. Words, I know, are wind.[12]

With kisses from Schnappy and myself and love from all. Believe me, your affectionate

KAKADOU

Thanks for all the letters and papers.

p.s. from Lafargue (in French)

We are leaving our little house on Monday or Tuesday and probably Paris a few days after that, for the Parisians cannot wait to see the uhlans arrive; although they cannot believe that the Prussians would be such idiots as to come and seek their deaths under the walls of Paris, you should know that the Parisians are reckoning more than ever on finishing off all their enemies in a single breath. Palikao[13] has, it's true, lied so well that they truly believe that Bazaine has beaten them [the Prussians] hollow and that Mac-Mahon is going to finish them off; it's not surprising. Louis Noir, the brother of Victor, has written a book called *L'Art de battre les Prussiens*; Louis Noir is an ex-Zouavian Figaroist, so you can judge how profound his book is. Trochu is now master of the situation — they say he's in the hands of the Jesuits.

1. The Marxes were in Ramsgate from 3 to 31 August. Marx's rheumatism had been troubling him.
2. "unproductive members of the population," lit., "useless mouths."
3. The Crown Prince of Prussia, Friedrich Wilhelm, nicknamed "unser Fritz," who had been charged with preparing the march on Paris.
4. Detachments of the Paris Mobile Guard, first billetted in Châlons and brought back to Paris by Trochu in mid-August.
5. Jules Johannard, an active member of the IWMA and corresponding secretary for Italy 1868–69.
6. "We can hardly *give* them to you." This passage refers to a Republican plan to invade the Legislative Body on 9 August. Many workers did in fact take part but the demonstration was a failure.

7. Amédée Combault, a member of the Paris federation of the IWMA who, along with the rest of the General Council, had been sentenced after Victor Noir's funeral on charges of belonging to a secret society.
8. A group of Blanquists carried out an ill-prepared attack on the fire station of the Boulevard de la Villette on 14 August, in which several people were killed and wounded, prompting the Government to make numerous arrests.
9. Robert Lowe, a *Times* leader writer from 1850 and Chancellor of the Exchequer from 1868–73.
10. The Prussian King, later German Emperor Wilhelm.
11. Napoleon III.
12. "Oaths are but words, and words but wind." (Samuel Butler, *Hudibras*, II, ii.).
13. The Comte de Palikao, an elderly imperialist general who had hastily been appointed head of a new Ministry after Ollivier had resigned. Several misleading reports about French military successes were published, notably in *Le Temps* and *The Times* of 23 August.

25. Laura to Jenny

[Bordeaux] 6 October 1870

My dear Jenny,

I was highly delighted this morning on the receipt of your letter, as I was beginning to fancy that you were angry with me for some reason or other and intended giving up writing to me for good and all.

The news of your continued illness was, as you may suppose, not calculated to enchant us; it annoyed us doubly from our being inclined to blame you a good deal for having managed to catch so horrible a cold, for no doubt, you were as careless as usual at Ramsgate. It is true that you do all you can to cure yourself when once victimized, but it would be better to keep out of harm's way. Your letters — Mama's, Tussy's and your own — were the most agreeable of surprises to me. We are cooped up in this place; in mourning for Paris, in such ignorance of what is going on there, that we look out for news with the utmost impatience. Our position here is rather an odd one. Paul is bullied by his father at every attempt he makes at being of some service to the International; while his Parisian friends are doubtless at the same time blaming him for his absence from Paris. The first paper he started in never had any life in it and I was a good deal annoyed at his engaging himself in it, as nothing beyond the anger of his father was to be expected from that enterprise. The small paper that he is now about to work at, may prove no luckier, but there are at any rate more chances in its favour. And you will admit that he cannot remain with his arms crossed at a moment like this.

You want to hear something of the old Lafargues. I really don't know what to tell you concerning them. They are very charming to Schnaps, who is admired by young and old. Madame Lafargue is as usual very amiable to us. She is much altered in appearance, her health seems to have suffered greatly since you saw her. And no wonder, for M. Lafargue's temper must make life in common with him very nearly intolerable. At present that we have no longer anything to fear from the danger threatening Paris, he is forging all kinds of *misères*, *grandes et petites*, for himself and others, out of every occurrence. He fears to lose his money . . . [letter incomplete]

While Paris remained under siege, a delegation led by Léon Gambetta, Minister of the Interior, escaped from the city by balloon to reorganize the defence of France in the provinces. It spent two months in Tours before establishing itself in Bordeaux in early December. The optimism shown by Laura toward the end of her next letter was inspired by Gambetta's success: new armies were raised, one to be led by Garibaldi, and France seemed to rally enthusiastically and patriotically to the Republic.

Paul Lafargue was active in the Bordeaux section of the International, and started a new radical news-paper, La Défense Nationale, *in which he called for a revolutionary conduct of the war. Arthur Ranc, a Blanquist who was chief of local security with Gambetta in Bordeaux, offered him a prefecture but Paul refused.*

Laura, meanwhile, was as usual beset by domestic problems.

26. Laura to Jenny

[*Bordeaux*] 12 *December* 1870

My dear Jenny,

I wrote you a letter a week or so ago which I did not send you, for on second thought I preferred suppressing a good deal of all the disagreeable news contained in it.

The fact is that I have from *divers* reasons so long put off sending you an account of what has being doing here that at this moment I don't know how to set about it. To give you some notion of past events, I should be obliged to rake up a deal of retrospective nasty matter, which just now I have not the least mind to. I hope some day to talk to you on the subject at length, as some of the details are highly grotesque. At present I am still so much under the impression of all the annoyance and vexation we have had here and were I to go into particulars, I should no doubt give you an exaggerated notion of the whole affair. To be as brief as I can, you must know that never in my life have I been so abused as here by my venerable mother-in-law — since M. Lafargue's death,[1] *bien entendu.* Paul was treated in the rudest manner possible by her, and having on one occasion — the only one — taken the liberty to answer her after her having insulted him, she told me in not the politest manner of the world to hold my tongue. All this would have been nothing had hostilities ceased there. But nothing of the kind took place. To prevent your charging us with being unjust, let me give you an instance or two of the way in which she set about treating us from that time forth.

Schnaps and myself having caught very bad colds — Schnaps in particular coughing a great deal — I begged that a fire might be made in the parlour for luncheon (the weather was bitterly cold and there was no fire in any other room). She at once gave orders to the servant-girl that no fire was to be lighted for us, in that or any room; declaring that her servant was not there to serve *us* and that if we wanted *fires* Paul might light them himself. She further prevented the girl from making our bedroom — the room in which Schnaps and myself were obliged to remain the greater part of the day — and as Paul would not let me make the bed myself the girl had to slip up at 7 o'clock in the evening and hurriedly make it — Schnaps being kept up behind his time in consequence.

I cannot go into details: suffice it to say that she got to grudging us the food we ate, the wine we drank, the oil we burnt and the wood consumed by our fires. *I am really* ashamed for the sake of Paul's mother to give you further examples of the mean and petty warfare she waged against us — the Lord knows why.

So disgusted had we grown to be with our existence here, that we resolved to bear it no longer, but to move into furnished apartments somewhere in the neighbourhood. No sooner had Paul informed his mother of our intention than she declared that she had no mind to stop in the house by herself; that she had decided on moving long ago and that she would do so at once. She in fact set off a week or so after, leaving us just barely what furniture we can manage to do with. We have had to buy several things, but had we changed apartments the expenses would have been much greater still.

Not that this was the arrangement I should have pre-ferred, but having no money, I hadn't much chance of being fastidious.

Talking of money, you have no doubt found out long ago,

that the great question of *cash* was at the bottom of all this. Had
we had that important ballast nothing of what has happened
would have occurred, or happening would have been a very
easy matter to settle.

I might say much more on this subject but reserve doing
so for another occasion. I have been bewildered and perplexed
by all that I have seen and heard here: I thought that nothing
of the kind existed out of Paul de Kock's novels,[2] but Truth, I
see, is stranger than Fiction.

At present we have the house to ourselves and nothing to
complain of; it is true, we are in a very denuded condition as
regards furniture, linen and kitchen utensils, but all this we
can manage to bear with very philosophically: we need only
fancy ourselves having undergone sundry inquisitions on the
part of the Germans and console ourselves with having come
off with our skins safe.

Paul has received answers to the letters he had written to
Marseilles and Brest. The news from Marseilles are good
enough. According to Bastelica[3] the International has a firm
footing in the whole of the South of France. At Brest matters are
less brilliant. It appears that there is a strong reactionary party
there that proceeds with the utmost rigour against the workmen. Le Doré,[4] to whom Paul's letter was addressed, is at this
moment in prison condemned, together with several other members of the Int[ernational] to three years' imprisonment for
complot contre la sureté de l'Etat.[5] His brother,[6] who writes,
gives no very favourable account of the dispositions of the working class at Brest. He intends sending a detailed account of the
state of things there to Dupont,[7] whose address he has asked for.
Paul is going to write him to send all his communications to
Challey, who will then be able to forward them to Dupont. Letters to Le Doré are to be addressed to Jean Prétequin, *poulieur*,
Rue du Coat-Arguévin, 31, Brest.

The Bordelaise section of the International is going on very
well.

I am glad to hear that there is a chance yet for France in
the war. The French are, I believe, just now more down-hearted
than they had been up to this time. It is curious that they should
have succeeded in organizing so considerable an army in so
short a time, and that without having any real heart to the
work, for a large proportion, at any rate, of Frenchmen have

given proof of not being precisely enthusiastic *pour la résistance à outrance.*[8]

I have hardly room left to give you news of Schnappy. That little man whom we call *le franc-fileur*[9] from his propensity to take to his heels at the sight of danger, is in a most flourishing condition in spite of a bad cough he has caught. He is the sweetest-tempered little fellow imaginable, prattles all day long and thinks nothing of taking a walk of an hour or two. The Bordelaises, who are greatly smitten by him, call him *Peau-de-Satin.*[10]

We were very disagreeably surprised to hear of your continued illness. I hope to hear of your perfect recovery in your next letter. I have to thank you for your last which gave us much pleasure.

Give my best love to all and all sorts of good wishes for the New Year. I hope you will enjoy your Christmas as much as is possible in so dreary a time as this is.

You must excuse me for my past silence. I have had such a deal of needlework on my hands and Schnaps to look after and the house to see to which after Mme. Lafargue's removal was in an awful state of dirt and confusion.

Goodbye dear Jenny,

Believe me to be your affectionate

LAURA

Kisses from Schnappy to all of you and our love, once more to all. Is Whisky alive? How is Challey? And is Helen better? I will write to Mama shortly. Thanks for Tussy's letter.

1. M. Lafargue had died on 18 November 1870.
2. French novelist who ridiculed bourgeois society in his salacious novels.
3. André Bastelica had founded the Bouches du Rhône section of the IWMA in January 1870 and was a leading member of the first Marseilles Commune.
4. Constant Le Doré was an eccentric clerk who had founded the Brest section of the IWMA in September 1869. After instituting his own Committee of National Defence and attempting to take over the town hall, he had been condemned on 28 October to two (not three) years' imprisonment and a 50-franc fine. He was reprieved the day after this letter was written.
5. "treason-felony."
6. Joseph Le Doré, also a member of the Brest section of the IWMA.
7. Eugène Dupont, corresponding secretary for France.
8. "about resisting to the bitter end."

9. A complicated play on words implying both cowardice and speed of movement. *Franc-tireur*, an irregular soldier or sniper, was currently being used to describe the armed inhabitants of Paris; *fileur* means someone who takes to his heels.

10. "Satin-Skin."

Paul's letter below describes the growing discontent at the inertia of General Trochu in Paris. Trochu's critics were calling for him to make a massive sortie *against the German lines, but he delayed doing so for two reasons: his low opinion of most of the troops at his disposal (civilians in the Paris National Guard) and his fear that military failure could lead to revolution. According to Marx, Trochu considered it more important to suppress the "Reds" than to defeat the Prussians. Finally, after pressure from Gambetta and the popular clubs of Paris, an unsuccessful* sortie *was attempted on 19 January, fully a week after Chanzy's army, advancing toward Paris, had been defeated at Le Mans.*

27. Paul Lafargue to Karl Marx
(in French)

[*Bordeaux, about 15 January 1871*]

My dear Mr. Marx,

You must know more details than we do about the sad defeat at Le Mans. The anger at Trochu is at its height, his stupidity is now patently obvious to everybody; for everybody realizes that the bombardment of Paris was only a tactic to conceal the withdrawal of the troops around Paris, thus allowing Frederick to mass over 180,000 against Chanzi [*sic*].[1] I was talking to Ranc about it, telling him that people thought Trochu was a traitor, but he said Trochu didn't have enough energy to play such a role, that he was quite simply a perfect ass, and that most people in Paris couldn't stand him. J. Favre,[2] he said, wrote to Gambetta that everyone in the government was furious with him [Trochu] and was pushing him towards an offensive, but he refused in case it would look as if he were abandoning Paris to the mob. Gambetta, as it was his duty to do, replied to Favre: your letter is your own condemnation. Ranc is desperate and furious. We must hope that the combined action of the members of the government in Paris and of the provincial delegation will force Trochu into action; for there's no point in hoping that in Paris they will ever have the necessary energy to send Trochu packing. There are several factors which explain the panic of the Bretons at the Tuilerie: first they were equipped with ancient guns without bayonets instead of quick-firing ones; and then their leaders, who were appointed at the election, couldn't be worse — the soldiers, who are very good, could do with having their officer *cadre* transformed.

The Lyons affair seems so far to be a mystery to everyone;[3] but the rage of the reactionaries is really beyond the limit. One of the accused, who had been consigned to the care of two National Guard officers, was assassinated by them while they were taking him to prison. This alone will show you what a pitch their anger has reached. When Gambetta was in Lyons a deputation from the National Guard came to request the removal of the red flag flying above the town hall. Gambetta replied that he couldn't do it, for that would create a riot. Well, so much the better, that's just what we want, we'll crush it! they replied. At this Gambetta dismissed them.

The Bordeaux section of the International has been going better for some time now: for their instruction I read them the excellent work by Beesly[4] which I'd translated — and which they appreciate. There are several very competent and keen men here; when they're briefed they will do admirably. We also have one absolute freak, a Proudhonian, a special friend of Proudhon's, and the author of a mass of highly comic pamphlets. This individual, who like his master keeps going on about law, justice, truth, morals, etc., gets in the way because he has written on every subject that comes up, and we are obliged to swallow his indigestible opinions. We are going to start a library; no doubt he'll stuff it with Proudhon. As an antidote I'm going to include *The Poverty of Philosophy*.[5]

If we could have the addresses of the other sections in other towns we could open up communications and establish a kind of centralization which after the siege of Paris could be taken up on a much bigger and more active scale, but unfortunately we only have the names of Bastelica and his substitute, Prenez,[6] in Marseilles and of Le Doré in Brest. I was counting on Ranc, but he told me it was impossible for him to do it, as he could only get hold of them through the superintendents of police, who would then think that they ought to be keeping an eye on the members of the Inter[national] — something that he quite rightly wants to avoid at all costs. So do ask Dupont for the list of all the corresponding members that he had, and Robin for the list of the correspondents that he had in Paris; he must surely have brought one with him, and in any case he must know a great many of them by heart. Get on to this and send me your answer through Jenny.

Now we're going to talk business.

My accounts have been settled, and Laura and I find ourselves in possession of the sum of 100,000 francs or £4,000, from which my father used to pay us the annual revenue. Some of that money is invested in property in New Orleans, in treasury bonds on the town of New Orleans and in American state debentures; the rest is in France, in mortgages on properties, and in shares in the Orléans railway.

I have spoken to my lawyer about the mortgages and he has told me that it would be possible to sell them, but at a loss of 3 per cent. Do you think it would be a good idea to make this change, for we'd prefer to have our money invested elsewhere than in France. Engels told us that when we wanted to he could make some investments for us in England; could he still do it today? If so, could he let us know so that I can have the mortgages sold and get the money to him.

I have spoken to you of some work I took on for the Bordeaux section, on the butchers' and bakers' trades.[7] After waiting for a very long time my research has been dealt with and a résumé made of it. I'm sending you a journal which contains it.

Little Schnaps is fit as a fiddle, he's livelier and prettier than ever. I wish you could see him, you'd be mad about him. He's already starting to lie: the other day he was given some bread and forbidden to give it to the dog; he immediately proceeded to do just that, and when we asked him what he'd done with it, he replied, "eaten it, eaten it."

We no longer get a London paper; might the freedom of the press have been suppressed in England — are no more papers published there? We are very anxious on this score — we beseech you to keep us informed.

Love to all.

Cordially,

TOOLE the 1st

1. The German victory at Le Mans was prepared by the capture of the Tuilerie which controlled the approaches. It was defended by General Le Bouëdec, who had hastily assembled about a thousand poorly equipped and ill-trained conscripts, most of them Bretons.
2. Jules Favre, one of the leaders of the moderate bourgeois republicans and Minister of Foreign Affairs in the Government of National Defence.
3. The long-standing division between *haute bourgeoisie,* radicals and workers in Lyons had flared up with the proclamation of the Republic: many outbreaks of violence had occurred, and the town hall was occupied several times. Finally, on 7 and 20 December, there were riots when a Commander of the National Guard, who had been accused of treason, was executed. Gambetta came to his funeral to re-establish order in the city, but the red flag that had been erected on the town hall remained there until 2 March.
4. Edward Beesly, "The International Working Men's Association," *Fortnightly Review*, November 1870.
5. See page 34, note 1.
6. Joseph Prenez, foreman and town councillor, member of the Bouches du Rhône section of the IWMA.
7. The Bordeaux section sent a long letter on the subject to the municipal council, which was published by *La Tribune de Bordeaux* on 20 March 1871.

On 28 January Jules Favre, the Foreign Minister, and Bismarck signed an agreement on the armistice and the surrender of Paris. This could be ratified only by an elected Assembly, which would have the power to negotiate the terms of the peace treaty with the Prussians. Elections were set for 8 February.

In the following letter Lafargue reports to Marx on the confused and disputatious atmosphere in Bordeaux during the election campaign, and on Gambetta's capricious behaviour. As the elections drew near many republicans became apprehensive about their outcome. In an attempt to reduce the influence of the Right, Gambetta published a decree disenfranchizing the "accomplices of the Empire" (31 January). The representative of the Paris government, Jules Simon (who had arrived by train rather than by balloon), first remonstrated with him then, following a telegram from Bismarck to Gambetta demanding "free elections" (2 February), issued his own decree that voting should be without restrictions (4 February). The Bordeaux delegation attempted to prevent the publication of the second decree and even threatened to have Simon arrested. On 6 February, however, Gambetta gave in.

In the midst of these historic events Laura gave birth to a son, Marc-Laurent. On hearing the news Marx wrote to Lafargue (in a letter which must have crossed with this one): "We must create some new defenders of France. You and Laura seem to have acquitted yourselves seriously and successfully of this patriotic duty." The baby lived for only five months.

28. Paul Lafargue to Karl Marx
(in French)

[*Bordeaux, 4 February 1871*]

My dear Steam-Engeen [*sic*],

You must have heard about the utter shambles we're in here. The delegation which came by balloon is at complete odds with

the delegation which came by train via Versailles: a matter of
modes of transport! One of the Jules from the Paris government[1]
has been cornered by the reaction, well and truly locked up and
given all kinds of seasonings to induce some warmth into his
heart; after a good deal of hesitation this Jules Simon made up
his mind to unsheath his famous decree. Next, Léon [Gambetta]
had the newspapers seized, and for a moment there was talk of
arresting Jules himself, but when the time came Grandbêta
lacked the courage and was content to send old Bizoin[2] to Paris
instead, to tell people what's going on here.

Since the armistice a mass of political agitators — I've no
idea where they've come from or how they got here — have
invaded the square in Bordeaux, to the considerable dismay of
the local orators, who see themselves being outshone by the
newcomers; but since our orators are well-brought-up fellows,
they have managed to control their anger by claiming that all
these strangers are Bonapartist agents sent to Bordeaux to sow
discord and force respectable people into civil war. I don't doubt
that there are Bonapartists among them disguised as demagogues — one of them was totally destroyed in the midst of a
meeting by little Delboy — and that Bonaparte might well attempt a repeat of the 1848 episode;[3] but to generalize in this
way you'd have to be a Bordeaux radical, quite surprised and
annoyed to find yourself taking up a reactionary line in front of
these agitators. One of them is a capital man, he's an Englishman by the name of Milleton,[4] an *aide-de-camp* of Garibaldi's
sent on a special mission by the old general. He speaks excellent
French and is extremely talented as a speaker and as a tribune:
he can speak on foot or mounted — I've seen him haranguing
the crowd perched on the shoulders of the people next to him.
It's mainly thanks to him that the population of Bordeaux has
been stirred up to the extent of demanding a continuation of
the war and suspension of the elections.

When Gambetta first arrived in Tours he seemed to want
nothing more than to command the adulation of the people: he
was always addressing the crowd on this and that. Today, however, now that the movement even at Bordeaux could become
serious if he wanted to declare himself forcefully, nothing an-
noys him more. Last Wednesday people had to seek him out
in three different places; yesterday, Sunday, he didn't want to
receive a deputation from the people: then Milleton, always on

top of the situation, appeared at a balcony right opposite Gambetta's and harangued the crowd from there. After him another stranger arrived and said that the people ought to force Gambetta to emerge from his disdainful silence; the crowd cheered his words. Gambetta received the deputation and gave an evasive reply in writing. But that evening he ordered the closure of meetings and the dispersal of the crowd by the National Guards.

It's fortunate that Bordeaux is one of the most reactionary towns; in Marseilles even the Prefect, the famous Gent, these days known as Esquiros II,[5] has demanded that there should be no elections. There will probably be some towns which won't vote. At Bordeaux delegates from over seventeen departments have strongly declared themselves against the vote. The Republican Committee of Propaganda in Bordeaux, for its part, has declared itself in favour; it's true that it is pledged to the prefecture from which it receives its orders; I shouldn't speak too badly of it, for I belong to it myself.

Ranc is desperate, he wanted to hand in his resignation; I think his influence diminishes as the situation deteriorates. Laurier, one of Gambetta's faithfuls, calls him a demagogue: and yet without Ranc and Steenackers Gambetta would have been able to do nothing.[6] It was Ranc who had his police remove all obstacles from his path, and Steenackers who suppressed all telegrams which it wasn't important to convey to the other three members of the delegation.

What's going to happen? Looking generally at the facts, opinions and trends, I think that the nation will be very disappointed if the Assembly doesn't carry on with the war: the fall of Paris seems to have produced a new fervour. All those who are truly Republican realize that peace would mean the death of the Republic. But what does the countryside think? *Nescio.*

You have heard about the three demonstrations of the International at Bordeaux. What a pity that we only have four or six sections and a thousand members here! What's this business with Otway, who you've made president, according to the *Telegraph?*

Marc-Laurent, still the Silent One, drinks, sleeps and pisses in an enviable manner. Laura is well, she would be quite recovered if she hadn't got it into her head that she should feed him; luckily *Coco-bel-oeil* (he has magnificent eyes) also sucks cow's milk, otherwise she wouldn't be able to stand it, for he's a *guzzler*. The illustrious Schnaps is full of beans and fat enough for four.

Love to all. Affectionately,

TOOLE the 1st

Have you received the two photographs of Schnaps? I forgot to mention your last letter, I've taken due note of its contents and will follow your advice.

1. A scathing allusion to the moderate bourgeois leaders of the Government of National Defence, several of whom were named Jules (e.g., Favre, Ferry and Simon).

2. Paul is referring to Glais-Bizoin, then aged 71, a member of the Government of National Defence who had followed Adolphe Crémieux to Tours (see note 6).

3. A reference to the demagogic campaign conducted by Napoleon III after the revolution of 1848. He was elected President on 10 December.

4. Possibly Robert Middleton, author of *Garibaldi: Ses opérations à l'armée des Vosges*, 1871.

5. Alphonse Gent had taken over from Henri Esquiros as Prefect of the Bouches du Rhône. Esquiros was a radical republican who, with Gaston Crémieux, had founded the *Ligue du Midi* in Marseilles with help from the local section of the IWMA. (See Stewart Edwards, *The Paris Commune: 1871*, p. 96.)

6. Just before Paris was invested Adolphe Crémieux, 74-year-old Minister of Justice, had been sent to Tours as a government delegate, accompanied by Laurier, Director of the Ministry of the Interior, Steenackers, Director of Posts and Telecommunications, and other ministers.

The elections of 8 February 1871 brought to the National Assembly a sweeping majority of conservatives and monarchists: it was a vote for peace and against the policies of Gambetta. Thiers was elected Head of the Executive. However, in Paris a number of left-wing and even revolutionary Republicans were elected as Deputies, among them Victor Hugo, Louis Blanc, Félix Pyat, Henri Rochefort, Millière and Delescluze.

The conditions of peace were harsh. France was to cede Alsace and Lorraine and to give an indemnity of five thousand million gold francs to Prussia. The Assembly nevertheless voted to accept them, on 1 March, by 546 votes to 107. The opposition included thirty-four of the forty-three Paris Deputies.

Some of the National Guardsmen wanted to resist the triumphal entry of the Prussian troops but in the end the advice of the International and the recently formed Central Committee of the National Guard prevailed. The troops were received with silent hostility only.

29. Paul Lafargue to Jenny

(in French)

Bordeaux, 28 February 1871[1]

My dear Jenny,

.　.　.

I don't know if London thinks of me as a great man, but I assure you that here in Bordeaux I have absolutely no perception of my greatness; so don't think that it's the clouds of glory that have prevented me from writing to you. Though my letters were addressed to More [sic], I knew that all the family *enjoyed* them: but your remark is so flattering that I must devote a few lines to thanking you for it.

At last we know the conditions of peace: the bourgeoisie must be proud of its leader, for it's to be hoped that it's thanks to his [Thiers's] nature and his political and diplomatic skill that we have succeeded in obtaining such lenient and honourable conditions. It seems that some strange things are taking place among the majority groups: it's claimed that the Legitimists[2] will not vote; it's also worth noting that all their leaders, Cathelineau, Charette, etc., have refused the mandate on the grounds that they couldn't make up their minds; and it's said that the Orléanist party is hesitating, and that many of its members do not want to assume responsibility for the peace; the bourgeois Republicans, on the other hand, will sign with four hands. Vacherole[3] the philosopher, after invoking the god of Duty, cried out: Ah well, I will have the courage to risk unpopularity, I will sign in full.

After greeting the rumours of peace with enthusiasm the people are reacting differently: the amount to be paid out frightens them. That's also the only thing that concerns our honourable Deputies: on reading about the conditions, they smiled ingratiatingly at the surrender of territory but were disagreeably surprised by the five thousand million. There's a legend in France which is probably going to have quite an influence on the situation: among the people it's claimed that ever since the First Empire Prussia has owed France several thousand millions, that it was to recover this debt that Bonaparte went into the war, and that now the debt will be diminished by the five thousand million. This legend must be widespread because I've come across it in Paris and again in Bordeaux: where does it come from, did Bonaparte start it, how did he get it around? That would be miraculous! Speaking of Bonaparte, his influence grows daily in the country areas, in almost all departments. His name, though it was not to be found on any electoral list, has attracted votes which were as good as lost; it seems that in the Charente he had up to five thousand votes in one canton; no doubt we shall now be seeing him putting up a hue and cry for a referendum. These worthy peasants say: our emperor has been betrayed by these rogues of Republicans, in the Chamber there are at least thirty leaders who are acknowledged Bonapartists and who influence fifty others. For a while the question of deposition was discussed: Thiers wanted it, the Legitimists clamoured for it, and the necessary measures had started to be put in motion when they were halted because it was clear that there would be at least two hundred abstentions in the Chamber. The Corsican Deputies, all Bonapartists, are as insolent as executioners' valets, publicly claiming that Corsica has supplied France with two glorious emperors.

Since the lifting of the siege Parisians have been coming here in droves. Bordeaux now has the privilege of containing the revolution's full count of lost children and remarkable men, so there is a rather amusing atmosphere here. All of them have come with the idea of attempting a coup, but they are beginning to see that there's almost no way. Serraillier[4] must have spoken to you at length about the state of Paris — so I'll skip it; but has he kept you up to date with Millière's accusation of J. Favre: it has been revealed today that Favre, after having co-habited with a married woman separated from her husband, in order to make the children he had by her legitimate and to grab a large inheritance, committed a forgery in the public register.[5] These things are absolutely staggering. I was talking to Ranc about it and he maintained that the most outrageous aspect of it is that he's been kept on as head of the government. In fact — I would have liked to have been able to send you a copy of *Le Vengeur;*[6] but I haven't had one for myself; I saw Millière's accusation in a copy brought by someone from Paris.

Favre, Thiers & Co. have just played a trick that's typical of them: in order to carry the vote by catching people at a moment's notice Thiers demanded urgency; when the polling stations were set up yesterday evening — Tuesday — at 9 o'clock, each presiding officer pulled out of his pocket a telegram which, he said, had just been delivered to him, in which Jules Favre, who was still in Paris, reported that agitation in Paris was increasing, but that Vinoy[7] was answerable for law and order, and that Bismarck had agreed not to occupy Paris if the [peace] preliminaries were agreed upon yesterday — Tuesday. The ploy failed. We had been informed about the telegram by Tridon,[8] who in his capacity as an important landowner has been elected in the Côte-d'Or, his own district: he considered the telegram to be an infamous hoax; the presiding officer of the polling station pointed out that the expression was not a parliamentary one. I've never learnt parliamentary government, and it is not the majority which will be able to teach me its language, for it is really very coarse.

Malon is here;[9] and he's one of the best members that the Left counts among its ranks. The illustrious Tolain[10] has finally reached the apotheosis of his dreams, to become a Deputy; this means he thinks only of hanging on to his position; and as he's a representative of the International and the word worker sounds bad to bourgeois ears, he is anxious to replace it with

another, less revolutionary word. He's held forth on the subject
to Malon several times; but hasn't yet been able to persuade
Malon of the need to change it; on the contrary, Malon holds
him in the deepest contempt — warn Dupont,[11] because he has
developed a passion for Tolain. Tell him also that his name was
on the International register — how are his business affairs
going?

Rochefort is here, Bohemian as ever. Malon, who travelled
down with him, asked him what he thought of the Chamber —
nothing, he replied, besides I don't give a damn, my *Mot
d'ordre*[12] has a circulation of 70,000. ·Gambetta is waiting for
someone to attack him to make use of the documents he has
against the Paris government; there's even an indictment drawn
up by the Left, and he's supplied them with some supporting
documents — it's very funny, in '48 the provisional government
was arraigned by the Right, today it's by the Left.

I'm anxiously awaiting the edition of the *Fortnightly* with
Papa's article in it — I'll do some extracts from it. Why are you
so mean with the *Pall Mall*, Engels could give you a subscription, if he's well in with the journal. A thousand thanks to
Mother for her letter, I'll reply in a day or two. Monsieur
Laurent is fattening up, and managing to sleep up to seven
hours in a row.

Goodbye — love to all —

TOOLE the 1st

Have you received the photographs?

1. Misdated; clearly written on 1 March.
2. The Royalists consisted of Legitimists such as Cathelineau and Charette, who
   supported the Comte de Chambord, and the Orléanists, who supported the
   Comte de Paris, grandson of France's last king, Louis Philippe, deposed in
   1848.
3. Lafargue means Etienne Vacherot, Bordeaux Deputy and philosopher.
4. Auguste Serraillier, a member of the General Council of the IWMA who was
   acting as a liaison between the General Council and the Paris federation.
5. Marx later used Millière's revelations, along with other charges against the
   moderate bourgeois Republicans—"Favre, Thiers & Co"—in his *Civil War in
   France*. He accused them of colluding with Bismarck against the people of
   Paris in order to protect their own interests and to conceal crimes and indis-
   cretions.
6. *Le Vengeur* was a daily paper published in Paris in 1871 under the editorship
   of Félix Pyat.

7. General Vinoy had replaced Trochu as Governor of Paris in January.

8. Edmé Tridon, a Blanquist journalist and historian.

9. Benoît Malon, a member of the IWMA and of the Government of National Defence who later founded *La Revue Socialiste*.

10. Henri Tolain, a member of the Government of National Defence, one of the founders of the French section of the International but later expelled for opposing the Commune.

11. Eugène Dupont, a member of the General Council of the IWMA.

12. Daily paper edited by Rochefort and intermittently suppressed on the orders of General Vinoy.

Significantly, the new Assembly had its seat at Ver-
sailles rather than in Paris. Anti-government feeling
among the people of Paris, who had suffered appalling
conditions under the siege, was brought to a head by
Thiers's provocative action in attempting to remove
the four hundred guns held by the National Guard on
18 March. (Almost the whole male working-class
population of Paris had been enrolled during the war
to defend the city.) Riots ensued and rapidly devel-
oped into a full-scale insurrection, forcing Thiers and
his Ministers to flee from Paris. On 26 March a Com-
mune was elected, in part a municipal government, in
part a revolutionary challenge to the Assembly at Ver-
sailles.

On 2 April, once again, Paris found herself under
siege — this time surrounded by fellow citizens: the
Versailles army, in collusion with the Prussians. Esti-
mates vary, but in the bombardments and street-
fighting that took place over the next two months at
least twenty thousand Communards and one thousand
Versaillists were killed. Several of the Marxes' closest
friends took part in the fighting, including Gustave
Flourens, a member of the Commune, who was killed
on 3 April.

Lafargue was in Paris from 7 to 18 April: hence
Laura's concern in the following letter. She does not
elaborate on the reason for his journey: he may have
been attending a meeting with delegates of the Inter-
national, or seeking powers to organize a revolutionary
army in Bordeaux.

30. Laura to Jenny

[*Bordeaux, between 7 and 18 April 1871*]

My dear Jenny,

I have no news from Paul up to this moment. To make matters
worse my poor baby has been so ill that during eight or ten
days I expected every moment to see him die. He is much better

since a day or two and I think will continue to improve. For the last week I carry him up and down the room nearly all day and rock him in the night so that I could not find time to write you even a few lines.

As to Paul, I don't know what to think. He certainly did not set off with the intention of remaining so long. But perhaps he cannot get back even did he wish to, or perhaps the sight of the barricades have tempted him to go in for fighting. I should not wonder, and I should not mind if I were with him, for I should have fought too. I intended starting for Paris but knew no one here to whom I could have trusted the children, and then the baby's illness made my leaving out of the question.

Now, my dear Jenny, I don't know what to say on the subject of your voyage.[1] If the boat started more frequently I should almost advise you to postpone it, for we shall not be able to start for the Pyrenees by ourselves and Bordeaux is a tedious place. I don't wish you to come over here to annoy yourselves[2] and our home just now is not very amusing.

As to my feeling lonely, I am used to being alone. Paul since many months is hardly ever at home and I have hardly stirred out of the house for the last six or eight months.

But I leave you to decide for yourselves. Give my thanks to Tussy for her letter. She is a good girl, for she writes me two letters to one of mine. As for *yourself* you snub me a good deal; fortunately I am rather used to that too.

Goodbye, dear Jenny. Should I hear from Paul, I shall let you know at once. My love to all.

Your affectionate sister

LAURA LAFARGUE

1. Lafargue had invited Jenny and Eleanor to stay with them in the Pyrenees, where he planned to write a book.
2. Laura is thinking in French: *s'ennuyer* = "to be bored."

31. Jenny to Laura

[London] 18 April 1871

My dearest Laura,

On the reception of your letter, I wished at once to start for Bordeaux — but since then have found out that it is impossible to do so, those damned Prussians of Versailles and Berlin having between them cut off the Orleans railway line. The other lines are monopolized by German and other troops, so that a journey by rail would be one series of interruptions and might take from eight to ten days. Consequently, we are again obliged to turn to the slow but sure steamer. The London boat is unfortunately overfilled with goods and the Captain refuses to trouble himself with the conveyance of passengers. The Liverpool boat does not start before the 29th. That seems a long time to me, for I cannot bear to think that you should be all alone and your baby ill! I hope that in case he does not rapidly improve you will *at once* make up your mind to get a nurse for him. Do follow Mama's advice in this respect, she speaks from experience, for you know she saved my life by going to Trèves to get a nurse for me where all other means failed.

As regards Paul's prolonged absence and silence, I am inclined to think that the irregular and interrupted railway communications are the cause of both. The letters he writes may not reach their destination. I hope and trust he will return home in a few days.

Do not worry yourself about the journey to the Pyrenees. It will be a great pleasure for me to stay with you at Bordeaux. I am looking forward so much to see again my own little *soeur* and the baby!

Even the foul London press has to admit that the people of Paris fight gloriously — that they are more than a match for the trained cut-throats of Versailles, for the hero of Sedan. If it were not for the Prussians who glory in their vocation of doing the police business for all the governments of Europe, all would go well!

Kiss your dear children for me and believe me, my dear Laura,

Your affectionate sister
JENNY

The following letter was written four days before the fall of the Commune, during the most brutal and heroic days of its short life. Jenny and Eleanor, now aged sixteen, arrived in Bordeaux on 1 May, travelling under the name of Williams. Paul had returned from Paris, but as a supporter of the Commune he was liable to arrest or even execution by the police; at the end of May he escaped to Luchon in the Pyrenees. On 26 July the Lafargues' baby, Marc-Laurent, died; Schnaps was sick with dysentery. Soon afterwards, warned by Marx in a carefully worded letter from London, Paul crossed the border to Spain. He was later arrested at Huesca at Thiers's request, but was released for lack of evidence.

The house in which they were staying in Luchon was searched by the police; Jenny and Eleanor were submitted to rigorous interrogation and taken into custody. They finally returned to England in September 1871.

32. Jenny to Karl Marx

[Bordeaux] 24 May 1871

My dear Nickey,

According to the Bordeaux papers the *tricolore* is flying on the *buttes Montmartre* — the wild beasts of Cathelineau and Charrette, the hired cut-throats of Pietri, are masters of Paris.[1] Outside the city the bold Prussian warriors are acting as the police-agents of Thiers — are capturing the Parisians that attempt to escape. All hope is dead. It is also rumoured that Dombrowski[2] has fallen into the hands of the Prussian policemen! Do you not think that the sudden success of the Versaillists is the work of foul play? Cluseret and Rossel[3] first disorganized and then betrayed the National Guards. If the members of the Commune had heeded your warning against the American adventurer,[4] all might have gone well. It is fearful to think that there was so much chance of success and that it has been thrown away. When the butchers will have done their bloody work in Paris,

101

it is very likely that they will wage war against the International leaders in the Provinces. Every provincial paper denounces the assoc[iation] in one way or the other. The miserable dwarf Louis Blanc has also raised a piping voice against the International. In answer to a deputation from Toulouse, he gave to understand that among the agents of the Int[ernational] who form the *Comité Central*, "*les influences Bonapartistes et Prussiennes se font sentir. Enfin*," *dit-il*, "*L'insurrection parisienne est tout-à-fait condamnable et doit être condamnée par tout véritable républicain. Le Comité Central préoccupé d'intérêts cosmopolites se souvient fort peu des intérêts parisiens et français.*"[5]

Yesterday Paul procured himself a Spanish passport so that we may be enabled to decamp as soon as possible. As Paul is a very active organizer of the I[nternational] he is by no means safe here. He has formed a new section with the *verriers*,[6] some of whom are very intelligent and devoted men. Last Monday we went to their factory. We felt as if we had been transported into Dante's Inferno on entering the building. The heat was unbearable. The tortured spirits ran about, without a moment's peace, a crowd of emaciated, deadly pale men and boys. The work is almost all night-work and yet children of seven, eight, nine years of age are employed. The poor little fellows are the first in the factory and the last to leave it. Their master has found out a capital way to exploit them. They are paid by the day and the men by the piece, so that it is in the interest of the men to make children work as hard as possible. Paul picked up many interesting facts, and is going to write an article on the subject. I fear however that in his capacity of *gens de lettre*, he will cut up the facts in order to thicken his own sauces (on them). Unfortunately, he is too fond of literary gravy.

I have just received Mama's letter. My best thanks for it. I was very happy to have news from home, and particularly glad to hear that you, my dear Mohr, have made up your mind to go to Brighton so soon as the address is printed.[7] By the by, is the address to be translated by Paul or Tallandier?

I was much amused to have a detailed description of the teacher of the *précieuse amie*. So Lavroff[8] is a Comtist? Woe be to him and to his friends! These Comtists are sad dogs. Prudhomme is a striking example of the deadly influence of Comte. Laura was perfectly right when she said that he is *abruti*.[9] It is almost impossible to recognize the Prudhomme of four years ago. At present the high priest of the Comtists, Laffitte,[10] is at Bordeaux. I have read his pamphlet on Comte. As a polity economist, the whole theory seems to me to come to this — *la classe capitaliste n'a pas le* DROIT *mais le* DEVOIR *d'exploiter les prolétaires.*[11] As to the famous *altruisme*, it is only another version of the *chacun pour soi* principle. *Seulement au lieu de dire — chacun pour soi et* DIEU *pour tous, ils disent chacun pour soi,* l'HUMANITÉ *pour tous!*[12]

With many kisses to all at home.

Believe me, my own dear Nickey,

Your affectionate

JENNY

Please address letters to *Williams* and not Mary.

I have read Engels' article[13] on Vogt. It is most witty. Remember us all to the General.

1. Cathelineau and Charette were legendary Royalist leaders; Pietri had been Napoleon III's Chief of Police.
2. A Polish officer, commander of the right bank forces of the Commune, Dąbrowski (Dombrowski) was mortally wounded on 23 May at a Montmartre barricade.
3. Delegates of War in the Commune: Gustave Cluseret from 3 April to 1 May, Louis Rossel from 1 to 9 May.
4. Cluseret had taken part in the War of the Secession as a Northern general. After the victory he became an American citizen.
5. "Bonapartist and Prussian influences are making themselves felt. In fact," he said, "the insurrection in Paris is totally reprehensible and should be condemned by every true Republican. The Central Committee, preoccupied by cosmopolitan interests, takes little note of Parisian and French interests."
6. "glass-makers."
7. On 30 May, three days after the fall of the Commune, Marx read his *Civil War in France* to the General Council of the International. It appeared first in London on 13 June 1871, signed by all the members. Marx claimed authorship in an open letter to the *Daily News* of 26 June. He did not leave for Brighton until 17 August.
8. Peter Lavrovich Lavrov (Lavroff, Lawroff), a Russian socialist and friend of the Marxes, who lived in London.
9. "an idiot." For the influence of Comte, see page 73, note 1.
10. Pierre Laffitte, a well-known philosopher, lecturer and Comtist.
11. "The capitalist class has not the *right* but the *duty* to exploit the proletarians."
12. "Only instead of saying — every man for himself and *God* for us all, they say every man for himself, *humanity* for us all!"
13. Vogt, a secret agent in the pay of Napoleon III, had been denounced by Marx in his *Monsieur Vogt*. Engels's article appeared in the *Volksstaat*, edited by Liebknecht, on 10 May 1871.

PART THREE

April 1872 – January 1883

After the Commune

Fᴿᴼᴹ 1872 ᴛᴏ 1880, in the aftermath of the Commune until the amnesty was declared, all branches of the family were based in England — though Marx could now afford to travel to Carlsbad for his cures instead of to the English seaside. The correspondence for these years, when Jenny married and bore four children, Laura lost her last child and Eleanor embarked upon her first serious relationship, is accordingly sparse and, in the main, of a domestic nature.

The quantity of letters increases for the years 1880–83, which was a period of continuing illness, crisis and tragedy for them all. By April 1883 Mrs. Marx, Jenny, Marx and Harry Longuet were all dead. Most of the letters written in these years are intimate ones from Laura and Eleanor to Jenny in France, where she spent the last wretched phase of her life. Those from Eleanor, who was unaware of the seriousness of Jenny's illness, amount to a confessional of her hopes and ambitions, and are perhaps the most revealing of all the letters reproduced here.

It took some time for the relationship between Laura and Eleanor to recover from the Lafargues' coldness towards Eleanor's fiancé Lissagaray, as recounted in letter 35, and their opposing natures — Laura calm, sensible, laconic, Eleanor impetuous and high-spirited — often led to strains and minor disagreements in later years.

After the fall of the Commune many of the exiled Communards fled to London. Often arriving without money or belongings, they were unwelcome refugees and Marx and Engels offered advice and support.

One of the refugees who frequented the Marx house was Charles Longuet, a Proudhonian journalist who had edited the Commune's Journel Officiel *and was a member of the General Council of the International. He and Jenny, then twenty-seven, became engaged in March 1872 and the first few letters from Jenny in this section were written soon afterwards, while Longuet was in Oxford hoping to find work teaching French.*

By February 1872 Laura and Schnaps were in Madrid with Lafargue. But in July Schnaps — who had been ill for some time — died at the age of three and a half. On 1 September the Lafargues left Spain to join the Marxes and Eleanor at The Hague for the 1872 Congress of the International, where Paul represented Spain and Portugal.

In the wake of the Commune the International had suffered from a widespread campaign to diminish its influence. At the Hague Congress, Bakunin was expelled, the powers of the General Council were extended, and its seat was transferred from London to New York. Most of the national federations rejected the General Council's authority, however, and the "Marxist" International was finally wound up in 1876.

From October 1872 the Lafargues lived in London. With the death of his three children Paul declared that he no longer believed in medicine and tried to earn his living as an engraver and photolithographer.

33. Jenny to Charles Longuet

[*London, April 1872*]

[The first two paragraphs of this letter were written in French.]

My great revered Charles!
I still love you a tiny bit, but I don't at all love telling you so in letters. I would rather kiss you once than write you a whole book, and I'd rather have just *one* of your kisses (you admit that you'd need *four* of mine) than four pages of your prose. This is undeniable evidence that you deserve the title of man of letters more than I do blue stocking. Let impartial observers judge between us! But so as not to provoke your morbid, man-of-letters' sensitivity I must confess — when I cannot kiss you my greatest happiness is to read you. So, imagine my delight this morning when I came down to discover your letter on the table. I had spent almost an hour longer than usual in bed for fear of having been mistaken in my hope that there would be a letter from you. What moral courage — it's worthy of that heroine with whom you're acquainted, is it not?

I am very happy to hear that you are enjoying Oxford more — Papa is calling me — he wants me to read through the second part with him, which has just arrived.[1] It's very hard, I promise you, to tear myself away from you — BUT DUTY FIRST — PLEASURE NEXT.

Engels has just interrupted us after three hours' work, so I may write you a few more lines. I regret to say that the translation of the first part of the second *livraison* is most negligently done — very carelessly indeed. It is necessary to make many corrections. Papa is very sorry he cannot consult you as to these corrections and almost feels inclined to go to Oxford on purpose. However, as you are coming to London on Saturday there will be some time for you to look them over with him. You *must* come over to London on this *first* Saturday. By and by you will get more used to Oxford and I to Hampstead — without you!! I see from your letter that you did not receive my letter early yesterday, though I sent it off the first thing in the morning. From it you will have seen that I at once wrote to your mother — I am being called again — Excuse this hurried scrawl and believe me as EVER

Your

JENNY

Unfortunately I cannot find *Le Neveu de Rameau*.[2] Somebody or other has walked off with it. I will get a copy in town.

1. A reference to the French translation by Roy of the first section of *Capital*, published in 1872 by Lachâtre.
2. Novella by Denis Diderot (1762).

34. Jenny to Charles Longuet

[London] *1 May 1872*

My own dearest Charles,

I am grieved to hear that my worst misgivings are being fulfilled, and that you are quite as ill at your ease at Oxford as I feared you would be. This small world of English university men and professorial shopkeepers must indeed be hopelessly dull. The British philistine is at his best *un triste sacco* — therefore what must the sad dog be at his worst, after he has gone through a regular academical training of his sadness! My poor Charles! How I wish I could take part of this burden of dullness off your shoulders. And to think you are enduring this most uncongenial life for my sake. That thought makes me feel quite angry with myself — but you — you, I love you more and more for it. How have I deserved so much true affection?

But to speak of business matters. Let me prove to you that I am very "practical," notwithstanding your assertions to the contrary. With regards to the exorbitant prices of lodgings at Oxford — I think that fact is not so alarming as it appears to be at first sight. Prices being high at Oxford, the tutors will have to pay accordingly, which will square matters. I think you ought to ask more than 5s. for an hour's lesson. However, the best plan will be to enquire of Beesly's friend, Mr. Richards, what the usual terms at Oxford are before fixing a price. In the meantime, however (perhaps the tutors do not pay at once), I hope you will write me a line to let me know whether I may send you an order for a few pounds, of which, by the by, no one at home will know anything as I have the money ready in my desk. At the same time I warn you that like Shylock and the rest of my *tribe* I do not lend out money *gratis*, as that would bring down the rate of usance — even like Jacob I shall take interest when you repay me. Write at once about these business matters.

Papa has read the preface and first pages of *Das Kapital* with Mützchen who, it appears, has thoroughly studied the book. He found fault with some of the first sentences in the preface which certainly are not so well translated as the rest.

This morning I was roused out of my sleep by Helen, who congratulated me most warmly. Wherefore do you think? Because I have grown a year older. A strange cause for congratulation, *n'est-ce pas?* Do you also feel inclined to congratulate your old woman? For my own part I should have forgotten all about my birthday if all these people hadn't taken the greatest pains to remind me of it in true German fashion. As I am anxious you should have this letter in good time I will say goodbye.

With many kisses, believe me

Your loving JENNY

Best remembrances from all at home. I wrote to your mother yesterday.

Jenny and Charles Longuet were married on 9 October 1872. They lived in Oxford for a while; the Lafargues stayed in London from the end of the month.

In March 1872 Eleanor had become secretly engaged to Hippolyte Prosper Olivier Lissagaray, a flamboyant Communard twice her age who had fought on the Paris barricades and was now helping with the rehabilitation of French exiles in London. Though not enamoured at the prospect of Lissagaray as a son-in-law, Marx was greatly to admire his History of the Commune of 1871 (*see page 115, note 3*).

35. Eleanor to Jenny

1 Maitland Park Road
7 November 1872

My dear Jenny,

Laziness, as you know, is the root of all evil (no allusion, Charlie) and laziness is at the root of my long silence. Every day last week I sat down with the intention of writing to you, and every day I got up again without having done so.

I suppose you expect to hear all the cancans, etc., and so as far as I am able I will report all that has happened "faithfully and to the best of my knowledge." Of the Lafargues' arrival Mama has given you all the particulars, so of them I will tell you nothing, except that I find Laura looks much better than she did at Luchon. I don't know whether you heard that *Lissagaray* called the same night as they came, but as we were all gone to hear Papa's lecture of course did not see us. Some days later he came again, supported by Richard. Laura and Paul had gone to hear Vermersch's[1] lecture, so with a certain amount of excitement Mama and I awaited their return. At last they came. I, of course, told them who was there. They went in, shook hands with Richard, and treated Lissagaray to a very cold bow. We thought this odd, but attributed it to a certain *gêne* on first meeting. But afterwards, when they went away, the same ceremony was again gone through. Last night Lissa came again with Wroblewski[2] and again Laura and Lafargue shook hands

with everybody (Serraillier was there) and not with him! Altogether they behave most oddly. Either Lissagaray is the perfect
gentleman Paul's letter and his own behaviour proclaim him
to be, and then he should be treated as such, or else he is no
gentleman, and then he ought not to be received by us — one
or the other — but this really unladylike behaviour on Laura's
part is very disagreeable. I only wonder Lissagaray comes at all.
He told me, too, that he would come one day this, or early next
week, to read me some extracts from the second edition of his
book which is shortly to appear.[3]

The latest event here is Plantade's death.[4] Very odd scenes
occurred at his funeral. For instance, Dupont carried a huge
cross, all the way, and it seems that the cemetery was an immense distance — much farther than Finchley. You may imagine how he has been plagued about it. In fact what business had
he to carry this cross all the time. Arrived at the cemetery an
altercation took place between the authorities, who wished the
coffin to be taken to the chapel, and the *Communeux*, who were
bent on an *enterrement civil*. At last they were told to take off
"their *bonhomme*." What a way of speaking of a corpse!

At Madame Plantade's where all the people assembled odd
things happened too. Lissagaray told us yesterday that when he
got there he went up to Madame Plantade to speak a few words
of condolence, when the latter turned round and begged him to
take *un petit verre de vin blanc*. The tables were covered too
with cakes, and biscuits, and oranges, and nuts, and all sorts of
things — much more like a wedding than a funeral, and Madame Plantade all the time saying *"Voyons, mes enfants,
mangez donc!"* Just fancy a disconsolate widow handing round
sweets!

You have received the celebrated document of the Blanquists, I believe.[5] What do you think of it? There are a few
phrases put in by Vaillant but the whole is done by Cournet.
The Martinists, as they are now called, are very proud of their
work. We have seen nothing of them. Paul intends calling on
Vaillant.

We heard from Outine yesterday, that a delegate from
Lyons and Paris had called on him to ask with whom they were
to hold — with the Jurassiens[6] or with New York — with Geneva
or Vaillant and Ranvier. Outine told them the Geneva and New
York were one, and all the rest enemies!

I think this is about all the news I have to tell you, for nothing particular has taken place. It is possible that Papa will go over to Oxford tomorrow,[7] and he will tell you all that remains to be told.

Goodbye then — are you coming up soon? Let us know if you are.

Your affectionate sister,

TUSSY

1. Eugène Vermersch, founder of *Le Père Duchêne*, who had fled to London.
2. Walery Wróblewski, a Polish émigré and Communard.
3. A reference to *Huit Journées de mai derrière les barricades*, written and published in Brussels in late 1871. This was a first draft of *Histoire de la Commune de 1871*, Eleanor's English translation of which appeared in 1886.
4. Jean Louis Plantade, an ardent socialist, belonged to a French-language branch of the International in London during the 1860s. After the Commune, he lodged many refugees in his hotel and restaurant in Ryder's Court, Leicester Square.
5. A pamphlet entitled *Internationale et Révolution. A propos du congrès de La Haye, par des réfugiés de la Commune, ex-membres du conseil général de l'Internationale*, which attacked the decision taken at The Hague to transfer the seat of the International to New York. The signatories, who included Martin (hence Martinists), Vaillant, Cournet, etc., all former members of the General Council, resigned from the IWMA.
6. Influenced by Bakunin, the members of the Jura Federation of the International took the lead in rejecting the resolutions of the Hague Congress.
7. Marx was in Oxford from 15 to 18 November to discuss the French translation of *Capital* with Longuet.

In 1873 the Marxes, the Longuets and the Lafargues were all living in London. In September Jenny gave birth to her first child, Charles-Félicien, who died the following July. She was very shaken by this experience and soon afterwards was taken by Engels and Lizzie Burns on visits to Ramsgate and Jersey; she returned to London on the day Eleanor wrote her this letter.

1873 was also the year that marked Eleanor's first bid for independence: in March, she took up a teaching post at a girls' boarding-school in Brighton. It lasted only a few months. Still involved with Lissagaray, but distressed by her family's evident disapproval, it was in Brighton that she suffered the first of her bouts of nervous depression.

In August 1874 Eleanor accompanied Marx to Carlsbad, where he was taking a cure: Marx's friend Dr. Kugelmann was also there, with his family. The Marxes returned to London in early October, after stopping at Dresden, Leipzig, Berlin and Hamburg, where Marx visited his publisher, Meissner.

36. Eleanor to Jenny

Germania, Carlsbad
5 September 1874

My dearest Jenny,

I cannot tell you how glad we were to hear from you. I should have written to you long since only I did not know where to address my letter.

As to Carlsbad, I have already told Mama, and she has no doubt told you, how much we like the town, and indeed one must be very *difficile* not to be enchanted with such admirable scenery. Less grand of course than Luchon, there is something lovely in this pretty little valley which is almost more "taking" than Luchon.

But I wish to speak to you a little about the people — all descriptions of the country will fall far short of the truth. The

Kugelmanns have been a *great* drawback to Papa in his cure. You have no idea, my dear Jenny, what an impossible person "Wenzel"[1] is, if you had you could easily understand that it was inevitable that he and Papa *could* not help quarrelling. At present they, indeed *we* are not on speaking terms. As to his wife she is a charming little woman, and Fränzchen,[2] though she has many unpleasant qualities, can only be admired for not being worse than she is. I am very intimate with Mrs. Kugelmann, and indeed it is impossible not to like and to pity her when one sees the life she leads. It's a hard thing when a woman has no money of her own and her husband tells her every minute that she is ungrateful for all his *Wohltaten*[3] to her and the child! You cannot imagine how brutish Kugelmann is and how shameless. He made Papa the unwilling listener of a most abominable scene (for the rooms are only separated by a door) after which he played the offended for a week because Papa and I of course sided with her and the child. You can fancy how unpleasant it was for us when Fränzchen came to us half in fits and her mother almost in the same state. I cannot of course in a letter give you a good account of all these affairs, but when we return to London you will see how much poor Trautchen[4] must have suffered during the seventeen years of her marriage, for he turned out his amiable side a week after the wedding. Of course had it not been for this scene, we should probably never have heard all these details, but both she and Fränzchen were so exasperated that out it all came. She says you had no real idea of all these things, for at that time her husband took care not to show off before Papa,[5] and secondly because he has got still worse in these last five years. As to Fränzchen she positively hates him, and it's no wonder. She adores her mother and has since she is a mere baby seen nothing but these continual quarrels — and always about nothing. The grand scene began because Mrs. K. didn't lift up her dress on a dusty day! As I told you he sulked for a week, then, not daring to say anything to Papa, took the pretext yesterday of a bad joke I made (one by the by that all concur in saying was nothing at all) to declare himself mortally offended. Fränzchen, who is a very critical little body, has told us many things that do not do much credit to her Papa. In all this of course Papa has had much bother but we shall take no more notice of him now. I cannot tell you how much I pity poor Trautchen. She says she well foresaw that this would happen, but that she had half-hoped Papa might have a little influence on Wenzel and thus procure her — to use her words — "at least four weeks of peace."

So much for Wenzel, but there are many things I shall tell you which, if it were not that his wife and child suffer, would be highly comical.

All this is a great nuisance, but still I think Papa is better, and the waters are sure to have a good effect. We are very exact indeed in all our "duties." Fancy Papa being ready dressed and at the *brunnen*[6] by six o'clock, frequently still earlier! We take long walks, and altogether get on very well here. You know of course about our *rencontre* with Deutsch.[7] He is a most amusing fellow, and he's known [by] and knows *everybody*. We shall have some odd tales to tell you — *entre autres* about poor Flourens. We have made another very nice acquaintance, that of the painter Knille. A charming fellow, whom Kugelmann looks down upon as not having such a deep mind as his own. We had also been introduced by Deutsch to an awful Frenchman who thank heaven is now gone away. A perfect idiot, who however as *agent de change* manages to earn from two to three millions (francs) a year! The most unbearable example of the bourgeois species that it is possible to imagine. He is at present a Mac-Mahonist and his greatest hope and desire is that the septennate will *never* change![8] Another person Deutsch introduced to Papa was Count Plater, a Pole who has also now left Carlsbad. A good fellow enough in his way. A regular old aristo and Catholic, but [a] good Pole and Russia-hater. He was described in the local paper here as "*chef* of the Nihilists" (you may suppose how horrified the old fellow was) and was announced as being here with the *chef* of the International.

Rochefort's *Lanterne* is much read here by the numerous Russians and Poles who take their headquarters here at Carlsbad during the season. Of course we always read it, moreover we have a subscription for the reading-room where *all* papers, French, English, German, Russian, American are to be obtained. We look over them as we read very little else. Indeed it is wonderful how the time goes. A day is gone before you manage to find time to read a paper or to write a letter.

The Kugelmanns are here three weeks tomorrow and only stay one week longer. We shall not go to Hanover but I do not know yet which way we shall return. I should like to see more of Trautchen, for I really like her, but as little as possible of Wenzel, but Hanover is out of the question. I have forgotten to tell you that one of Mrs. K's brothers spent two days here. I cannot tell you how much we liked him. He is the kindest person you can see. His sister says she always hides her position from him as much as possible as he is so very unhappy about her relations with her husband.

I see I have got to the bottom of the page, so I must needs say *adio*, besides it is dinner-time — a most important event here.

Give my best love to all at home not forgetting the Engels.

Papa sends his love and will also write soon.

I am, dearest Jenny,

Your affectionate sister,

TUSSY

Please address all letters to *me*.

1. Nickname of Kugelmann (allusion to "Good King Wenceslas").
2. Nickname of Franziska, Kugelmann's daughter.
3. "Kindnesses."
4. Nickname of Gertrude, Kugelmann's wife.
5. Marx and Jenny had stayed with the Kugelmanns in Hanover in 1869.
6. "Pump-room."
7. Austrian journalist with whom Marx had quarrelled during their mutual exile in Paris.
8. In 1873 Marshal Mac-Mahon accepted the presidency of the Republic, a term of office then as now running for seven years, but he resigned in 1879.

In 1874 the Lafargues moved to 27 South Hill Park, Hampstead, and the Marxes, early in 1875, to a smaller house at no. 41 Maitland Park Road.

Charles Longuet was teaching French at King's College and Jenny teaching French and German at St. Clement Danes Parochial School. In May 1876 they moved to 30 Leighton Road, Kentish Town. On 10 May Jenny gave birth to a son, Jean, nicknamed Johnny, who many years later became Jaurès' faithful companion and played an important part in the French socialist movement.

In August 1876 Eleanor again accompanied her father to Carlsbad, from where this letter is written. Jenny and the Lafargues were on holiday in Hastings; Mrs. Marx was in Ramsgate with Engels and Lizzie Burns, who had become an intimate friend since the Engelses' move to London.

37. Eleanor to Mrs. Marx

Germania, Carlsbad
19 August 1876

My dear Mama,

I am afraid you have not received my last letter, so I send this one to "Mrs. Williams" with slight variations in the address.

Still you may have had my letter, so I won't repeat the adventures of our journey — suffice it to say that we have recovered from our twenty-eight hours' journey and are now enjoying Carlsbad. Before continuing I must however remind you how proverbially stupid one gets at Carlsbad — so don't be surprised if I seem rather incoherent.

We go through exactly the same routine that you have heard me speak of so often. Everything seems just as it did — except that it's much pleasanter without the grumbling and quarrelling of Kugelmann. We see "the doctors," especially Fleckles,[1] a good deal. He is really a very witty and a very good fellow. He has a great deal of worry and trouble just now. Just fancy, Mme. Wolman's husband has lost every farthing he

Karl Marx in London, aged forty-three

Jenny von Westphalen,
who married Marx in 1843

Jenny Marx in a photograph
taken a few years before her death in 1883

Jenny, Eleanor and Laura in 1864, with Engels and Marx

Laura
and her husband, Paul Lafargue

Eleanor and Edward Aveling, with whom she lived from 1884 until her death

Jenny (wearing a cross she was given by Polish patriots) and Laura

Jenny's husband, Charles Longuet

Jenny with her father

Jenny and Charles Longuet's house in Argenteuil,
where Marx visited them several times in 1881 and 1882

possessed as well as his wife's entire fortune. She and all her and his relations were perfectly ignorant of his speculating and it was of course a great blow to a woman accustomed all her life to being immensely rich. Fleckles I think does everything he can for them — he is even working very hard.

Besides the doctors we see also two of the professors of Breslau — two nice old fellows — one is married and his wife is also very amiable. Kowalewski is not here, and I miss our old friend Deutsch, who I hear from Fleckles is also very badly off.

Carlsbad is still very full. There are as many Jews as ever, and more anxious than ever to get as much water as possible. Still, an American has outdone them. He came to Carlsbad but being unable to stay more than two days took forty-two glasses a day! It's a marvel he didn't die of it.

I see from the papers that it is very hot in London. Dear Mama, I am so sorry for you to be in that horrid close atmosphere. Do let us know how you are.

Have you seen or heard anything of *Cara mia*?[2] How are Ludovic Lormier and Mrs. Lormier? Give them my love when you see them and tell Mrs. Lormier I will write to her as soon as possible — but indeed you cannot imagine how the time goes doing nothing. What with drinking and eating, and walking, it is bedtime before one has well managed even to commence a letter.

I wrote to Jenny yesterday, and I hope to hear the boy is getting on. Is Helen at Ramsgate? If not, give her my love.

I think Papa will write too, so today I will say goodbye. Please send me the last *Hornet*,[3] and next week's too.

With many kisses,

Your affectionate

TUSSY

P.S. I went out the other day with a pair of very wide stockings. The consequence was a fold just on my little toe — producing quite an inflammation, which prevents my wearing my new boots!

Adio!

---

1. Dr. Ferdinand Fleckles, son of Dr. Leopold Fleckles, one of the leading proponents of the Carlsbad cure.

2. Nickname of Harry Juta, Marx's nephew, who arrived in London in September.

3. Possibly a reference to *The Beehive*, a union journal initially sympathetic but later hostile to the IWMA.

By 1878 both Mrs. Marx and Lizzie Burns were seri-
ously ill. On 12 September 1878 Lizzie, after having
been legally married to Engels the previous day ac-
cording to the rites of the Anglican church, died of
cancer of the bladder. Mrs. Marx was told by a spe-
cialist that she was suffering from an incurable dis-
ease: it was cancer of the liver.

A total amnesty for the French exiles was pro-
claimed in July 1880. Lissagaray was one of the first
to go back to France, followed shortly afterwards by
Charles Longuet, who left his family in London while
he established himself and found somewhere to live.
Jenny, who had given birth to two more sons, Harry
(Harra) in July 1878 and Edgar-Marcel (Wolf) in
April 1879, did not join him until April 1881. The fol-
lowing letter was written soon after his arrival in
France.

Paul Lafargue returned to France in April 1882
and Laura in July of the same year.

38. Charles Longuet to Jenny
(in French)

Sunday afternoon
[Paris, late 1880]

My dear Jenny,
I'm writing this on a café table, out of doors, on the boulevard!
You must think I'm feeling very happy. Well, it depends. Certainly Paris is much more lively than London and this morning,
a few hours ago, going to the top of a tram to visit my mother in
Ménilmontant, I felt a genuine pleasure, almost an emotional
experience, at finding myself among *faubouriens*.[1] I went up to
the top deck on purpose — besides, I hardly looked like a member
of the Commune and everyone took me for an Englishman.
What a come-down! I'll return to my impressions in a moment,
or tomorrow at the latest, because I'm sure I'll have new ones
every day. But first I must tell you the main outlines of my

odyssey — in search of a mother! Our boat didn't arrive at Boulogne until 6 o'clock in the morning. They'd made us wait at
Folkestone until 2.30 or 3 in the morning in a huge room, on
benches. And I was very lucky to get one, I slept on it for almost
two hours. Most of the travellers had nothing at all and had to
walk about.

First MISHAP. But it was paradise compared with the boat
The second-class cabin was a horrible, narrow little hovel the
very sight of which was enough to make you seasick! But I
think that on this occasion people would have been sick even on
a transatlantic liner. It was a horrible crossing. At around 5
o'clock I went up on deck. Not being a great expert in nautical
matters, I thought we were going to sink at any moment. Luckily most of my fellow-passengers broke into peals of laughter
whenever I was on the point of taking fright at a slight swaying
of the boat which had made me think we were about to be ship-
wrecked. So I managed to put a good face on it, having already
got rid of most of my bile in the cabin. The most dismal part of
it was the cold. When I got off the boat at 6 o'clock I didn't at all
feel like getting on to the train that was about to leave. Also I
felt obliged to go and see Mlle. Basset. I took a room at a hotel
near the station. I was woken at 10.30 and went to the rue
Belterre (note the spelling — it must be deliberate, so as to baffle the etymologists like Lafargue — the road is one of the ugliest
you ever saw). Mlle. Basset struck me as very friendly — an old
Boulognaise but very anglicized. She told me that my mother
had stayed in Boulogne for three weeks and that she expected
us there with the children, but when we didn't come she had
allowed Mlle. Basset to let someone else have the rooms and had
gone to Paris. I found her there this morning at 71 (note, not no.
64) rue de Ménilmontant (it used to be called "causeway"). I
had warned her of my arrival in a letter from Boulogne. She
was expecting me this evening and was on very good form. She
has two pretty rooms with enormous windows of the kind she
likes overlooking a street which teems with all the working people of the district, especially on Sundays. I am sure that you
would really enjoy the area — as a visitor. I had slept at a hotel
near the station. She has just been there with me and brought
back my luggage to her place while I went about my business.
I'm going to see Humbert[2] and his wife — he was at the station
yesterday. It was very kind of him because he has just lost one

of his little twins and I fear that he may lose the other one too. He has a nurse who must not have milk because the child is made to drink . . . [incomplete]

1. People who live on the outskirts of the metropolis.
2. Alphonse Humbert, a friend of Longuet's who had been sentenced to deportation for his part in the Commune and, like Longuet, had now returned to France.

39. Charles Longuet to Jenny
(in French)

Friday evening
[Paris, late 1880]

My dear good wife,
I'm writing you a few words just so that you don't have to wait till Monday morning. I wanted to write you a long letter but I had an invitation to lunch, which I'd put off for ages, and which took up the whole day. And don't start thinking that I'm reduced to not putting stamps on my letters. I left the stamp I bought on the *tabac* counter and it's too late to get one now. I had half guessed what you tell me about Melotte[1] from a letter he sent me two days ago. He really has a nerve to imagine that he's going to go behind Gaborit's back. For one thing it would be most unjust and I'd feel obliged to do all I could to prevent it. And I'm going to tell Melotte what I think of it.

I want to come back to the Irish question one of these days — it looks as though things are getting worse. But I must have at least one of the Irish papers. And you must help me, and if necessary send me pieces yourself, as you used to do for the *Marseillaise*. I'm sure they'd go down extremely well. You're always sending me extracts of strongly worded articles in your letters — but it's no use. You'd do much better to follow my advice.

I'm very busy with getting together the reports of the Marseilles Congress[2] and other supporting documents that I need for the rest of my series on workers' organization. Your friends the collectivists are beginning to make all sorts of friendly gestures towards me. Today Massard described me in the *Citoyen* as one of the nicest editors of *Justice*[3] and paid me all sorts of compliments simply because I mentioned him yesterday.

Kiss our little ones for me and tell me what you think of your condition.[4] They're throwing me out of the café, it's about to close. Roy has written an enormous article on Littré[5] which hasn't appeared yet because it's so long. He's promised to do *Capital* and I'm counting on him.

Your letter to my mother came via Paris. I've sent it on to the right address which I'll give you in my next.

Hello to all and twenty kisses for you.

CHARLES

Ireland article sent this morning. At least I gave the order.

---

1. Possibly a reference to Georges Melotte, who had played an active part in the Commune and whom Longuet had known when he was in exile in Britain.
2. The third Socialist Congress of Marseilles had been held in October 1879.
3. *Citoyen* and *Justice* were both socialist dailies.
4. Jenny was pregnant.
5. Emile Littré (1801–81), disciple of Comte and author of *Dictionnaire de la langue française*.

Charles now had a job, as joint editor of Clemenceau's
Justice, *and a house, in Argenteuil, where Jenny*
joined him shortly before giving birth to her fifth
son, Marcel-Charles (Par). She was in poor health,
burdened by housework and nostalgic for Maitland
Park Road.

40. Jenny to Laura

11, Boulevard Thiers,
Argenteuil
Thursday [April 1881]

My dear Laura,

Though I feel awfully knocked up, I do not think I have ever
felt so tired, I must write you a line to tell you that we have just
had the great pleasure of seeing Lafargue, accompanied by
Mesa. He is looking very well and gave me hopes soon to have
you over here. I think he intends returning to London tomorrow.

I suppose you have already heard from the people at Maitland Park that we arrived safe and sound, notwithstanding the
terrible disaster of finding the house shut up after having travelled during twelve hours with the poor babes, whose conduct
was admirable up to the very last. I think the *vie de Bohème*
is very congenial to children, the Wolf was so happy that he forgot the use of his fingers and was all eyes and ears. The worst
difficulties here are an impossibility to get anything settled — the
people of this place being the greatest dullards I have ever come
across. One case in point will suffice to make this clear to you.
Three different men have now tried in vain to fix the wheel of
the perambulator and it still comes off after a few minutes. So
it is with everything else, the consequence of which is that all is
pell-mell in the house and one has nothing to do but to pick up
litter right and left.

It was a mad idea to come to this unfurnished house with
the three children, I ought to have come over by myself.

Mrs. Longuet is going to bring me an Alsatian servant in
some days, as it is scarcely safe for me to be alone in the house

at night (the woman leaves at 7) with Emily, who does not know a word of French and could not even find her way to the doctor. Last night for instance, Longuet, who has been too unwell of late to go to the *Justice*, missed his train and did not turn up until this morning. The worst of this Alsatian servant is that she does not know French well, having only been in the country since two months, and that the children will have strange instructors and will pick up an execrable accent.

It is post time and so I must leave you, my dear Laura, for the present. Kiss Papa and Mama for me and give my best love to Engels and to Pumps.[1]

Your affectionate sister
JENNY

I think everything over here is awfully dear.

---

1. Mary Ellen Rosher, known as Pumps (Lizzie Burns's niece), who had lived with Engels and Lizzie since 1878 and on Lizzie's death took over as mistress of his household.

41. Eleanor to Jenny

London, 7 April 1881

My dearest Di,

We are glad to see from your letters that at least the dear little men seem to get on in their new quarters. Of course we know without telling what an awful time you must be having, in a strange house with three babies and no proper servant. The water trouble too seems a rather serious one. In what way are you going to remedy it? If you've been having cold weather, here it has been terrible. Such east winds as I cannot remember having felt before, and lasting not for a day but for two weeks. Of course Papa had to stop in altogether, but even with that precaution he has a bad cold. As to Mama we all find she is looking much better than she was, though she is not really any better. This new doctor[1] has pleased both her and Mohr extremely — *reste à savoir* if he'll do any good. He seems to incline to Gumpert's opinion, though he is still very doubtful as to the real nature of Mama's illness. If Dr. Donkin has pleased Papa, he seems to be immensely taken with Papa. Mr. Rose[2] knows him well and told me he was "delighted" with Papa, and very anxious to know him more. Is it not odd how all the people one meets know someone else you know? After all what a small place the world seems to be.

It certainly would be a great pity if you had to give up writing but by and by when you've settled down and have a good servant you'll find more time. Just now naturally every moment is occupied with the house or the children, but that will only be for a time. Have you seen what is going on in Ireland?[3] Two men shot and many wounded, and now a girl of twenty shot and several women hurt. Verily they are getting on. No doubt you'll get all details about these frays from the Land League. Most's[4] arrest is making quite a stir here: it is most unfortunate — for the government are doing Most a great service. The few followers he had were beginning to desert him, but now he is once more a great man. As to the government they have blundered frightfully in the matter and shown they were even greater asses than they were supposed to be.

We've not heard much more about the newest "New Party"[5] — but I don't think it will come to much. Meanwhile Shipton and Weiler are about to start a workingman's paper — the *Labour Standard*[6] — and Hirsch's[7] head shines again with excitement and busyness. The spirit of the paper will, I daresay, be willing, but the pens, as far as I can see, will be decidedly weak.

A few days ago Beesly called: the Comtist idea is that very shortly — in a few months in fact — Germany will take Switzerland and Holland — and that a European war will ensue. With regard to Ireland Beesly thinks Home Rule a necessity. The poor devil has had a lot of trouble: his eldest boy had typhoid fever and since then one illness after another, so Beesly was not in a very cheerful frame of mind.

Little Jollymeier is here on account of that case in which he is a witness and also to take part in the dinner given in honour of Helmholtz. He is particularly nice — and not at all silly — at least he wasn't a few nights ago, but in the interim he has no doubt been demoralized by continual intercourse with Chitty's bottles and with that "British Philistine" Moore.[8]

I saw the Lormiers yesterday. Ludovic has had a photo from the Queen which he is to paint in oil — it is one of the Duchess of Edinburgh's children — a pretty child enough. Of course Ludovic is in the seventh heaven of bliss, though why he calls painting a photo painting a "portrait" I do not quite see. Mrs. Lormier is always the same and sends no end of messages and good advice to you. The only thing worth repeating is to tell you to find out if there's not a regular "market day" at or near Argenteuil, as you would get everything at that so cheap, and having such splendid cellars you could get in a good store.

I am more happy than I can say to know that my Harra is in a skilful doctor's hands — and I am glad you are at last to consult a specialist. You may imagine how anxiously we shall await news of the darling. I am very pleased to hear Johnny is in good spirits. I so feared he would fret. That that dear little Wolf would be all right I knew, he's such a little brick. Tell Jack his Auntie sends him heaps of kisses for him and his brothers.

I wish I could give you some interesting news, dear, but there is none. How is poor Longuet? I hope better.

With best love and many kisses from us all,

Your affectionate

TUSSY

1. Bryan Donkin, a free-thinking doctor who was much in demand in political and literary circles; he later treated (and proposed marriage to) Eleanor's close friend Olive Schreiner.
2. Edward Rose, a friend of Eleanor's who was both an actor and a playwright.
3. The agricultural crisis of the late 1870s and the ineffectiveness of the 1870 Land Act had further aggravated the need for land reform in Ireland. In October 1879, under the presidency of Parnell, the National Land League was founded. However, claiming that the restoration of law and order was an essential prelude to further reform, Gladstone introduced a Coercion Bill early in 1881, which became law in March despite Parnell's efforts to obstruct its passage through the House of Commons. The Bill led to many outbreaks of violence and increased Nationalist resistance to new legislation.
4. In his journal *Freiheit*, published in London, the Anarchist Most had applauded the assassination of Tsar Alexander II. In June 1881 he was sentenced to sixteen months' hard labour.
5. The Democratic Foundation.
6. Trade Union weekly which appeared from 1881–85, edited by George Shipton.
7. Carl Hirsch was a German journalist and friend of the family's, whose proposal of marriage Eleanor rejected the following year. He was involved with

many radical journals and corresponded with both Eleanor and Lissagaray on publishing and other matters.
8. Jollymeier = Schorlemmer; Chitty = Engels; Moore = Sam Moore.

42. Jenny to Laura

[Paris] 22 *April 1881*

My dear Laura,

It seems to me a century since I left dear old England and you all, an endless century the days of which resemble each other so much that it seems impossible to distinguish one from the other, except that some days contain extra doses of the wretched small miseries *de la vie du ménage*, which weigh more heavily upon me than great troubles. The free, independent, active though monotonous existence I lived for some months in London has spoilt me and made me unfit for [illegible] and all that sort of thing. It all is so unbearable to me now that I feel as if some years, nay months, of this existence in a strange country, among strange people, would make an incurable idiot of me, an idiot after the fashion of Madame Arnaud[1] — I feel wretchedly hopelessly nervous — ill at ease mentally and physically. One of the three children generally keeps me awake at night, and added to this our poor Johnny has been very ill. He has had another attack of fever — a sort of gastric fever — and has been in bed for more days than when ill in London, the doctor coming to see him every day. His only joy is to see his brothers, upon whom he dotes now that he has no other friends. He does not get on with the French children whose acquaintance he has made here as he did with the Nayments[?]. He is longing for the time when you will be here and is constantly asking me when will Aunt Lolo come. Lolo answers when? When do you think you are likely to leave London? If soon I should like you to bring me some glycerine — good-sized bottle, and half a dozen tablets (small ones) of Pear's soap. I fear Mama will feel most lonely when you are also gone. It is indeed cruel that ill and old she should thus lose all her children — when she has most need of them. Do you think it at all likely the latest acquisition in the Esculapian line[2] will do her any good? And how is Papa — the weather must be very trying to him. Here we have had a spell of intense cold after some days of exceptional heat.

What do you think of the Land Bill and of Dizzy's exit?[3] I am quite cut off from all news — and daily long for the placards of the London newspapers which keep one in communion with the beings who live and struggle outside the prison called home. Pardon this wretched letter and attribute it in some measure to a pen that cannot be coaxed with moving on. Give my love to Paul and believe me ever

Your affectionate

JENNY

I cannot send you Charles' regards because he is not here at present.

1. Mme. Angélique Arnaud (1799–1884) was a well-known French radical, writer and feminist. It seems more likely, however, that Jenny is referring to a family acquaintance, Mme. Antoine Arnaud, whose husband had been on the staff of the *Marseillaise* and had spent the post-Commune years in England. Longuet spoke at his funeral in 1885.
2. Presumably a reference to the new doctor, Bryan Donkin.
3. The second Land Act, granting fixity of tenure, free sale by the tenant and fair rents, eventually became law in August 1881. Dizzy = Disraeli, who had died on 19 April.

Eleanor was now twenty-six and in search of a career. She had joined the New Shakespeare Society, one of the many literary organizations inspired by F. J. Furnivall, an energetic man of letters whose other ventures included the Early English Texts Society, the Browning Society and, in 1884, the Shelley Society. Furnivall also helped her to earn money by employing her to do research work for his various societies at the British Museum.

Out of the New Shakespeare Society emerged the Dogberry Club, an amateur dramatic society whose chief members were Clara and Dollie Maitland, Ernest Radford (later to marry Dollie) and the playwright Edward Rose. Encouraged by her success at these readings as well as at poetry recitals elsewhere, Eleanor decided to take acting lessons from Mrs. Hermann Vezin, a retired actress.

43. Eleanor to Jenny

London, 18 June 1881

My dearest Di,
I have to thank you for two letters and feel quite ashamed of myself. The fact is I did not want to write till I could tell you something definite about my new plans for studying with Mrs. Vezin, and that I could not do till now. Of that, however, anon. First let me tell you how very, very happy we are to hear our dear little men are so well. It is always such a joy to us to hear of them though it does make us long sorely to see them. The affection of those children for one another is simply beautiful. Dear little Wolf — I can imagine how bright he is — for you know the darling quite won my heart — his love for Harra is delightful. You must tell us as much as possible of the boys — of little grandfather Jack and of the *petit dernier*. You don't know what a treat it is to us to get any little story or anecdote about them. We had been terribly anxious at getting no news, and for the future, dear Di, if you'd send us just a *postcard* we should be glad — only don't leave us without all news. We

know well enough you haven't time for long letters and we don't ask for them — just one line to say you are well is what we want. As to my visit I'm afraid, dear, that cannot be just now. You see while we thought you ill in bed and no one to help you I should have managed to go — but I fear I must for the present give up all hope of doing so. I don't think Papa would like me to go away at this moment — and moreover I have some work to do — and if you knew how difficult it is to get work of any sort you'd not wonder that I stick to the little I have.

As to Mama, the doctor saw her yesterday and strongly advises both her and Papa to go to Eastbourne. I heartily hope they will — especially on Mohr's account, for after those coughs he has had all the winter he wants the change sadly. I think too it would do Mama good — but you know how queer she is and she doesn't seem much inclined to go. As soon as anything is really settled I'll let you know. Lina[1] has been with us since Monday. She is as amiable and sweet-tempered as ever — but alas! so deaf that it is well-nigh impossible to speak to her at all. She is almost as bad as poor old Allsop, so that it is quite painful to be with her.

And now Di, about myself. You may well suppose that all the difficulties you speak of have not been overlooked by me, and I do not feel at all sanguine about success — still I am going to take the lessons. Even if, as I fancy will be the case, Mrs. Vezin finds she has much overrated my powers, the lessons will still be useful to me, and I can always make the recitation venture. That you know was my object when I went to Mrs. V., but as she seemed so opposed to that I shall say nothing to her, but just let time show what I really *can* do. Till Monday I could not write to her as Papa hadn't the necessary money — but then I wrote and have received a nice letter in reply. Mrs. Vezin is just moving to our immediate neighbourhood (Highgate Rd.), which will be a great advantage to me, but after her moving, as she is unwell, she leaves town for a month. Then I am on her return to begin work. I feel sorry to cost Papa so much, but after all very small sums were expended on my education, compared at least to what is *now* demanded of girls — and I think if I do succeed it will have been a good investment. I shall try, too, to get as much work as I can so that I may have a little money by the time I need it. In this a new chance has luckily been given me. Just fancy that this morning I met Mayall[2] in the 'bus. He started the conversation by asking me to come and have my photo taken "in that pretty hat (my old brown one!) and Mother Hubbard cloak." He seemed quite anxious I should, so I've promised to go on Monday. Then he said the scientific journal with which he is connected requires a précis writer and asked me if I would try. I suppose you know that in literary slang a précis writer is one who summarizes articles, books, etc. It is a mere trick to do it — but as I told Mayall, I have never tried it and don't know if I can do it. He will let me try, and if I can I shall earn £2 a week, and not have much work — about a quarter what I'm doing now. I hope I shall be able to do it — it would be such a comfort. Well I'll try anyway — if I fail, I fail. You see, dear, I've a goodly number of irons in the fire, but I feel I've wasted quite enough of my life, and that it is high time I did something.

I don't remember whether I told you that we — i.e., Dollie, Mr. Radford, Harry Moore, Mr. Stoner and myself — are getting up two little plays which we are going to perform at the theatre of the Dilettante Club on the 5th July.[3] I of course enjoy it immensely and I feel besides that it is good work for me. Both the plays we are to do are pretty and I fancy will "go" tolerably. Details about them I will send you another time. I have a racking headache this morning and find it difficult to write at all. This evening I'm going to see Irving in *Hamlet*. There were only two seats to be had and I got them, but as Mama is going with me to see the German troupe on Monday she thought two days would be too much — and so Mr. Radford has taken the ticket and I shall go with him. He is a very nice young fellow — we all like him very much — and he has one great virtue — he is wonderfully like Irving!

Goodbye, my dearest Di. I kiss you and the dear little ones with all my heart.

Your
TUSSY

1. Lina Schöler, a nurse who had been engaged to Mrs. Marx's brother, Edgar von Westphalen.
2. Probably John Edwin Mayall, who had published a series of "photographic por-

traits in character," including one of Eleanor's teacher Mrs. Vezin, entitled *Celebrities of the London Stage* (1867–68).

3. Two one-act French plays: *First Love*, by Eugène Scribe, and *At a Farm by the Sea*. The Dilettante Circle, which had its headquarters in Aberdeen House, Regent Street, offered entertainments "of a semi-private character."

In spite of her illness Mrs. Marx was determined to visit Jenny and her grandchildren, whom she sorely missed, in Argenteuil. After their return from Eastbourne, where she and Marx spent most of July, she was examined by Dr. Donkin and advised that the trip might do her good. They had been in France only a matter of weeks before a telegram arrived from Eleanor's friend Dollie Maitland informing them that Eleanor was seriously ill (she was suffering from nervous depression and what is now termed anorexia). Marx left immediately, leaving Mrs. Marx, who was in great pain, and Helen Demuth to make the return journey in stages.

In October it was Marx's turn to be ill, with a serious attack of pleurisy. Eleanor's letter below is in reply to one from Jenny, untraced, declaring her intention of coming to London to be with him.

44. Eleanor to Jenny

London, Tuesday 18 October 1881

My dearest Di,

We had your letter this morning. You must not dream of leaving the children. It would be the merest madness and would cause Papa more anxiety than your being here could give him pleasure or do him good — much as we all wish you were here.

Dr. Donkin was here this afternoon and finds Papa better. The attack he has had was a serious one, so the doctor tells us he cannot get over it in a day — but all is going well. Since Saturday I have not left Papa's room — day or night. Tonight however Helen will be with him as the doctor wants me to have a night's rest. There is of course continuously something to do — though from today there will be rather less as Papa need not inhale so frequently nor take any more medicine. Engels is of a kindness and devotion that baffle description. Truly there is not another like him in the world — in spite of his little weaknesses. I have also had a charming letter just now from our good Mme. Lormier, begging me to let her come and

137

help us. My friend Miss Black has also asked to come and sit up with Mama should she need anyone. Isn't it kind of people to take such an interest? Mama however is no worse, and has such good nights that no one need be with her.

I send you a *Standard* so you can follow up the movement in Ireland. Never even in '67 during the Fenian rising, has the Government tried so hard to drive the people into a revolt. Therein lies the great danger — for an open rising would be crushed and the movement thrown back for years. Notice the conduct of the police in Dublin, Limerick, etc. It is simply outrageous. If only the people will keep firm but quiet the government will find its hands full.

My dear old Di, I am really very tired this evening (as Donkin didn't come till 5 o'clock I couldn't write by the early post) so you must be content with a short letter.

Don't be anxious. I am writing you daily *exactly* how matters are — though Papa (who is a terribly cranky patient!) is furious that I wrote you at all. I felt though that I must — I had no right not to let you know. Only dear, do not worry uselessly. I promise you that I will tell you quite faithfully how dear Papa goes on.

Kiss those little darlings for me.

Your affectionate

TUSSY

45. Laura to Jenny

[*London, October 1881*]
Thursday evening

My dear Jenny,

I am behindhand again in my letter-writing but I am so in spite of myself. I have so little time.

Of our invalids, Papa is in the fairest way of getting better, poor Mama is slowly growing worse. She can scarcely be thinner or weaker than she is, but her energy and her spirits are undying.

You do wrong to fret so much about her separation from

her grandchildren. At this time of day their presence here could do very little for her: she is unhappily too far gone to derive much comfort from the prattle and the pretty naughtiness of children and it says much for her fine nature that with such poor services as I am able to render she should still be so touched and pleased. It requires quite other behaviour to give her pleasure now than any, the very best, children can have. And although a glimpse of them every now and again would be a great thing, I am sure that the impossibility to get that is more than compensated for by the opportunity their absence gives her of thinking about them, and planning and plotting for them in their new home. Your own letters are a never-failing source of pleasure. She has got all your house-arrangements by heart and is for ever busying her mind with ways and means of adding to your comfort.

I was more deeply grieved than I can say to hear that what was probably her last letter never reached you. She would be inconsolable if she knew it. It had cost her such an effort to write and she had put so much into it to which she looked for an answer from you that the loss of the letter is irremediable. The posting of it had been entrusted to Tussy, into whose hands it was placed before being put into an envelope. Helen had expressed her doubts to me respecting your receipt of the letter, wherefore I asked you to let me know the rights of it.

Mama imagines that you replied to all her questions in your supposed letter to her and consequently doubly regretted the loss of it. I cannot find out what her questions were, but fancy there was something asked about your method of lighting your rooms, lamps, candles or what; and of heating them. Also, I think, something about certain little knickerbockers of Johnny's: did they fit or not?

At any rate, my dear Jenny, you cannot be too circumstantial when you write. She is never too ill to take the deepest and warmest interest in the least of the little things that make up your daily life. It is her one preoccupation, for she can neither read nor write and her never-idle needle is beginning to rust at last. She sees no one beyond the members of her own family.

I thank you for the information you gave me about you and yours. Clemenceau being *the* man of the moment I should think that the *Justice* could now raise a prouder head than ever. It strikes me that your Lord and Master's contributions to the paper are somewhat few and far between. May I ask how that is?

Hirsch has some soap in charge for you. With the wonderful traveller's tales he will bestow upon you take as many grains of salt as you can.

I am afraid my handwriting is becoming illegible, but, as I told Engels, a pen is too slight a thing for a hand used to the handling of turks' heads and carpet brooms!

With affectionate remembrances from all to all,

I am, as always, my dear Jenny,

your affectionate

LAURA

46. Eleanor to Jenny

London, 31 October 1881

My dearest Di,

First of all will you please send the enclosed letter to old Lawroff? Papa can't find his address, but wants this sent to him, and says even if you do not know his whereabouts you can find out through the Jaclards.

I hope, dearest Jenny, that you have quite understood that if I have written less often it is not *neglect* — but simply that Papa being much better there wasn't anything to write about. He now gets up a few hours every day, and will soon, Donkin tells me (he has just been here), be able to go down, or at any rate to go next door and see Mama. She is much the same — though weaker — and since two days has been in more pain. The doctor says he thinks he will soon have to give cutaneous injections of morphine — in which case we shall probably want a nurse. He says *I* could do it, but really I should not like to undertake doing it. By the way, Mama wrote you quite a long letter some five days ago and is *very* anxious at not hearing if you've had it. As my letters to you once or twice have not reached you she is fidgeting fearfully — it would give her so much pain if you'd not had it — that I almost think, dear, it would be better if you *said* you'd had it even if it has not reached you. If it has *not* tell me on a *private* slip of paper and

I'll write about it to the Postmaster General — not that that does much good though I don't think there was any *special* news in Mama's letter — so you can answer in a general sort of way. I still hope though that you've had it and that the return of Longuet has taken up so much of your time you've not been able to answer it. How dear Mama could write it I don't know. She is so thin and weak now it is a miracle. She has not left her bed at all now for many weeks, but in order to give her a *little* change Dr. Donkin says we are to lift her — in her sheets — from her bed to the chair bed.

Papa, as I have already told you, goes on well — in fact is improving more quickly than we had ever hoped he could. Unfortunately I'm beginning to feel very seedy — now the excitement is over a reaction is setting in. The doctor has given me iron to take and ordered me to go on more regularly again with my Turkish Baths and to get out more. This I shall do, as on the days Sarah is here Helen can well be up here with Papa and Mama, and I can go to the Museum, and shall not work there *long* — but get two or three hours work and the walk there and back. You see I had some work to do when Papa got ill. Dr. Murray[1] — though I hardly know him at all personally — has been most kind in waiting till I could resume my work (it has been a *great* inconvenience to him too), which I am thankful for as I did not want to lose it. You don't know how many people — most far better qualified to do the work than I am — try to get what I've been doing, and if I once give it up I may whistle for something else.

Dear Di, I'm talking to you a great deal about myself but believe me, all my thoughts are with you. *Do* give me news of how matters really are. You must know me well enough to be sure that I am discretion itself, and that anything you say to *me* I shall repeat to *no one* else.

Goodbye dear. How I wish I could see you and the dear children again! I long to make Par's acquaintance.

I kiss you all.

Your

TUSSY

Love from all here to you all.

I enclose *two* photos of Willa[2] and myself. We have only

a *very* few copies so I can only give you *one* — but I want you to choose which you like best. Do so and return me the other.

Yr

T

1. Sir James Augustus Murray, editor of the Oxford *New English Dictionary*, with which Furnivall was also involved. Furnivall had employed several of his personal friends to undertake research for the dictionary which, not surprisingly and to Murray's later annoyance, greatly exceeded its budget.
2. Willa Juta, a cousin.

Mrs. Marx died on 2 December 1881 and was buried three days later. The funeral was, as she had wished, a simple ceremony. Engels delivered a brief eulogy, which is reprinted in Appendix 1, pp. 305–07.

47. Eleanor to Jenny

Sunday 4 December 1881

My dearest Di,

I must write you a line though I am sick of writing — I have had so very many letters to write — but I must just speak to you. I do *so* miss you just now. I send you, dear, some of her dear hair — it is as soft and beautiful as a girl's. If you could but have seen her face at the last — the look in her eyes was simply indescribable. Not only that they were so clear — clear as one only sees *children's* eyes — but the sweet expression as she saw and recognized us — which she did to the end. The last word she spoke was to Papa — "good." She added something else, and indeed she before that said many things but we could not hear them. Oh! Jenny, she looks so beautiful now. Dollie [Maitland] when she saw her said her face was quite transfigured — her brow was *absolutely smooth* — just as if some gentle hand had smoothed away every line and furrow, while the lovely hair seems to form a sort of glory round her head.

Tomorrow the funeral will be. I do dread it — but of course Papa cannot go. He must not yet leave the house, and I am glad of this in every way. We have asked all the people Mama liked — and many just because on *Thursday* afternoon she still spoke of them.

To the *very last* she thought of you and the children more than of anyone, and she was *only on Thursday* saying what she would send them at Christmas.

Dear old Di — I can't write more now — I will write again tomorrow evening.

Kiss the dear little ones for me — and for Mama — she loved them so.

Your
TUSSY

After the death of his wife Marx went to Ventnor, on the Isle of Wight, on doctor's orders, taking Eleanor with him. They stayed until 16 January 1882, Eleanor's twenty-seventh birthday.

At Ventnor Eleanor underwent the second serious crisis of her life. The following letter offers a revealing analysis of her own mental condition, and her mistrust of conventional medical advice. She was tired out by the strain of caring for two sick parents, distraught at the death of her mother, still uncertain about her relationship with Lissagaray and above all impatient to "do something" before it was too late.

48. Eleanor to Jenny

*1 St. Boniface Gardens
Ventnor, Isle of Wight
8 January 1882*

My dearest Di,

Many thanks for your nice long letter. We are very anxious about the box though.[1] It would be really awful if it were lost.

Since we have been here the weather has been simply awful. Much colder than in London, and with the exception of two days it has rained continually. We hear it is the same all along the South and South West Coast. It is dreadful for Papa — as he hardly can get out at all. Indeed if the weather does not mend we shall, he says, return to London. As far as rooms are concerned we have been *most* fortunate — having two *large, airy, warm* bedrooms and a charming and very large sitting room, just below the cliff (i.e., well-sheltered) and with a view of the sea and hills. Our landlady is charming, a good cook, and most attentive in every way, and we pay only two guineas! *How* attentive they are you will see from this — that I *never* have to remind them to light Papa's bedroom fire morning or evening — it is done with the punctuality of clockwork. Since Friday evening Dollie Maitland has been here (she leaves early tomorrow), but by her coming there hangs a tale. I must tell you that if Papa is on the whole better at Ventnor I have been really ill ever since we came. In writing last week to Miss Black[2] and in a note to Mr. Radford (he is about to publish his translations of Heine which he wants to dedicate to Papa, and about which he consulted me) I happened to say I was feeling too ill to write or do anything and that, seeing how anxious I am to be able to look after Papa, I was terribly afraid of breaking down altogether, as I had done before. This seems to have alarmed my friends so much (they really *are* good friends to me, Di, as I will tell you one day when I *see* you — it is too long a story to *write* about) that Miss Black wanted to start off at once and see me and if need be stay with me, but having an engagement that binds her to London she could not. Mr. Radford thereupon rushed off for Dollie and went to Helen — (frightening poor old Nim, I've no doubt) and begged *her* to go to Ventnor. Helen could of course not leave the house — so Mr. Radford packed off poor Dollie! A very foolish thing to do as had I really needed some one Dollie would have been worse than useless. This accounts for Dollie being here (it was *very* good of the child to come) but she must return to her pupils tomorrow. I have been *much* annoyed by all this — of course I'm grateful to Clemmie and Mr. Radford and Dollie — but I wished they had let me alone. It only made Papa angry and anxious and can do me no good. He was angry that I had written I was ill and not told him. It was rather hard — for of course I'd only said nothing (and as I am really ill it was, to say the least, trying) in order to save him from any anxiety! Moreover I do not ever like to complain — and I hate to do so to Papa — he bitterly scolds me — as if I "indulged" in being ill at the expense of my family — or gets anxious, and that worries me most of all. What neither Papa nor the doctors nor anyone will understand is that it is chiefly *mental worry* that affects me. Papa talks about my having "rest" and "getting strong" before I try anything and won't see that "rest" is the last thing I need — and that I should be more likely to "get strong" if I have some definite plan and work than to go on waiting and waiting. If I really were needed just now to nurse Papa — as for instance when he was so ill — I should not feel this — but he does not really want me now, and it drives me half mad to sit here when perhaps my *last* chance of doing something is going. If I only had a *little* money I should distinctly say this; go in for hard work with Mrs. Vezin — and then *see* (you may be sure I will make no rash plunge) what I can do. I am not young enough to lose more time in waiting — and if I cannot do this *soon* it will be no use to try it at all.

But I've no money (I mean not enough to begin my lessons even) and it *is* hard. Really, Jenny, I think I *could* do something. I cannot believe Mrs. Vezin would have spoken as she did, nor offered to bring me out had she not thought I had *some* chance of success. For she could have no object in bringing out a failure. You know, dear, I'm not a bit vain — and that if I err it is not from over-confidence but from distrust in myself — but in this I think I could get on. I have seen too often — and with such different people — that I can *move* an audience — and that is the chief thing. (I wish very much I could do something before you — I'd like to know what *you* think.) Well, all this naturally worries me. Like yourself I suffer very much from insomnia — and once I get thinking I find it impossible to go to sleep. (For a long time I tried various drugs — this quite *entre nous*, and am loth to try them again — it is not much better, after all than dram-drinking, and is almost if not quite as injurious.) *Since I have been here I have not slept six hours.* You may imagine — even without counting other things — that this is killing — and I really do fear a complete breakdown — which for Papa's sake I would do anything to avoid. What I most dread is the consulting of doctors. They cannot and will not see that mental worry is as much an illness as any physical ailment could be.

I have said all this to you, my dear Di, because I want you to *understand*. I so fear too that my darling Mohr may think me disagreeable and dissatisfied — but I *can't* explain to him.

I think I told you that Papa has some idea of returning to London and then going somewhere else. The only objection is (and really this place is *frightful*) I don't quite see where we could go. Devonshire — indeed the whole coast on a level with the Isle of Wight — seems from all accounts to be equally badly off for cold and wet. A longer journey I should fear — and so would you if you had seen how *very* tired and knocked up Papa was even after coming here — a distance of only a few hours. I sometimes think perhaps if he could go to you to begin with — but then I don't suppose Paris is better than London — for you know we have had a perfectly marvellous winter. During the whole of November there was not only no fog — but we had the brightest sunshine — and till we came here the weather was lovely. Indeed it is too tantalizing that while here it is so cold we shiver in the warmest clothes, we daily get letters from London saying: "What beautiful weather you must be having for *even here* it is glorious!" It is too bad, isn't it?

If we *do* stay on here I shall go, as I told you, to London for that recitation — and I shall not feel the least anxiety. Papa *could* not be better looked after than he will be here.

Now, dear, I must bring this endless (and *very egoistic*) letter to a close (Dollie positively *groans* when she is left five minutes unentertained). I hope you won't be *much* bored by it. I am fearfully tired.

Papa kisses you all. *Do* send us much news of those darling children. It is really our greatest delight to hear about them and we talk of them continually. Poor Mama! How she used to talk of them! I think of Mama so much just now. It seems so strange to know we shall never see her more. Does Johnny talk of her so much still?

Goodbye, dearest Di. Forgive my bothering you with all this. I only wish you'd tell me of *your* troubles — for alas! I know you must have plenty of them.

Always your
TUSSY

1. A case of Christmas presents that had failed to arrive.
2. Clementina Black, sister of Constance, both friends of Eleanor's.

49. Eleanor to Jenny

Ventnor
15 January 1882

My dearest Di,

Papa told me you had written to him about me — and from what he has said I see how kindly you have spoken of me. After I wrote you last Sunday I almost regretted it — for it seems selfish to worry you with my affairs, when you must assuredly have worry enough of your own. Still more selfish does it seem that I think at all about myself — instead of think-

ing only of our dear Mohr. How I love him no one can know —
and yet — we must each of us, after all, live our own life — and
much and hard as I have tried I could not crush out my desire
to *try something*. The chance too of independence is very sweet.
But if all this has been troubling me it is not all. There has
been *much* else. For a long time I have tried to make up my
mind to break off my engagement. I *could* not bring myself to
do it — he has been very good, and gentle, and patient with me
— but I have done it now. Not only that the burden had become
too heavy — I had other reasons (I can't write them — it would
take so long, but when I see you will tell you) — and so at last
I screwed my courage to the sticking place. And now, dear, I
have a *great* favour to ask of you — namely that you will if
possible see Lissa sometimes, and treat him just as an old friend.
Remember *he* is blameless in this. I hope we shall continue the
best and most intimate of friends — and to do this nothing will
help so much as if you and Longuet continue to see him. You
will, I am sure, understand my feeling in this. Ah! it has been
a terrible struggle. I sometimes wonder how I have lived through
it all. I firmly believe that owing to my long intercourse with
cats, I have acquired, like them, nine lives instead of one.

Dear old Di, I wish I could talk it all over with you. I have
had so much worry of late. One friend after another I have
found false and treacherous — till even Dollie comes here and
tells Papa she believes me to be *secretly married* and a lot of
other cock and bull stories, that do far more honour to her
imagination than to her veracity. But this is over: I mean to
try hard by dint of hard work to make something more and
better of my life than it has heretofore been. After all *work* is
the chief thing. To me at least it is a necessity. That is why I
love even my dull Museum drudgery. You see I'm not clever
enough to live a purely *intellectual* life, nor am I dull enough
to be content to sit down and do nothing. Tomorrow is my birthday — if I keep but half my good resolutions for the coming
years I shall do well. But enough of myself. I *hate* to speak of
myself — and you too will be, by this, tired of the subject.

The weather in this "genial" place having gone from bad
to worse, Mohr has made up his mind to leave here tomorrow
(Monday). He had determined not to outstay the three weeks
up on Thursday — and as I am going tomorrow it is better he
should start at once than wait two days, and have me back

again for one. That Mohr is really much better and stronger I see from the fact that he hasn't got worse here. We have had days with icy winds, and days with fogs that would not disgrace London — and yet *on the whole* Mohr has stood it well. Then I feel too that he has had in me a most disagreeable and trying companion. I was really ill and, as you may guess, terribly preoccupied with my own thoughts which were none of the pleasantest. I feel heartily ashamed of myself now for having worried him. I *did* try not to let him see — but I succeeded very badly, and then Dollie's advent made further efforts at concealment useless.

We were more than glad to hear you had had news of the box — and we are now waiting anxiously to know whether you have it — I could hardly get over the disappointment were it lost. To begin with there are dear Mama's things which we so much wanted you to have — and then the toys for the children! In my mind's eye I have many a time gone over the scene of their unpacking their box and finding the various things.

News of any other kind I have not to give — for Ventnor is not exactly an exciting place, and the greatest events of each day have been my morning interview with butchers, poulterers, etc., and the various "meals."

Mohr and I have been saying for the last few days that when he feels up to it we shall both come to see you (I for a little while of course as I hope to get to work without loss of time) and also that in the spring or summer you *must* come to us with all the boys. Par will by that time be quite a man (from all I heard he was almost an independent gentleman six months ago) and either Helen or I would go over to help you on the journey.

And now, goodbye, dearest Di. Kiss my dear little boys for their Auntie, who also kisses you.

Your

TUSSY

p.s. Engels wrote about the box. He says you are to let him know the names of the Companies you have applied to and what they said to you.

From 9 to 16 February 1882 Marx and Eleanor stayed with the Longuets in Argenteuil. From there Marx travelled to Algiers, where he hoped the climate would be good for his chronic bronchitis. Eleanor stayed on for a few days and saw Lissagaray. The engagement was now finally off.

50. Eleanor to Jenny

London, 25 March 1882

My dearest Di,

Your little note has made me feel heartily ashamed of myself for leaving you so long without a letter. The fact is for about a week or so I had neuralgia frightfully (and you know from Longuet what that is!) and since then I've been in one of those disgracefully lazy moods when one simply dreads writing letters. I promise you, dear, I will not be so lazy again. Meantime I have made the petticoats for the boys and shall send them off on Monday. I fear you won't find the making very brilliant — you know needlework is not my *forte* (*entre nous* it isn't yours either) and you must take the will for the deed, remembering that if the buttonholes are weak the spirit has been willing.

I can't tell you how anxious Mohr's last letters have made us, though there does *now* seem a decided change for the better. Still I am very anxious and I do wish Mohr would not leave us so long without news — if he only wrote two lines it would be enough.

There is really *nothing* to tell you. *The* event has been *Romeo and Juliet*[1] — which is just on the stage in a manner so exquisite that it baffles any attempt at description. I've never seen a Shakespearian play so satisfactorily played "all round." The most disappointing feature is the "Juliet." Charming in the early scenes — comedy scenes, so to say — Ellen Terry gets weaker and weaker as the tragic element appears, till in the potion scene she collapses altogether. It is of course very interesting to me, as since my return from Paris I've been grinding at Juliet with Mrs. Vezin. She seems extremely pleased with it — and says, despite my absolute ignorance of stage business, she would like me to try it publicly. She now has, I fear, not many relations with actors, but she wants to get me a chance if it is possible. What I should prefer would be to go to some small provincial place and get some *practical* knowledge of the stage to begin with. But all these are dreams, and ten to one, my dear, nothing will come of it all.

The General is much absorbed just now in Pumps (the young one hasn't come even yet!)[2] and in Dr. Beust — a brother of the Beust whom you knew. This one — a dull dog he seems to me — has come over to see the English hospitals, and thanks to the remarkable kindness of Dr. Donkin he has seen everything here that is worth seeing.

By the way, Di, don't leave your letters about. Your sweet Emily[3] reads them, as we know from the things she writes home. Moreover in her last she informs her mother that she has been offered thirty-five francs a month to go into an English family, but she wants her to "leave on the quiet." That looks very odd, doesn't it? Then she says she wants to come back to see her Mother *first*, then winds up that she wants to go to a "religious house." Don't let her *know* you've heard this, or her people here won't tell us anything more, but keep a sharp look out — and don't let her out after dusk if you can help it. You *must* get someone else. I am going to that immense agency in the Strand with Mrs. Furnivall where I *may* hear of someone that would do for you.

I am so glad to hear those darling boys are well. If you only knew how I long to see them all. Don't let Johnny quite forget his Aunty. The little ones of course must forget.

Goodbye, my dear. Forgive my not writing. Kiss the sweet little men and give my love to Charles.

Yours always,

TUSSY

P.S. Did the noble Massard ever answer Longuet's excellent snub?[4] You know I don't see the illustrious *Citoyen* — and I find I can live remarkably well without it. Best love from our old Nim.

---

1. *Romeo and Juliet* had opened at the Lyceum Theatre, with Henry Irving and Ellen Terry, on 8 March.

2. Pumps (Mary-Ellen Rosher) gave birth to a daughter, Lillian, the same day.
3. The Longuets' English maid.
4. The socialists were divided about the education laws then under discussion in the Senate. Emile Massard, a socialist journalist on *Citoyen*, called in the *Egalité* of 26 March for "Revolution — and education afterwards"; Longuet replied in *Justice* (29 March) that the laws would involve "reform of the first order."

51. Jenny to Laura

Argenteuil, Wednesday
[end March 1882]

My dear Laura,

If you could but see me at this moment (half-past 9 P.M.) more than half asleep, you would understand why I have left your last letter unanswered until this moment. You would indeed not only forgive me, but bless your stars that I do not oftener favour you with my drowsy mutterings. Those blessed babies, though really charming good-tempered little fellows, put such a strain upon my nervous system by day and night, that I often long for no matter what release from this ceaseless round of nursing, and think with a pang of the dark underground, to Farringdon Street, where when I was not stifling with asthma, I could at least indulge in my morning daily, and on alighting could run down the muddy Strand and stare at the advertisements, which I miss more than I can say in this Argenteuil waste, where I hear and see nothing but the baker and butcher and cheesemonger and greengrocer. I do believe that even the dull routine of factory work is not more killing than are the endless duties of the *ménage*. To me at least, this is and always has been so. Some women I know, such as Mrs. Lormier for instance, glory in this home drudgery — but we are not all made of the same stuff. You have always accused me of being somewhat of a misanthropist — *now* I have lost all my animal spirits — man delights not me nor woman either.[1] But dear Laura, the truth is, all joking apart, I write so much about myself to get you to pity me and to forgive my apparent neglect. I think of you very often and often miss those visits of yours so dear to me and to the little ones, who always looked forward with special

delight to the arrival of Aunt Lolo. Only the coming of their beloved Granny was hailed with equal joy.

I wrote on the arrival of the box to Papa asking him to
thank you for the charming blue dress you have sent little Par.
It is most elegant. Do you know, my dear Laura, that the children, when they go out in gala anywhere, always wear your
presents. Johnny shone at the Jaclards this Christmas in the
famous velvet suit, somewhat lengthened in arms and legs, and
at Caen, everywhere presented himself in the sailor costume
which I have just had cleaned. You have great taste in dressing
children. I (or perhaps my purse must answer for this), generally turn out poor Johnny as a *bourgeois gentilhomme* — as
poor Mama used to say.

I sent Engels yesterday a letter received from Algiers, according to which the weather is still bad there. Is not this unfortunate? Papa was so much in need of sunshine. I cannot get
over the impression his state of health has made upon me. I
think of him by day and night. I found him so terribly changed
in every way since last summer. I did not know he had had
pleurisy, Tussy having always written of bronchitis.

Thank Lafargue for thinking of me, and tell him though
I read nothing else I read him. Have you followed the great discussion in the *Citoyen* and *Justice*?[2] Massard I think behaved
impertinently and stupidly.

Hirsch is making a stir in the world. I have not seen him
since he has grown to many riches. His article[3] will no doubt
do good in France, he said what he could say in such a revue as
is Madame Adam's. Kiss Nim for me when you see her and
give Paul a hearty shake of the hand for me.

Yours

JENNY

Johnny sends lots of kisses. Do write *soon* to tell me how
you are.

1. "Man delights not me — no, nor woman neither" (*Hamlet*, Act II, scene ii).
2. See page 152, note 4.
3. "Le socialisme en Allemagne," *Nouvelle Revue* (ed. Juliette Adam), March–
   April 1882, signed "Un socialiste allemand."

After his unsuccessful visit to Algiers, where bad
weather brought on another attack of pleurisy, Marx
decided to leave for the South of France: he passed
through Monte Carlo and Cannes before rejoining the
Longuets in Argenteuil. At the same time he took a
sulphur cure at nearby Enghien. Helen Demuth ar-
rived to help Jenny out, and toward the end of July
Eleanor came too, returning to England on 21 August
with Jenny's eldest child Jean.

By now Laura was back in France with Lafargue.
Eleanor had become a member of the Furnivalls' lit-
erary circle, and the night before her next letter to
Jenny had given a recitation to the Browning Society
at University College.

52. Eleanor to Jenny

London, 1 July 1882

My dearest Di,

The General has just sent me on Mohr's letter[1] — and precious
glad I am to have got it. I intended sending a telegram today
if I got *no* news. I really think it rather shabby of you people
to leave me all this while without so much as letting me know
you were not ill or anything of that sort, and that Helen had
reached you safely. I have been frightfully anxious — conjuring
up horrors of all sorts. For heaven's sake invest in half a dozen
postcards — write "Well" or "Not well" and send them off.

On Sunday I was at the General's; so I am out pretty well
all day the General can't see me so I looked him up on Wednesday, and dined with him and the Roshers[2] at the Adelphi on
Thursday. Last night our Browning affair came off. The place
was crowded — and as all sorts of "literary" and other "swells"
were there I felt ridiculously nervous — but gone on capitally.
Mrs. Sutherland Orr (the sister of Sir Frederick Leighton, the
president of the Royal Academy) wants to take me to see Browning and recite his own poems to him! I have been asked to go
this afternoon to a "crush" at Lady Wilde's. She is the mother

of that very limp and very nasty young man, Oscar Wilde,[3] who has been making such a d.d ass of himself in America. As the son has not yet returned and the mother is nice I may go — that is if I have time, for I am also going to Toole's benefit, where the beloved Henry recites.[4] Ellen Terry does the "Bridge of Sighs,"[5] which I look upon as a personal injury, that being one of my stock pieces. Mrs. Kendal[6] recites also, and other "stars" appear. Tickets I could not get so I'm going to the pit — Pumps wants to go too, and the Blacks and others will go also. Doors open at 1.30 and we are to be there at 11! What a fine thing enthusiasm is! Next Tuesday I am going to see Ristori[7] (I've never seen her) as Lady Macbeth, which she acts for the first time in English. Last Tuesday I went to see Modjeska in *Odette*[8] — and liked her more than ever, but the piece is vile — simply idiotic, in fact, in this English version. These dissipated evenings have not interfered with my daily work — and I'm rather hard at it just now.

Tell Helen that her two setting hens are a subject of continual anxiety. Since her departure neither of them have left their nests. Tell her I feed "Fooley," who eats out of my hand — but "Blacky" resents such familiarity, and though I put all kinds of food before her nest I fear she eats nothing at all. The cock is amiable — but feels lonely since Helen is gone. I positively dread next Monday — when some of the chicks are *supposed* to come out. What I'm to do with them goodness knows.

I think I have told you pretty well all I have to tell. Oh! if, without offending our good old General (whom I am going to see tonight) I can "get off" my Sunday with him, I am going for a picnic down the river with the Furnivalls.

Emily arrived here — as I heard from "Ep" — on Sunday morning. Of course she tells a tale of unspeakable horror; of hardships endured, of overwork (!), injustice, etc., etc. Her chief rage seems directed against Mohr — who she declares "called her all the names he could lay his tongue to." The finest thing though was that she informed her family she now intended teaching children French! However, as she had very little money after the first gush it appears her Mother's feelings are growing cooler, and Emily has begun looking for a place. To her profound astonishment she has not yet got one! I need not say that she has not, nor will not show up here.

I do so long for some news of the boys — but at least I know nothing is *wrong* and so can wait with more or less patience.

Goodbye. I kiss you all heartily.

Your

TUSSY

1. Letter from Marx to Engels, 24 June (*Marx-Engels Werke*, vol. 35, p. 74).
2. Pumps and her husband, Percy Rosher.
3. Wilde was in North America from 2 January to 27 December lecturing on the Aesthetic Movement and contributing useful publicity for Gilbert and Sullivan's *Patience*.
4. Toole's Theatre was founded by J. L. Toole, an actor friend of Irving's, who produced popular plays and also contributed to the Ibsen debate. Henry = Henry Irving.
5. A poem by Thomas Hood.
6. The actress Madge (later Dame) Kendal (1848–1935). Mrs. Kendal and her actor-manager husband were celebrated, like the Bancrofts, as a fine example of theatrical partnership.
7. Adelaide Ristori (1822–1906), an Italian actress whose interpretation of Lady Macbeth won her great critical acclaim, most famously from Mrs. Kendal.
8. Helena Modjeska (1844–1909), a Polish actress, immensely popular in spite of her poor English, who specialized in Shakespeare and contemporary French drama. She had opened in Sardou's *Odette* at the Haymarket Theatre on 25 April 1882.

In September Jenny gave birth to a daughter, also named Jenny but nicknamed Mémé. Marx returned to London early in October.

53. Eleanor to Jenny

[*London*] 2 October 1882

My dearest Di,

I have just put my boy — (I am getting so used to and so fond of Jack that I forget he is *your* boy) to bed; Helen is gone with the interesting Pumps to the theatre, and before I begin my evening's work at the glossary I will just send you a line. There isn't anything in particular to tell you. We are looking forward with the pleasure you may imagine, to seeing Papa here. I should look forward still more if I weren't so horribly afraid of his getting cold on the journey. I daren't hint at such a fear here — for Engels — with that terrible optimism of his — resents it as a sort of outrage. Meanwhile I wish Papa would come *at once*. Today the weather was lovely — it can't last long, and it would be such a blessing if he came before wet and fogs set in again. I see Mohr writes to Engels that Dourlen[1] thinks he could winter in the Isle of Wight or *Jersey*. But if *wet* is bad for him Jersey certainly would not do. Its winters are as mild as those of Southern Italy — but it rains *continually*. It is, if possible, more rainy than Devonshire.

There has been quite an excitement at the Museum these last few days on my account. This is the so-called "closed week" — when the Reading Room is shut, and the books are dusted, re-arranged, etc. Now, I am, as you know, very hard pressed for time, so I asked Mr. Bond, the Principal Librarian, to allow me to go all the same to work. Mr. Garnett,[2] Mr. Bullen (the chief man in the Book Department) and some half-dozen of the head men very kindly went to Mr. Bond and also asked him to let me come — and Mr. Bond actually gave the permission. It is an immense favour, which I was told today had been extended to no one since some years ago Gladstone was allowed to go and finish his pamphlet on the "Atrocities" there![3] Of course I can't work in the turmoil of the cleaning in the Reading Room, so I am either in the "Large Room" or in one of the "private" rooms belonging to the head men. This morning I was with Garnett — tomorrow I shall probably be with Bullen. It is a great boon to me, as I was desperate at losing so many days.

Schorlemmer turned up last week and today left again. Yesterday I really *had* to stay at home — and I was not sorry to have an excuse. I *do* enjoy my Sunday at home — as only those who are out every day can.

What do you think of the rival Congresses?[4] They are more suggestive to me of the Kilkenny Cats than of anything else.

Jean is very anxious to hear about his little sister. Having got over the shock he is taking more interest in her now. Do you know he is getting on *very* well at school? Knows all his letters — large and small *perfectly*. What troubles me most is his English. The way he speaks is awful — but I suppose in time he will grow out of it. I've no doubt we spoke Helen's English sometime. The worst is when I correct the boy Helen is either offended or laughs — which is not exactly pleasant.

Have I told you that *great* event — the early production (on the 11th) of *Much Ado* at the Lyceum? I feel much excited — as you may imagine.

Goodnight, my dear old Di. I think of you so very very much — oh! I do wish I could do something better and help you a little! Kiss baby for his aunt.

Your

TUSSY

Where is Papa? Is he with you — or in Paris? I should write him if I knew. If he is with you this letter will do for him too. I am too tired of writing to send him a separate one, especially as I've nothing to say. I am too hard at work to go anywhere or see anyone.

---

1. Dr. Dourlen, the Longuets' doctor, who had also attended Mrs. Marx in Argenteuil.
2. Richard Garnett, who later became Keeper of Printed Books.
3. *Bulgarian Horrors and the Question of the East* (1876).
4. The Saint-Etienne Congress, which had opened on 25 September, had confirmed the split between the Broussists (Possibilists) and the Marxists (led by Guesde and Lafargue). The Marxists henceforth adopted the name *Parti Ouvrier Français* (French Workers' Party) and set up their own congress at Roanne on 26 September. Eleanor's "Kilkenny Cats," according to legend, fought until nothing was left of them but their tails.

For almost a year Jenny had been suffering from acute abdominal pain, which she initially attributed to her pregnancy. She was stoical about her illness and only when she was dying did she reveal to Eleanor the extent of her pain and the misery of her life at Argenteuil. The following letter arrived the day before Jenny's death, probably from cancer of the bladder. She was almost thirty-nine.

54. Eleanor to Jenny

London, 9 January 1883

My dearest Di,

Hearing nothing from you, and only very little through Engels, I am *very* anxious on your account, and should be most grateful if Charles would send me a postcard now and then to tell me how you are. Are you sure Helen would not be of use to you just now at least for a little while? You know how good she is as nurse. *Do* think it over. I wish with all my heart I could go to you for a while — but I can't get off. Besides the Early English Texts work[1] I have so many lessons.

Your boy is wonderfully well — and in the highest spirits. Yesterday he had a great treat. Mrs. Bircham (where I teach at Kensington) invited Jean to a party. We went and had a "real good time." Mrs. Bircham had engaged a conjuror who did the most clever things, and you can imagine how the boy enjoyed that. Then the games and "refreshments" were welcome, and the numerous servants were also a source of wonder and interest to Johnny. He behaved admirably, and the Birchams were delighted with him.

Moore and Schorlemmer have now returned to Manchester after the "festivities" — which grow sadder every year.

From Mohr I heard this morning. He seems better — and if only he could get a little fine weather would soon be all right — so at least the doctors say.

By the way, my dearest Di, while you are so ill it seems to me that it would be *folly* to have over Johnny. Your hands are too full already. You had *much* better let him stay on for the present. He is well and happy, and we are only too happy for an excuse for keeping him. If you think this, Helen wants me to lose no time in *sending* the box. She fears the cakes and puddings else will quite spoil, and after the trouble of making them that would be a pity. If I don't hear to the contrary from Charles (you must not trouble to write) I shall send the box this week.

My dear dear Di — I can't tell you *how* your illness troubles me. I think of you day and night, and only wish I could *do* something. Tell Charles he is to send me a postcard — for I am too anxious to go on waiting like this.

We all kiss you and the dear little ones.

Your affectionate

TUSSY

1. The Early English Texts Society had been founded by F. J. Furnivall in 1864, as an adjunct to the research for the *New English Dictionary*.

Eleanor had to break the news of Jenny's death to Marx, who was still at Ventnor. He took it badly: Jenny had always been his favourite, the one who was "most like him." Eleanor said she felt as though she were bringing him his death sentence. Marx insisted that Eleanor travel to France to look after Jenny's five children, while he returned to London. He was suffering from nervous coughing fits, laryngitis and bronchitis. In February he developed a tumour of the lung.

Eleanor arrived back from Argenteuil with Harra, who was very sick and had to be sent to a children's hospital. On 14 March 1883 Marx died, aged sixty-five. He was buried in Highgate Cemetery in the same tomb as his wife. A week later, Harra was buried there too.

PART FOUR

March 1883 – June 1889

International Socialism

P ART FOUR BEGINS with the aftermath of Marx's death and ends with the important Paris International Congress of 1889.

At Marx's death Eleanor, then twenty-eight, took on the dual task of preserving her father's practical and spiritual legacy. Laura did not attend the funeral and Eleanor, with Helen Demuth's help, began sorting out the papers — letters, manuscripts and drafts — at Maitland Park Road. Only the first volume of *Capital* had so far been published; the rest was still in rudimentary form. There are signs that Laura felt ostracized and away from the centre of things: her children all dead, often ill herself, and her own political activity essentially secondary to her husband's. Marx had died intestate, and Engels spared Eleanor the details of an unpleasant correspondence which took place shortly afterwards. Laura had expressed doubts about the manner in which Engels and Eleanor had assumed they were to be Marx's literary executors, and more or less accused them of having concealed from her the seriousness of his condition.

For Eleanor, the six years covered here set the pattern for the rest of her life: periods of elation combined with moods of deepest despair. Though deeply grieved by her father's death, the trauma seems also to have offered some kind of release, and a freedom that she could not contemplate during his lifetime. A year later she set up house with Edward Aveling, and found a place for herself in the revival of socialism taking place in both England and America. By the mid-1880s wage-cuts and layoffs were inspiring a new militancy among the workers, and many of these letters are to do with the arguments between the various factions of the socialist movement. For Eleanor internationalism was, as it had been for Marx, of central importance, and her facility with languages and her cosmopolitan background made her an important delegate at Workers' Congresses.

After Jenny's death the Longuet children spent more time with the Lafargues and the eldest, Jean, sometimes stayed with the Avelings in England. Jenny's last letters had revealed that Longuet had not given her much support and that in her hour of greatest need he had often been away from home. Eleanor, in particular, felt bitter about his behaviour toward their beloved Jenny and his refusal to answer their letters about the children, though others have testified that he was an affectionate, if unreliable, father.

In the first letter Eleanor emphasizes her reluctance to depend upon the generosity of "our good General" (a nickname Engels had acquired while reporting on the Franco-Prussian War), though she was well aware that she was the only member of the Marx family to have such scruples. She longed for independence, and seems at times almost to have resented Engels's patronage.

55. Eleanor to Laura

41, Maitland Park Rd.,
London. N.W.
26 March 1883

Dear Laura,

I need not tell you that I shall take the *utmost* care to prevent our good General from seeing anything that is likely to give him pain. Indeed *all* the private letters I shall put aside. They are of interest only to us, and can be looked to any time. The other papers — Mss., International correspondence etc. — is what we must look to now. Would you like me to send you all your and Lafargue's letters? If so as I find them I will put them together. This sorting of the papers will be terrible work. I hardly know how it is to be got through. I must give certain days in the week to it *entirely*. Of course I cannot sit down and do *only* that. I must keep up my lessons, and get all the work I can. I know Engels is goodness itself and that I shall always have all I want, but I think you will understand that I am more anxious than ever now to earn my own living. In time I shall be able to get on quite well, I hope. The house we have for another twelve months — but if we can get a tenant sooner we may leave. For the next six months, however, I don't think I *could* leave — as the papers *must* be settled before I can do anything. I suppose Engels has told you that we have at *least* 500 pages of the 2nd vol. [of *Capital*] — probably the whole. That is good, isn't it?

Till I leave the house I think everything had best be left as it is. Afterwards we will see about dividing the things—that is, if you don't mind.

You will have heard from Engels about little Harry. It is best so — but Longuet's conduct has *quite* decided me as to Jean. I cannot, now Helen and I are all alone, take the responsibility of keeping the boy! I have therefore written to *le père* — (but have as yet no answer!) that as soon as it is convenient to him Helen or I will take Jean to Calais where he can meet us. Since writing this I have had another idea — of which I wish to speak to you. Poor old Nim really needs a holiday after all the terrible work and trouble of these last awful months, and it has occurred to me that instead of taking Jean to Calais she should take him to Paris, and then, if it suited you, have a little stay in

Paris. I've said nothing about it to her as yet, as if nothing comes of it she would feel disappointed. I can manage quite well. Carry comes in the morning, and she could do all that has to be done, and she might look in in the evening to see if I wanted anything, and for my meals I should manage as I have before when alone. I *do* want Helen to have a little holiday — and I don't know how else to arrange it. I cannot leave London, and she would not enjoy going anywhere alone. Of course if it were in *any* way inconvenient to you, you need not mind telling me, as Helen has heard nothing of it so far.[1]

I have just written Meissner to get the 3rd ed. of the 1st vol. out as soon as possible, and then we'll get on to the 2nd vol. Beyond that I can, as yet, tell you nothing. I shall, by and by, publish the "*Tribune* articles."[2] Don't you think that would be well?

Schorlemmer is still here, and he and the General are dividing their devotion between whiskey and Pilsner. Pumps is still keeping the world waiting for number 2. She *looks* as if she were, like Mrs. Lessner, going in for triplets!

Yours

TUSSY

Let me know about Helen, as in case Longuet writes we may know what to do: also if the arrangement about the house will suit you — I mean with regard to furniture, books, etc.

1. This visit took place in April, when Helen took Jean Longuet back to France.
2. *New York Daily Tribune*, to which Marx had been a regular contributor. See page 281, note 4.

This is the second letter in which Eleanor mentions Edward Aveling. Atheist, science lecturer, doctor and journalist, Aveling shared Eleanor's passion for the theatre, and had himself written and adapted several plays. She had known him for over a year, but their relationship did not become public until the summer of 1884. In the meantime Eleanor had taken lodgings near the British Museum, at 32 Great Coram Street, and Helen Demuth had moved in with Engels as his housekeeper.

Since 1881 Aveling had been a Vice-President of the National Secular Society, the most prominent members of which were Charles Bradlaugh and Annie Besant, and he contributed to its newspaper, The National Reformer. *In 1883 he became editor of* Progress, *a monthly with "advanced ideas," and asked Eleanor to write an obituary of her father, which appeared in the May 1883 issue, and an account of Marx's theory of surplus-value, which appeared in June.*

56. Eleanor to Laura

London, 14 September 1883

My dear Laura,

. . .

I spent last week — from Monday to Monday — at Eastbourne. Happily the weather was beautiful, and I got out each morning by 5 o'clock and wandered about till the breakfast hour of 9 — I had quite a "good time." The poor old General must have found it very dull. He is far from well and can't walk, and as it is against his principles to sit down outside — though Eastbourne is so well provided with seats in comfortable places — he remained indoors the whole day, merely sitting, "for a change"! on the balcony. Pumps was in an awful temper all the time, and poor Nym was not very bright either. On the whole, though I enjoyed my walks and bathing, I was glad to get back again.

I expect I shall be very busy shortly. I am going back to

the Birchams[1] to teach Mildred, and I am also going to have a
Literature Class there. Other classes I think — and hope — will
be got up elsewhere. I shall be glad — for I want the money. It
is *so* difficult to get work — or at least regular work. The kind
of lessons I give are not like teaching "all subjects" — and one
just gets pupils for a time.

Can't you and Lafargue send us something for *Progress?*
Tell Lafargue that this little magazine is beginning — to the
great annoyance of Bradlaugh — to have a really good circulation, so that articles such as he could send would be of use. Of
course Aveling is not *quite* a free agent, but he can do more or
less what he likes — as you see by the publication of (as I
think) Bax's excellent paper. If the good-natured Mesa could
be induced to send me some notes (anything — he need not
trouble about putting them into shape) about Spain, and if you
could get some of the Russian colony to send me any information, I would try and put the things together. Anyway I hope
the prisoner[2] will use his time to send something. His last article
delighted the people — from all I hear.

How are the little ones?[3] Drop me a line now and then —
and don't expect long answers. I have to write so much — I mean
just mechanical writing — that the sight of pen and ink make
me ill.

Dr. Aveling sends kind messages to you and Lafargue.

Yours
TUSSY

---

1. A school in Kensington run by a Mrs. Bircham, at which Eleanor had already
   given some classes.
2. On 25 April Lafargue had been sentenced to six months' imprisonment by the
   Allier Court of Assizes for incitement to crime, murder, and looting, after
   meetings held in the Allier following the Roanne Congress.
3. Jenny's children.

A number of socialist journals and magazines were founded in 1884. Eleanor became a regular columnist on Today, *later to be called the* Monthly Magazine of Scientific Socialism; *she reported on international workers' movements, and Laura sent her material from France. Aveling also wrote for* Today, *and it was there he published his first socialist article, "Christianity and Capitalism," in which he declared himself to be a disciple of Karl Marx. Charles Bradlaugh and Annie Besant were enraged: Besant, a former lover of Aveling's, blamed Eleanor for his "conversion" to socialism, and Bradlaugh charged Aveling with having misappropriated National Secular Society funds in his capacity as Vice-President. Aveling airily pleaded ignorance of all financial matters and the affair blew over, though it undoubtedly endorsed Aveling's reputation as a man who could not entirely be trusted.*

Eleanor and Aveling were also writing for the new weekly Justice, *organ of the Democratic Federation, which they had joined the previous year.*

57. Eleanor to Laura

32, Great Coram Street, W.C.
13 February 1884

My dear Laura,
I feel quite ashamed of myself for not writing long ago to thank you both for the pretty birthday card you sent me, and for the invaluable notes. The fact is when I felt inclined to write I had not time and when I had time I was too lazy!

In your last letter you asked me about the editorship of *Today.* The two editors are Bax and Joynes[1] — the two finding the money. Bax started the whole thing, and has put most into it (I believe) — but Joynes has just as much to say as the other, which I think a pity. Bax is all that is good. He only wants to be with people who keep him up to the mark. Joynes I am not so sure about. Not that I've anything particular to say against the man, but I don't quite like him. He is one of the people who always want to "avoid shocking" the sensibilities of the British public, and who always end by "shocking" the public just as much as if they spoke out frankly, and alienate our friends. Have you seen the new weekly *Justice*? If not I'll send you the four copies. Anyhow I send you one copy today as I want you to see a letter of Dr. Aveling's in it.[2] This letter is in answer to a paragraph (which I also enclose) published in the *National Reformer*[3] and written, as you will see, in Mrs. Besant's own chaste style. Dr. Aveling sent his answer to the *Reformer*, which with characteristic dishonesty and cowardice published only — (as you will see from enclosure) a most disingenuous note.[4] I've more than once of late wished like Beatrice that "I were a man";[5] and that I could inflict on Mr. Bradlaugh the sound thrashing he deserves. *A propos*, I saw that Clemenceau had met Mr. Bradlaugh when the latter was in Paris. Do you think Paul could in any way get the numbers of the *Justice* in which our poor Jenny's letters appeared? I very much want them, but I know asking Longuet for them is useless. I *did* ask him months ago, but naturally, heard no more about it.

The General told me the other day that the poor little men have all got whooping-cough. *Do* let me know how they are, for I am very anxious about them.

I am so much obliged to you for the papers you send me. It is such a worry having to get together news for *Today*. Tell Paul that I shall be *very* grateful for any little scrap he sends me. You'll think I'm like the man in Mama['s] old story: *"Und nun geben Sie mir noch'ne Tasse Kaffe und dann sind sie wirklich eine gute Frau."*[6]

As yesterday was the 12th I went up to Highgate and took some flowers. I couldn't take many because I am so hard up. I am going one day this week to see a gardener about the grave. I did not get it done before because during the winter months we couldn't have got any nice flowers. I want it all nice though by the 14th March.[7]

The Jutas are still here, but I don't get time to see very much of them. It is frightfully dull for poor Willa. Aunt Emily has been very ill with inflammation of the lungs and it is just possible Aunt Louise may go over to see her. Of Aunt Sophie I've not had further news. Did you write at all to poor Lina?

You should, for she is very miserable, her little girl at school, and her mother at this asylum.[8]

Goodbye, my dear Laura. Many many thanks, and *please* keep Paul at note-sending point.

Yours

TUSSY

The General is much better,[9] and works now at Maitland Park looking over the books. He, no doubt, has written you what he is doing.

Every good wish to every good friend.

EDWARD AVELING

1. Ernest Belfort Bax was a philosopher and friend of Engels; James Joynes had taught at Eton.
2. 9 February 1884.
3. 3 February 1884.
4. 10 February 1884.
5. Beatrice in *Much Ado About Nothing*, Act IV, scene i.
6. "Now give me yet another cup of coffee, and then you'll be a really good woman."
7. Anniversary of Marx's death.
8. Louise (Juta), Emily (Conradi) and Sophie (Schmalhausen) were sisters of Marx's; Lina (Caroline) was Sophie's daughter, who was married and living in Maastricht.
9. Engels had had a severe attack of rheumatism which had confined him to bed for several weeks.

The Democratic Federation was the first coherent so-
cialist organization to have emerged from the revival
of the early 1880s. There were, however, many differ-
ences of opinion between its founder, H. M. Hyndman,
an energetic but opinionated socialist whom Marx had
been unable to take seriously, and the Marx-Engels
faction. For his part, Hyndman was suspicious of their
close links with the European socialist groups and re-
ferred to them as the "Marxist clique."

One of the most dramatic rows concerned the
preparations for a commemorative meeting, to be held
in Highgate Cemetery in March 1884, which was to
mark both the anniversary of Marx's death and the
proclamation of the Paris Commune thirteen years
earlier. Hyndman was strongly opposed to the idea of
the Democratic Federation taking part in the meet-
ing, and declined an invitation from the German
Communist Workers' Education Association to deliver
a speech at Marx's grave, on the grounds that it ought
to be given by a member of the working classes. In the
event the honour was accorded to Aveling.

There was similar dissension among the French
socialists: between the Reformists or Possibilists, led
by Brousse and Malon, and the Marxists, led by
Guesde and Lafargue. The VIIth French Workers'
Party Conference was due to take place at Roubaix
from 29 March to 7 April and the Marxists had in-
vited the Democratic Federation to send delegates.
Hyndman, as Eleanor explains in this letter, wanted
to refuse.

58. Eleanor to Laura

32, Great Coram Street, W.C.
17 March 1884

Dear Laura,
Very many thanks for your letter, newspapers, and other con-
tributions. I really don't know, what would become of my
Today notes without them.

You no doubt have seen from *Justice* both the "appeal" of the German Verein here to hold a commemorative meeting of the 18th March at Highgate, and also that Hyndman tried his best to prevent it. The reason for *that* is of course not far to seek — but it may interest you both to know more about it. Last Sunday week then two of the Verein committee (one of them, Weiler, you probably remember) came to ask Dr. Aveling to speak at Highgate, which he naturally said he would do. Hyndman's name had been put forward really through a mistake, but his public declaration on the subject was surely needless. Well, Dr. A. then decided to speak — but we wanted to make Hyndman declare either for or against the demonstration. On the Tuesday our friend Bax turned up, and (I being at Kensington) left me word with Dr. Aveling that I was to be sure and go down in the evening to the Democratic Federation, as Hyndman would try and stop the Federation from joining the procession, and also because the question of the Roubaix Congress was to be settled. I went — so did Dr. Aveling — and a very good thing we did. Owing to my being there Hyndman only said the Federation should take part, and even had to declare that Dr. Aveling would have their "entire sympathy."

This settled, the Roubaix question came up. Hyndman — who Bax afterwards told me had intended making a violent attack on the suggested Conference as a "family manoeuvre" of ours — did not dare to say much — but nevertheless objected to the Federation taking part or lot in the Congress. This was opposed by most present — and I gave him his *coup de grâce* by explaining, so far as I was able, the position of the Roubaix people *vis-à-vis* the Broussists, and carried all the committee with me by saying this was a necessary protest against the Broadhurst Congress.[1] Aveling also spoke, pointing out that Hyndman's exception to the *"parti ouvrier"* as being a small section could even better be applied to the Federation, and that we had here to consider the principles at stake, not the persons. This was a hit to Hyndman, who based his objections on Lafargue's indulging in "personalities." Morris,[2] who is a fine old chap, also spoke for us, and the workmen on the Committee being with us it was *unanimously* voted that the Federation should be represented. Then arose the question by *whom*. Hyndman tried hard to keep out Bax on the old ground of his not being a "working man"! Finally, after a good deal of discussion it was decided to send *two* delegates — a working man, Quelch,[3] and Bax. You see our going was of some use. Bax says that otherwise there would have been no chance of his getting the resolution (to send delegates) accepted. As to Quelch, I will write you about him fully one of these days. He is not a bad fellow at all. As to Bax, he is excellent in all respects, and I am *very* glad he is to go. Yesterday Hyndman began talking to me about the Anzin-Guesde-Lefèvre row — and wanted information.[4] Of course I could give none. Tell Paul he would do well to let me know now and then what goes on. It may be of use here. There are *admirable* elements in the Federation — but also endless difficulties, and as I foresee not the least of these will be Hyndman.

And now about yesterday. I never — nor indeed did any of us, for a moment — believe that we should have more than a very small gathering — but when I tell you that between five and six thousand persons assembled you will see that it was really a splendid affair. The procession, with band and banners, started in Tottenham Street, and we marched — I going with them too — along Tottenham Court Road, Hampstead Rd., etc., to Highgate. The cemetery authorities had had the gates closed — and inside them were drawn up *five hundred policemen with six mounted police!* As we were refused admittance, and we asked if I and some ladies bearing crowns could go in alone, we adjourned to the top of the street just by the reservoir. It was a really grand sight. From . . . [letter incomplete]

1. The Possibilists had held an international conference in 1883 which had been attended by a group of British Trade Unionists led by Henry Broadhurst, MP and Secretary of the parliamentary Trade Union group.
2. William Morris.
3. Harry Quelch, who was carrying on with his job as a wallpaper packer while voluntarily editing *Justice* and teaching himself French and German.
4. On 12 March a meeting was held in support of the miners' strike at Anzin. It was led by two miners, Lefèvre and Lacroix, with the support of Lafargue, Guesde, etc.

59. Eleanor to Laura

32, *Great Coram Street*
19 March 1884

My dear Laura,

• • •

I'm in the thick of a fight with the Austrian Anarchist (police-agent?) Peukert[1] — and I am beginning to find more and more that it is not all play *"dans le parti."*

I got the re[gistere]d papers and Paul's lectures[2] this morning. Many thanks. By the way, if I can make an arrangement with Champion and Foulger (the publishers of *Today*) would Paul mind my translating his *Conférences?* I think they would be *very* useful here. Don't you? The worst is I've so very little time, what with one thing and another. All the people who sent me notes for *Today* expect notes in return — and I am more sick of writing letters than ever.

By the way, I forgot to tell you *how* we got our "Baxie" elected for the Congress. One of the members of the Executive of the Federation is old Murray,[3] whom Lafargue and you must remember from the old International times. Well Murray is blindly devoted to Aveling, and obeys him like a child. Aveling — not being of the Executive — could not himself propose Bax. So he got Murray to do so. First Hyndman pretended not to hear, and went on discussing about Quelch,[4] but presently Aveling pushed on old Murray again, and as I had "caught his eye" — I mean Aveling's — and I saw what he was after, I "worked" Scheu, who seconded Murray's proposition and so Bax *had* to be put to the vote. I tell you all these little details because it is as well Paul should know with whom he has to deal. Keep me posted in all necessary news. I can always "work" some of the Committee, and Aveling and I together can do something. If you knew what admirable elements there are in the Federation, and the really immense stride the movement has taken, you would understand how important it is to keep the English connected with the right side. Much depends on that now. Bax is dying to get Aveling and myself on the next Executive. I've no ambition that way, and I want to keep out of it — especially as there's no chance of *both* of us getting elected.

I must off to the General's now to consult him about this Peukert business — and I'm dead tired as it is!

Yours

TUSSY

1. Peukert had fled from Vienna after the suppression of the Anarchists in January 1884.
2. Lafargue had given three lectures in February and March, the first called "L'idéalisme et le matérialisme dans l'histoire," the two others "Le matérialisme historique de Karl Marx."
3. James Murray who, together with his brother Charles, had been active in the Chartist movement and the IWMA.
4. i.e., whether or not Quelch should be sent to Roubaix.

In a letter dated 18 June 1884[1] Eleanor informed Laura of her decision to set up house with Aveling. She asked her to convey the news to her two brothers-in-law, Lafargue and Longuet. Engels characteristically accepted the arrangement with a good grace; he said that he and Helen had seen it coming. Eleanor also explained the situation to some of her close friends, leaving it to them to decide whether or not they wanted to continue their relationship with her.

In early August, before leaving for Derbyshire, Aveling attended the annual conference of the Democratic Federation. Though Eleanor was not present both she and Aveling were elected members of the committee, which from now on was known as the "Social Democratic Federation."

1. Housed in the Institute of Marxism-Leninism, Moscow.

60. Eleanor to Laura

32, Great Coram Street, W.C.
21 July 1884

My dear Laura,

I have been so busy with one thing and another that despite the best of intentions I could not find time to write. Yet I wanted to *very* much, both to thank you for your letter to me, and for what I know you must have written to the General. I am more than grateful to him for his generosity — but I also know that I owe it to you, although he has not said so. He has actually given us £50! Is it not much too much? I feel quite unhappy about it — though, as I need not tell you, it was *very* welcome.

The agreement for our rooms in Gt. Russell Street[1] is duly signed, and on Friday I had all my things — save my bed — taken there. Happily I can put my furniture there now, thus saving my rent while we are away, although we only have our new rooms from the beginning of September.

We leave London on Thursday at 5 in the morning! And very glad I shall be to get away.

Our reason for staying here till Thursday is that Edward is anxious to be present at the meeting, on Wednesday evening, of a new branch of the Democratic Federation. There has been no end to the petty intriguing within that body of late. Details you, who know the Broussists, will not need — your own large experience will supply them. Besides some very nasty personal affairs, which have resulted in the departure for Scotland of Scheu, Hyndman has also succeeded in getting poor old Bax turned out of *Today*, for Champion,[2] who takes Bax's place, is just a tool of Hyndman's, albeit a talented, and I think honest young fellow. Bax founded *Today*, spent a lot on it, and now he is left in the cold! I shall, of course, not go on writing for *Today* under these circumstances, and I hope Paul will not either. If the much-talked-of International Conference ever comes off it will be interesting to see how Hyndman gets on. So far he has things here much his own way, but he is playing his cards very badly — irritating everyone, and his little game will soon be played out. The sooner the better for our movement. It has *every* chance here at this present time if only we had better leaders than Hyndman and his henchmen. Early in August there is to be a Conference of the Federation, and as a new Council is then to be elected it will be of no little interest. I shall not be in London, but Edward will come up and see what goes on.

I don't remember if I told you that the Jutas had returned from Germany and are now at Brighton. They are, it appears, going to settle down here for good. I am now going to write and tell them of my plans, and if as you so *very* kindly suggested [you] will take some of the cousins and aunts off my hands — why I shall be most grateful. I have heaps of letters to write, and jump at the chance of escaping from some part of them. It *is* good of you to write for me!

The General tells me there is a chance of your coming over here. I *do* hope that is true. Edward sends his love and thanks you for all your kind messages.

Yours affectionately,

TUSSY

P.S. Our address will be: Nelson Arms, Middleton, near Wirksworth, Derbyshire. Don't forget the near Wirksworth, as else letters will not reach.

1. No. 55, opposite the British Museum.
2. H. H. Champion, an ex-army officer who later broke with Hyndman, and founded the *Labour Elector*.

*Laura visited London in October 1884 and returned to
Paris mid-November.*

*During the last months of the year the schism
within the SDF came to a head. In the important letter
that follows Eleanor recounts the latest developments
and gives a clear analysis of the causes of dissension:
Hyndman's tyrannical authoritarianism, his chauvinism, his conspiratorial and insinuating behaviour (he
had, in fact, conspired with the French Possibilists
against the internationalist Marxists). Yet, paradoxically, Hyndman remained one of the most influential
proponents of Marx's economic theories, and it was he
who introduced them to the writer and artist William
Morris. Now, Morris led the opposition against Hyndman, and the split was formalized at a stormy meeting
on 27 December. Though Hyndman was in the minority, most of the Executive Committee nonetheless resigned to found a new organization, the Socialist
League, led by Morris, which was to be essentially
international in its outlook. The Socialist League
started a new periodical,* Commonweal, *for which
Eleanor wrote the international news column.*

*Eleanor's letter reveals the simultaneously active
and clandestine role played by Engels in the preparations for the split in the party, and the close watch he
kept on the development of the new organization.*

61. Eleanor to Laura

London, 31 December 1884

My dear Laura,

I feel very guilty — and yet I am sure you would forgive my
long silence if you knew how little time I've had for writing
letters. But you *do* know — for you have been a good deal
"driven" too. I suppose you heard from Engels — he and Nym
will never cease chaffing us, I fear — how Edward and I waited
outside Charing Cross while you were *inside* the station. I was
so vexed not to say goodbye to you! We have been hoping that

something might "turn up" and that we should be able to run over to Paris for at least a few days — but nothing has turned up, and though the spirit is willing, the purse, as you well know, is very weak. However we haven't given up hope. Edward is a perfect Micawber in this respect, and still waits confidently for the "something" that is to set us up.

I know you'll be wanting to hear how things have gone at the Federation. Into all the details I need not go. You and Paul have had your Brousse — and we have simply had the same experience here that you have been, and are going through, with the Possibilists. Apart from the disgraceful vilification of everyone to whom he personally objected as not being a "follower" of himself, Hyndman forced things to such a condition that it was impossible to go on working with him. The personal question — inevitably personal questions will be mixed up in all such movements as these — is after all very secondary to the principal one (Ed. A.) — that of whether we were to sink into a merely Tory-Democratic Party, or to go on working on the lines of the German Socialists and the French *Parti Ouvrier*. In the motion brought forward by Morris of confidence in Scheu (whom Hyndman has been maligning most shamefully), and of want of confidence in Hyndman, we had a majority, although — a most unusual course — the chairman voted, and Hyndman had brought together all his "party." Having gained this point we next, in a body, gave our resignation as members of the Federation Council. Our majority was too small to make it possible for us to really get rid of the Jingo faction, and so, after due consultation with Engels, we decided to go out, and form a new organization. This is to be called the Socialist League. Bax is anxious that we should issue a weekly paper. But Engels is dead against this, so we shall probably, for the present, content ourselves with a monthly journal. The General has promised, now we are rid of the unclean elements in the Federation, to help us; many others who have till now stood aloof will come to us also; we shall of course (through Engels) have the Germans with us, and we also count on the *Parti Ouvrier*. A short statement will be drawn up and sent by us to the various Socialist parties, at once to explain our secession, and to ask their support. Hyndman will now, no doubt, be able to form the alliance he has all along tried to make, and been prevented by us from making — with Brousse — like will to like. I suppose

Paul saw the attack on himself and Guesde in last week's *Justice* by that arch-humbug Adolphe Smith.[1] Is he going to reply? If he thinks it worth while he should do so in our paper. *A propos*, he ought (perhaps Engels has already written about this — if so forgive the repetition) to write to Champion and Frost to ask them to withdraw his name from the list of their contributors to *Today*. Apart from all general questions he can't write for two men who deliberately accused you or me of forging a letter.[2] By the way, I "went" for Hyndman and his creatures about that. After trying, without exactly asserting it, to insinuate that the letter was forged, he was forced to withdraw his statement. I read your letter on the subject, and then told Mr. H. what I thought of him. Oh, dear! is not all this wearisome and stupid! But I suppose it must be gone through with. I comfort myself by recalling the long Schweitzer-Lassalle-Liebknecht quarrel in Germany, and the Brousse-Lafargue split in France. I suppose this kind of things is inevitable in the beginning of any movement. But enough of this. I am sure you, who know the Broussists, are sick of all this miserable bickering — and moreover understand it all without needing *further* details. *A propos*. Could Vallès be induced to send me the *Cri*[3] again? I *only* see the *Bataille*[4] — ergo I am considerably fogged as to what is really going on. You will also have to send us all your other papers, *Défense des Travailleurs*,[5] etc. These you should send to our "office," 27, Farringdon Street, E.C.

I heard about Longuet and the little ones through Engels. When you write *do* tell me about them, there's a dear. Poor little things! I do so long to see them. I need not say that I have not had a line from Longuet!

There is not much other news to give. We are all much the same as you left us. Edward and I dream of going to see you — but I confess I don't see how we're to realize our dream.

Meantime, dear, goodbye and a Happy New Year to you both. *Do* write.

Your

TUSSY

---

1. On 27 December *Justice* published a letter from Adolphe Smith entitled "France and the International Congress," in which he called on the SDF to recognize the French Possibilists as the principal French socialist organization and to have no more to do with the French Workers' Party (the Marxists).

2. Hyndman claimed that Eleanor and Laura had forged a letter to the Executive Council in connection with the dispute over the Roubaix Congress.
3. *Le Cri du peuple*, daily paper started by Jules Vallès, a journalist and novelist.
4. *La Bataille politique et sociale*, daily paper started by Lissagaray.
5. Guesdist weekly, organ of the socialist workers' groups of the North-East.

62. Eleanor to Laura

55, Great Russell Street, W.C.
12 April 1885

My dear Laura,

Many, many thanks for your letter (*very* welcome) and Paul's article. He really is a brick to help us all as he does. I feel doubly grateful just now, for help means the rest for Edward that Donkin declares "absolutely necessary." (Doctors are such "absolute" knaves!)

I am just now alone, Edward has gone off for a few days to Ventnor. He sadly needed it. We could not possibly afford to go away together: it was as much as I could do to get him off. He has been really *very* ill. Calculus in the kidney with a slight (and threatened serious) inflammation. Paul will probably know best how serious this may be. You know Donkin never fusses, but he frankly told me the matter unless attended to at once might be really very serious. There is no need to tell you how difficult it is for us to "rest entirely, not move at all, and do nothing"! Apart from the necessary work for getting a living — *tant bien que mal*[1] — there is the *constant* worry from the "Socialist League." From childhood we have known what it is to devote oneself to the "*prolétaire.*" It is superfluous to explain to you. I only say even this much to make you understand how grateful I am for Paul's help.

· · ·

I am very grateful to Paul for articles and so forth but I really *did* swear at you both — at him for telling you not to write about the children, and at you for being fool enough not to do it. Can't you understand that I am really anxious to know about those little ones? Remember how much I had dear little Johnny and Wolf with me and you *will* understand.

I did not forget the 2nd April. I told Edward it was seventeen years since you were married, and although we drank your health (in nothing grander I fear than our homely cask-ale!) and though he said the date *might* be correct, he loftily scorned my assertion about the seventeen years. He wouldn't discuss the matter even, but dismissed it with the advice "not to fool about"!!! He declared no woman *could* look as you do after seventeen years of marriage! Dear, I have thought so often in these days that your dear little one would be sixteen. I look at the sweet little golden curl that is very dear to me, and remember . . .

News I have none. Schorlemmer is here, and he, Helen and I dined in town yesterday, but that is about all I can tell you of them. They are just the same as always. Nym is none the worse for occasional word-battles with Pumps, and is looking extremely well.

On the 23rd we have a public meeting to protest against the Sudan War,[2] but of course this Russian business rather complicates matters.[3] Our meeting to celebrate the 18th March was a great success. Do you or Paul know anything of a Mdlle. Le Comte — now in Marseilles Prison for wounding another woman she accuses of being a spy? She is an Anarchist and has just written to me. If Paul *can* give any information I shall be much obliged. The Anarchists here will be our chief difficulty. We have many on our Council, and by and by it will be the devil to pay. Neither Morris, nor Bax, nor any of our people know really what these Anarchists are: till they *do* find out it is a hard struggle to make head against them — the more that many of our Englishmen taken in by the foreign Anarchists (half of whom I *suspect* to be police agents) are unquestionably the best men we have.

I am in the midst of a "whitewashing and cleaning" during Edward's absence, and am up to my neck in work of all kinds (not, alas! very remunerative). How I wish people didn't live in houses and didn't cook, and bake, and wash and clean! I fear I shall never, despite all efforts, develop into a decent *Hausfrau.* I am horribly Bohemian in my tastes. Dear, *do* write. I know I am a frightfully bad correspondent — but you should set me a better example!

Love to you both from
Yours affectionately,
TUSSY

1. "somehow or other."
2. British troops had been in the Sudan for two years following an insurrection against Egyptian rule. Khartoum had fallen in January.
3. A reference to the dispute between Britain and Russia over the North-West frontier of Afghanistan.

*The period between the last letter and the following
one — Spring 1885–86 — was very eventful. In England,* Commonweal *came increasingly under the influence of the Anarchists, and Aveling resigned from
the editorial committee, though both he and Eleanor
continued to write for it from time to time. Bax succeeded Aveling as sub-editor and William Morris's
daughter May took over Eleanor's international column. Before Christmas the Avelings left London for
Kingston-on-Thames, where Edward finished the English translation of volume I of* Capital. *Eleanor revised
her translation of the* History of the Commune *and
embarked on her translation of* Madame Bovary.
*Johnny Longuet, who had come to stay with them in
the autumn, was left in London with Engels.*

*On 8 February 1886, later to become known as
"Black Monday," a rally of the unemployed, supported by the SDF, met in Trafalgar Square and
marched on Hyde Park. The fact that there were almost no police present gave rise to accusations of government collusion in the violence which followed:
looting, fighting and destruction of property.*

*In France, the ministry of Jules Ferry, a Repub-
lican secularist whose colonial incursions into Tunisia
and Indo-China had made him profoundly unpopular,
was overthrown in March 1885. Lafargue, who was
on the editorial committee of a new weekly launched
by the French Workers' Party,* Le Socialiste, *took part
in the electoral campaign in the Allier. In the second
round of elections, on 18 October, the Republicans
gained 243 seats to the Conservatives' 25, and many
workers' representatives were elected.*

*1885 was also the year in which Engels brought
out volume II of* Capital. *Laura's French translation
of* The Communist Manifesto *was serialized in* Le
Socialiste *from 29 August to 7 November.*

*The following letter from Eleanor was written
soon after an assassination attempt on Bismarck, which
had prompted Bismarck to claim to the Reichstag that
his attacker, Ferdinand Blind, had been a pupil of
Marx's. Eleanor, always quick to rise to her father's*

defence, replied to his accusation in the 1 May issue of Commonweal, *pointing out that Marx had lost contact with Blind when Blind was twelve or thirteen. She also sent an open letter to the* Sozialdemokrat *and* Le Socialiste, *with a copy, signed by the two sisters, to Bismarck himself. Thinking that Laura would have no objection, Eleanor had signed on her behalf, though in Laura's opinion the best answer to Bismarck would have been a scornful silence.*

63. Eleanor to Laura

2, Parade Villas, Kingston
23 April 1886

My dear Laura,

I must first ask your pardon for having signed your name the week before last without your permission. The General, I think, told you I was to send you a second copy of the letter to Bismarck for you to sign and forward. Well, the General was anxious it should go at once, but the Monday (the day after the letter was written) was Uncle's funeral.[1] I was away from ten in the morning till past eight in the evening, so I could not get time to copy it. Therefore to prevent the delay of first sending on to Paris I copied the letter, signed both our names and sent it direct, with a little note to Bismarck. The note (merely stating that a copy of the enclosed would be made public) I also signed by your name as well as my own. I knew you would not mind signing and I thought it best not to lose a day or more for the mere formality of your countersignature. I hope you will not mind.

· · ·

I suppose you have seen that the *Commonweal* is to come out as a weekly — and an awful mess they'll be making of it ere long. By dint of much arguing the General and I induced Edward to give up the sub-editorship. This, I think, was necessary on more grounds than one. First he really has not the time: secondly, and more important, there is no one here really dependable to work with. Paul has five or six men whom he can depend on — we have *no one*. Bax, reasonable on many points, is quite mad on others, and both he and Morris are just now more or less under the thumb of the Anarchists. We should therefore have been held responsible for a paper that will constantly do things we should be bound to condemn, and yet have no power to prevent from appearing. The position was impossible. A propos of this! I *do* wish Paul would send a short article about Decazeville[2] and I should be glad if he would in it talk up the ground or the real work done there and the flash in the pan at Liège.[3] The Anarchists of course are glorifying the latter at the expense of the former: if *I* write there'll be a row and the article would in all probability not be printed, but Bax (who is sub-editor now) would certainly take something from Paul. I ask this (though I know how hard he is working already) because there are some really good men among us, working men who do not know the real facts, and for their sakes it would be worth while to set things straight for them.

Edward and I, as you will see from our address, have come to the river for a day or two. We get more work done here really than in London, and get some fresh air besides. I have (the Lord be praised!) finished my translation of *Madame Bovary*. It *has* been work! It will be out ere very long I suppose, and I am now working at an "Introduction" to it. By the by, that reminds me that there are one or two matters I must consult Paul about — certain law terms (I want to know exactly what they *are* and then Moore will find me the equivalent English terms) and three or four slang words of whose meaning I am not sure. I'll send them you when I get back to London. I also want to know if you will send me your translation from Chamisso.[4] I want to try and get it published for you. I suppose you'd not object if I can get you a few shillings for it.

We are now going out for our afternoon walk — we indulge in such luxuries when we're down here — so goodbye. It's Good Friday. I wish I could send you a bun!

Love from us both to you both

Yours affectionately

TUSSY

We go back to London on Sunday.

---

1. Carl Juta, Marx's brother-in-law.
2. On 26 January a strike had started at Decazeville, in the mining basin of Avey-

ron, to protest a cut in wages. Reporters from *Le Cri du Peuple* and *L'Intran-sigeant* were arrested, and later condemned, on charges of having supported the strikers.

3. After a rally in Liège in March, which ended in the looting of shops and cafés, the whole Charleroi basin came briefly out on strike.

4. Laura had translated Chamisso's poem "Salas and Gomez" into English.

In 1886 the Socialist Labor Party of North America (SLP), which was based in New York, invited Aveling and Liebknecht (co-founder of the German Social-Democratic Party and friend of the Marxes) to give a series of lectures in America. The party, dominated by emigré *Germans, was made up of a scattering of socialists from different European countries; the Secretary-General was W. L. Rosenberg. Eleanor accompanied Aveling on the trip, though her fare was not paid by the Party. Before they left she had checked the sources of all the English quotations in volume I of* Capital, *which appeared in January 1887 in the translation by Sam Moore and Aveling.*

Between their arrival in New York on 10 September and their departure on 19 December the Avelings spoke in over thirty-five towns, excluding New York and its environs. They had a particularly good response in Chicago, where indignation over the famous "Anarchists Trial" was at its height. In May, during a factory picket by some members of the Knights of Labor, seven men had been killed after police were called in. The next day a protest demonstration was held. A bomb exploded among the throng of police, who fired on the crowd, causing several deaths and many casualties. Eight militant Anarchists were subsequently arrested, four of whom were sentenced to death and hanged in 1887. They became known as the "Chicago Martyrs."

Eleanor made many rousing speeches on the subject, calling for a re-trial and making firm distinctions between socialism and anarchism. It was also in Chicago that she stressed the importance of the role of women in the socialist movement.

64. Eleanor to Laura

Adelphi Hotel, Liverpool
31 August 1886

My dear Laura,

In a few hours we are off, but I must send you and Paul a line of goodbye. There has been a fearful lot of work to get through these last days with packing, and moving, and finishing up the *Capital* work, so far as I am concerned. I have made a list of "books and authors" quoted (at Moore's and Edward's wish) which took me an awful time to get straight.

It has been a great disappointment to us that we could not see you before we start. But indeed, we *could* not get to Paris. You don't know what a chronic state of hard-up-ness we are always in.

Liebknecht turned up yesterday and we saw him at the General's, who came over from Eastbourne to meet him and take him back there.

I look forward to this journey with no little anxiety. We shall have a difficult time of it in many ways, especially since this Chicago business. I *do* hope you'll write and tell me how things go on. As we shall be constantly on the move I think it would be best if you always send to W. L. Rosenberg, 261 East Tenth Street, New York City. He will always know our where-abouts and send on. *Please* write and tell me of yourselves and the children. I never hear from Longuet!

Love and good luck to you both. Perhaps we shall see you at Xmas or the New Year.

Yours affectionately,
TUSSY

P.L.I. (please look inside).

Dear Laura and dear Paul,

My love to you both. I wish you were going with us. We shall be quite strangers in a strange world. *If* we make millions of dollars we will spend some of the very first of them in a Cook's ticket to 66 the Boulevard de Port Royal.[1] You don't expect us a tenth as much as we want to come.

Always yours
EDWARD

1. The Lafargues had moved to this address in August 1882.

65. Eleanor to Laura
(incomplete)

[New York, September 1886]
.   .   .

doing little and no serious damage, though it was an anxious half-hour waiting while a boat from our ship was lowered, rowed out and back again and reported the little vessel "all right." For all we could tell many a man might have been drowned even as we waited. Then a poor woman in the steerage, who was going out to her husband in New York, died and we saw her burial in the early morning at daybreak — the simplest and most impressive scene I have ever witnessed. But these events apart the days were very uniform, but very pleasant, and the seeing of whales and porpoises and, once or twice, vessels, created the greatest excitement.

When we got into New York — and the entrance up the bay to the harbour is a marvellous sight, I should say the most beautiful I have ever seen — we were met by some red-ribboned gentlemen, one of whom was Cuno,[1] whom no doubt you re-member. We were taken off to our quarters, which are in the German part of the city. I rather regret this, for the Vaterland, like the poor, is always with us here. The reporters were down upon us like wolves on the fold, and life has been one whirl these last days. Yesterday Liebknecht arrived, and after meeting dozens of people in the morning we were serenaded last evening and then taken off to beer and talk, and hand-shaking with so many delegates from so many organizations that we were fairly tired out.

Tonight Edward and I really start speaking at Bridgeport,

whither we go this afternoon, returning late at night. It will be very hard work, especially as we have so very much press work to do (you know I am bound to "keep myself," as the party only pays for Edward). Edward has about a dozen newspapers to write to, and I shall have a good many without counting letters, and callers. Every ten minutes someone or other turns up, and if I am very incoherent ascribe it to that. Edward sends best love and wants to say to Paul that the first moment he can get he'll send something for the *Socialiste* but he really has *very* little time. We both, dear Laura, send you our very best wishes for the 26th, and I will write shortly and tell you about the "party" here and about this very dirty, shoddy town.

With love and good wishes to you both, and should you see them a kiss for the children.

Yours affectionately,

TUSSY

Do write. I *long* to hear from home. (*Europe* seems home now.)

1. Theodor Cuno, German Social-Democrat who had emigrated to the U.S. in 1878.

Before leaving New York Aveling advised the SLP that its effectiveness might be increased if it were to align itself with the indigenous workers' movements now beginning to flourish in America. In this Aveling was at one with Engels, who was critical of the sectarian and theoretical nature of the German socialist émigré groups in the country. However, the SLP interpreted Aveling's report as a direct attack on the present Executive and its Secretary-General, and it prompted a swift response, in the form of assiduous scrutiny of the list of expenses that Aveling had submitted to the Executive. The expenses were indeed high, and the SLP singled out for criticism items such as corsage bouquets bought for Eleanor and theatre seats which had in fact been complimentary.

To the delight of his many enemies in England the Evening Standard *reprinted an SLP circular accusing Aveling of fraud. Whatever the truth of the matter, it is clear that the party's real grievance against Aveling was his recommendation that it should unite with the Knights of Labor, which constituted a genuine people's organization. Hyndman seized the opportunity to attempt to discredit Aveling, while Engels staunchly defended him against accusations from America, Britain and Germany. But in a letter to Sorge of 8 August 1887 Engels conceded that Aveling had provoked the situation himself, through his "ignorance of life, of people and of business and his weakness for romantic reveries."*

Soon after his return Aveling delivered several lectures on the political situation in the U.S., wrote a series of articles for Time, *which were published as a pamphlet under the title* The Labour Movement in America.

66. Eleanor and Aveling to Laura

Dodwell
Stratford-on Avon, 30 August 1887

My dear Laura,

I am ashamed of myself. I'm a lazy beast not to have written to you — and I tell myself so every day. But that doesn't seem to do much good. However, I can bear the reproaches of my conscience no longer.

Have you heard from the General of our *K*astle? If not — and I assume not — I must tell you how we happen to be here in Warwickshire, the heart of England, Shakespeare's country. A few weeks ago the North-Western started a cheap excursion from the Friday to Tuesday to Stratford. Edward, for one of his papers, got two "passes." We came down here, saw and were conquered. One day, walking from Stratford to Bidford (one of Shakespeare's well-known walks) we saw a farm — near the farm two cottages, one unlet. We inquired, found the rent was 2s. a week — and subsequently, after our return to London, we decided to rent this lovely little place. It is two miles from Stratford, and Dodwell consists of this farm and its two cots.[1] The farmer at first tried to explain these were only cottages for labourers — he could not understand our wanting to come. You would. Downstairs we have a large kitchen — stone-flagged of course, a back kitchen and washhouse in one, and a pantry. Upstairs three rooms — two, of course, very small. Besides this we have $\frac{1}{4}$ of an acre of garden, where we can grow more vegetables than we ourselves want. Edward goes out and digs up our potatoes as we need them and we have been sowing all sorts of things. Next Spring our garden will be not only ornamental but useful. And all for two shillings a week! Our furnishing has not cost more than two or three weeks at the seaside would have done (and our railway journey costs nothing), and I have already two or three people to whom I am going to sub-let when we are not here. The living is very cheap, and next Summer when we have all sorts of vegetables will be cheaper still.

We *do* so wish you and Paul would come over some time. There's plenty of room, without counting that the delightful family (two brothers and two sisters) at the farm will let me have beds for friends at any time. I can't tell you how charming this country life is after the hurry and worry and wear and tear of London. It is as Scott calls it — "*the* beautiful county"[2] — essentially English, of course, in character, as it becomes Shakespeare's home to be. Think of it, Laura, Shakespeare's home! We work two or three times a week at his "birth place" (by permission of the Librarian of the place) and we have been over his home, and seen the old Guild Chapel that stands opposite "New Place," and the old Grammar School — unchanged — whither he went "unwillingly to school," and his grave in Trinity Church, and Anne Hathaway's cottage, still just as it was when Master Will went a-courting, and Mary Arden's cottage at Wilmcote — the prettiest place of all. Now that I have been in this sleepy little Stratford, and met the Stratfordians, I know where all the Dogberries and Bottoms and Snugs come from. You'll meet them here today. Just near our "Kastle" is a bank — many think it Titania's, for it is covered with wild thyme and oxlips and violets (in the season). I never knew before how Stratfordian Shakespeare was. All the flowers are Stratford ones, and Charlecote I would wager anything is Rosalind's Arden. But you *must* come and see the place, and you will fall in love with it as we have done.

We are pretty hard at work here, though we do a good deal of walking and "lazing" (as the Yankees say). Edward is writing no end of things. Have you heard that a play of his, *Dregs* (a short one-act thing), has been accepted by a very popular and "rising" actress Rose Norreys, and is to be produced shortly? And that he will probably have two other plays, one an adaptation of the *Scarlet Letter*, accepted also shortly?[3] You'll have to come over and see them. We have just finished arranging our *Time* articles for a book that Sonnenschein is to bring out. We have added much new, and I think, useful material. We are also going to write a series of articles on "Shakespeare's Stratford" (it is for these that we work at the "Birthplace")[4] and I am translating some of Kielland's wonderful short stories from the Norwegian. You ought to read Kielland (most of his things are translated into German), for I am sure you and Paul would admire him immensely.

As we are settled here till our lessons and other work call us back to London, there is no chance of our getting to Jersey.[5] I remember St. Brelade well. It is, like all Jersey, a delightful place. You must be sure to see the other side too, though — the Gorey and St. Catherine side. In some respects I like that even better than St. Brelade. I envy you having the children with you. It must be so pleasant to have them about. We have nothing but our dogs and cats (whom we brought with us) and I long to see the little ones. I haven't seen Mémé since she was a wee baby three months old. Have you all four with you? If so tell Jean he should write to me. His last letter — the only one I've had — was no pleasure to me as it was all corrected and amended by *le père*.

Olive Schreiner[6] has been talking to me a great deal about you and Paul. Of course you know Mrs. Walters is translating Paul's *Matriarcat*[7] and should, I fancy, do it remarkably well. There is some difficulty in getting it printed. Magazines won't take an article translated from another magazine. I have suggested to Mrs. Walters to try Sonnenschein. He would, I am almost certain, bring it out as a pamphlet. Do you ever see any English magazines? If you can, at any library in St. Hélier get the *Fortnightly*, look at Olive's allegory on "Woman" in the August number.[8] As an allegory I think it perfect.

We shall, I think, be here till about September 10th. Then we go back to Chancery Lane to our teaching and usual dreary round of work. By the way, I don't think I ever told you anything of our new London quarters. We have three large rooms, and kitchen and a smaller room, and little boxroom, all on one floor — and that the fourth! But really the going up and down once or twice in the day is not nearly so trying as the constant running up and down in the usual houses and apartments. It is a great deal less trouble for me, anyhow, especially as I have given up having a servant and do my own work. Sundays, of course, we still spend with the General, and there is the usual round of dinner, drink, cards, supper and more drink. Pumps had a great excitement as Fritz Beust was staying at the General's. He has grown so big and fat you wouldn't know him. Poor Percy is deafer than ever. Nym is always the same, and the General has been better in health lately than he had been. I don't know how he has got on at Eastbourne.

Edward wants to add a few lines.

Give my love to Paul and the dear little ones, and if you can find it in your heart to treat me better than I do you write soon to

Your affectionate sister

TUSSY

My dear Laura,

I owe you and Philip Shun [illeg.]. This letter is not in quittance of that debt, which will be discharged when the plays begin acting and royalties roll in, or when I see something within my temporary means and your liking. But it is to say how charming this place is and how equally charming you and Paul would be if you would only come and see us at it. The last phrase sounds like an invitation to witness a family row, but is not so meant. Jersey is, I fear, out of the question. I think I could get passes, but you will be leaving before we leave here and at most we could only come for a day or so. Better luck next time, or the best of luck, that you come hither. I know Jersey wellish. Once there as a boy with a tutor and a hatred of him. Once again with the Bradlaugh people. And yet the place has a sweet smell in my memory. How are Paul's eyes? I trust not troubling him one-hundredth part as much as I am you with this letter. Good fortune to you both and to us that of seeing you soon!

Yours always,

EDWARD

1. 1 and 2, Dodwell Farm Cottages, built in 1873. Dodwell still consists of only the farm and its two cottages, but Stratford has spread to meet it.
2. In chapter 25 of his novel *Kenilworth,* Walter Scott refers to "the beautiful county of Warwick."
3. Aveling's adaptation of Hawthorne's *Scarlet Letter* was first performed at the Olympic Theatre, London, on 5 June 1888, with Charles Charrington and Janet Achurch; *Dregs* on 16 May 1889 at the Vaudeville, with Rose Norreys.
4. Not traced, possibly never completed.
5. After an operation on Paul's eye in mid-August the Lafargues went to Sainte-Brelade, Jersey, with Marcel and Mémé Longuet. Subsidized by Engels, they stayed until the end of the month.
6. South African author of *The Story of an African Farm,* one of Eleanor's most intimate friends.
7. "Le Matriarcat, étude sur les origines de la famille," *Nouvelle Revue,* March 1886. Mrs. Walters, a friend of Schreiner's, had done translations for Havelock Ellis's Contemporary Science series.
8. Olive Schreiner, "Three Dreams in a Desert," *Fortnightly Review,* 1 August 1887.

On their return from Dodwell the Avelings resumed their political activities, speaking in the Radical Clubs in the East End and rallying support for the Chicago Anarchists and the Irish Home Rule movement.

In the winter of 1887 large numbers of unemployed workers took to gathering in Trafalgar Square. There were several scuffles with police, and on 8 November the press published a warning from the Chief of Police, Sir Charles Warren, forbidding any further rallies and speeches from taking place. On 13 November, a day which has gone down in history as "Bloody Sunday," the Metropolitan Radical Federation and the Irish National League held a protest demonstration which was violently broken up by mounted police. Many people were wounded, two of whom later died; Eleanor was slightly injured. There were nearly three hundred arrests and about a hundred sentences, ranging from two weeks' to six months' hard labour.

On 18 November the Law and Liberty League, whose aims were to protest against police violence and affirm freedom of speech, was inaugurated. Its members included the Avelings, William Morris, the crusading journalist W. T. Stead, Hyndman, and many other leading Radicals and Fabians. On the same day a rally was held in Trafalgar Square which was again charged by mounted police. A passer-by, Alfred Linnell, was seriously wounded and died on 2 December. After an inquest to determine the precise cause of his death, his burial finally took place on 18 December; about 120,000 people followed his coffin, and William Morris wrote an elegiac poem, illustrated by Walter Crane, in aid of his family.

67. Eleanor to Laura

65, Chancery Lane, W.C.
31 December 1887

My dear Laura,

Just one line to wish you both from us both a happy New Year. Edward is away at Torquay to superintend the rehearsing of a little play of his to be produced there,[1] so I am writing for him as well as for myself.

I hear from the General that you have gone in for the house decorating and painting line. I wish I were there to help. Though I say it as shouldn't, I believe I have a genius for house painting. We have a most splendid enamel here now (if you like I'll send you some pots) which I find invaluable. I enamel chairs, tables, floors, everything. If the climate only permitted I should enamel myself.

Of course I have heard nothing about the children. I don't even know Longuet's address, and have had to send a few little toys — all I could afford — for the children to Longuet at the *Justice*. Heaven knows if the children will ever get them!

By the way I get the *Socialist*[*e*] in a rather eccentric fashion — sometimes two numbers of one week and then nothing for three! I enclose an extract, or rather a letter, that appeared in the *Globe* last week. It may amuse you. I have been told that "blank warrants" are out against Edward and myself so that we can be "run in" whenever the police choose. The Linnell funeral was *very* fine, and a great success. The streets were a wonderful sight, especially as we neared the East End. There was one very curious scene — we saw it because the horses of our drey had fallen, and so we were rather behind. In the Mile End Road (right out East) a large number of people stood ready to fall in behind the procession, when some omnibuses tried to drive through and break up the procession. They were called on to desist, but one man lashed his horses to a gallop, while a passenger outside had a long stick and lashed and struck out at the people. Then one man threw himself in front of the horses, clung to them and actually stopped them. In one second the traces had been cut, the passengers all taken down, and the beast who had lashed the people knocked down in fine style. He was howling to be "let alone." He will think twice another time before he strikes the people. Then, the 'bus turned out of the procession, the people quietly fell in and marched on in order as if nothing had happened. It really was fine to see. If only the Radicals were not so many of them cowards we could carry the square. As it is they are all "funking" more or less.

Tonight there is a solemnity at Pumps'! I envy Edward at Torquay!

With all good wishes to you both

Yours

TUSSY

1. *By the Sea* and *The Love Philtre*, Torquay Theatre, 7 January 1888.

The Avelings were now deeply involved in the theatrical world. They were ardent Ibsenites and were to take an active part in the controversy sparked off by A Doll's House. *Eleanor had learnt Norwegian and was working on several translations, including* An Enemy of the People; *she was also editing an Elizabethan play,* A Warning to Fair Women, *at the request of Havelock Ellis, and she and Aveling prepared two lectures on "Shelley's Socialism" for the Shelley Society, the most recent venture of Eleanor's old friend Furnivall. Aveling was writing drama criticism under the pen-name of "Alec Nelson" and was beginning to make a name for himself as a dramatist: several of his plays and adaptations were performed, with varying degrees of success.*

In the summer of 1888 the Avelings decided to try their luck in America. They travelled with Schorlemmer and Engels, who were on a private visit, but eventually joined them on their journey, Aveling's theatrical plans having largely foundered. They returned together on 29 September 1888.

68. Eleanor to Laura

S.S. City of Berlin.
Queenstown.
9 August 1888

My dear Laura,

In about two hours we shall be at Queenstown, and from there we can send you a line of greeting — the last till we reach New York. Of course you know that the "we" is the General and Jollymeier besides us. I should have told you this as soon as I knew it myself, but the General was so anxious to keep it dark I did not dare to. I thought if it leaked out we should get the blame. I can hardly realize that we are actually off to America again and that the General is actually coming too. I believe this sea-voyage and the perfect change, and perfect air and rest will do him a world of good. The boat is not very full — it is still rather

early for the Americans to leave Europe — but all the pleasanter. And we've *such* a lot of priests, and clergymen on board,
and some babies and no end of Amurcen twang. Both our old
men seem to be enjoying themselves and eat, drink and are as
merry as possible. Great excitement! A sailing vessel is passing
quite close and I must go and look at it.

As you know we shall be in Yankee-land three to four
weeks. We go to New York, Boston, Niagara, Pittsburgh certainly, and Edward and I to Chicago, but I don't know yet if
the others will go so far west.

The General tells us Paul is going to send us a play of
yours. That is good. If you can, Edward would be glad if you'd
send it to New York, as he might then work at it on the return
journey. I should be glad if something could be done with it. In
any case there are now three or four managers who will at least
read anything Edward takes them, and that is something.

There was such a scene when the General at last plucked
up courage to tell Pumps, but she went too far and the General
got cross and bullied her, and then she somewhat recovered.
Why she should be so wild, after her pleasant Continental trip,[1]
that the General is coming with us I don't know. How did you
find her? Nymmy has told us so much of your lovely house and
garden that Edward is frightfully jealous. You beat our Castle
hollow. But then I comfort him by reminding him that our rent
is only £5 a year, and we this year sold £3 worth of potatoes.
Why don't you sell some of your produce? You ought with such
a garden to make quite a little income.

I'm very disjointed, I fear, in my remarks, but it is awfully
distracting to write on deck, when something or somebody in-
terrupts you every moment. Let us hear from you. Send any
letters c/o John Lovell, 16 Vesey Street, New York City.

Love from all of us to you both.

Your affectionate

TUSSY

---

1. After a visit to Germany Pumps, Helen and Schorlemmer had spent several
days with the Lafargues, who had moved to Le Perreux in December 1887.

69. Eleanor to Laura

St. Nicholas Hotel, New York.
21 August 1888

My dear Laura,

Here we are in New York, and I can even now hardly realize that Engels is in America with us! Our voyage over was very jolly, though it was rough part of the time and rained. But we were well, and all in the best of health and spirits. I've not known the General to be so well — or so lazy — for years. Even his eyes are less troublesome. Unfortunately the great heat here (it is cooler, thank goodness, today) and a cold he caught knocked him up a bit. But it is nothing much, and on the whole he is wonderfully well. Indeed of the two anyone would think him ten years younger than Jollymeier, who is quite an old man compared with Engels. I fear that fall and blow on the head have hurt Jollymeier more than we or he supposed. You have no idea how he has aged. He walks, talks and looks like an old grandfather. Perhaps this trip will help to set him up again.

As we were not comfortable at the boarding house we first went to, we have moved. The General and Jollymeier are staying at Hoboken (Engels at Sorge's, Jollymeier next door) and we came to this hotel. We must be actually in New York. This city of iniquities strikes me as more hideous than ever — and yet it might be so beautiful. I don't believe there is any large town in the world so exquisitely situated as New York — and commerce has made of it a very hell.

Our plans are not yet settled but as soon as Edward can get away — which will not, I fear, be till Sunday — we take a steamer up the Hudson to Albany, from there we go on to Lake George, then to Boston, Niagara, up the St. Lawrence to Montreal, and Pittsburgh. We sail again probably on the 19th.

Our fellow-travellers were, on the whole, a very dull lot — about twenty of them I should say were clergymen. We had priests, a Bishop of the American Church, dissenters and heaven knows what else. Oddly enough too, three people on board had heard us speak in different towns two years ago. The least stupid people we had with us were a lawyer, a doctor and a young actor.

Old Sorge is, as you may fancy, overjoyed to have Engels

here. He is so glad that he hardly grumbles at all. Edward is just off to Hoboken, and I expect they'll all come back together. Edward, however, will have to spend the next few days seeing after rehearsals.

Goodbye. Love to you both.

Yours affectionately,
TUSSY

I hear poor little Johnny is not very happy. I'm glad he is to have his holidays with you. He will be so delighted at your garden. If only Edward does well with his plays we want to try and have Johnny with us for good. We both liked to have the child and we never had the least trouble with him.

Good luck to you!

In the late 1880s socialism had steadily been gaining strength throughout Europe. In July 1889, the centenary of the storming of the Bastille, two rival workers' congresses were held in Paris which led to the emergence of the Second International. As described in the following letters from Eleanor, the preparations for the congresses revealed the extent to which the international socialist parties were at loggerheads during this crucial period of their history — as often for personal as for political reasons.

The main schism was between the French Trade Unionists, supported by Lafargue and Guesde, allied with the Marx-Engels-Liebknecht faction, and the International Trade Unionists, supported by Brousse and the Possibilists, allied with Hyndman and the SDF and some of the British trade unions.

The Possibilists refused to attend a meeting in the Hague in February to prepare for the centenary, claiming that they alone had the right to convoke the Congress. Lafargue made the tactical error of inviting William Morris of the Socialist League to the Hague but not the more representative SDF.

By April 1889 it was clear that amalgamation of the two sides was impossible. Eleanor, recognizing the desirability of a single united Congress, attempted to rally the trade unions. Meanwhile Hyndman published some vicious attacks on "the Marxist clique" in Justice. Engels joined the fray by writing a statement of the Marxist case, signed by the German Social Democrat Bernstein, of which three thousand copies were printed and distributed throughout England. From then on Hyndman adopted a more conciliatory tone, expressing his desire for a united international congress which would transcend differences of opinion.

Eleanor and Bernstein decided to visit Hyndman to deliver Bernstein's reply, to be published in the 13 April issue of Justice, in person. As the Congress approached, Eleanor's chief concerns — as revealed in the following letters to Laura — were the unnecessary

208

*delay in sending out invitations, which lost them sup-
port, and the absence of a newspaper which could be
relied upon to support the Marxists against the Possibilists. Even Massingham of the* Star, *usually sympathetic to the Marxists, proved susceptible to per-
suasion from their rivals.*

70. Eleanor to Laura

65, Chancery Lane, W.C.
11 April 1889

My dear Laura,

I know exactly what you're saying of me. I deserve it *nearly*
all. Not quite. For last Saturday I actually wrote you a letter
of some 8 pages. I was to meet Edward at the Crystal Palace
(whither we went to hear Berlioz's *Faust*) and took the letter
as he wanted to add some lines. I put it in the book I was reading (one of Meredith's!) and lo and behold! when I got to the
Palace the book was in my hand but the letter was gone. I had
faint hopes a conscientious person might find it, and seeing the
address on the paper send it me. But no such luck. I'm doubly
sorry. I'd told you "all about" what's going on, and one doesn't
care for such a letter falling into any hands.

I got Paul's letter for the *Star* but as there were new developments we did not take it to Massingham. Hyndman had
meantime practically caved in, and as, after all, a single Congress is desirable we must do our best for that. To this end
Bernstein and I saw Hyndman on Monday. I send you no account of the interview as I know the General will tell you of it.
Hyndman looked green when he saw me, and knowing what
an awful temper I have, did his best to irritate me. But though
I'm a bad temper I'm not a fool. I saw his game and would not
play up to it. I remained quite polite and amiable, even when
he began with the usual calumnies against us and Paul. I only
remarked (I couldn't for the life of me resist *that*) that if Lafargue was accused of all manner of sins to the party, he, Hyndman, too, was so accused, and that it all came to a question of
personalities rather than facts. "You say Lafargue has ruined

the French movement and is etc., etc., etc., etc. Well, Champion and Mann,[1] and others innumerable, say *you* have ruined the movement here. They may be right or wrong. But what's that to do with the Congress?" Then came up the old sore of our *family*. You and I should feel proud. *We're* supposed to be doing it all! About twenty times Hyndman informed Bernstein and me that I was a "bitter partisan." I am, and I'm not ashamed of it. However the upshot of it all is (you could trust me and Bernstein, Jews that we are, to drive a bargain) that Hyndman will, we think, do all he can to bring about some sort of "conciliation." He evidently was staggered when he heard that all Socialist Europe is practically with us. The Belgians, however, are playing a double game,[2] and the Broussists are, I am convinced, lying to Hyndman, and taking *him* in. It would all be very funny if it weren't very sad. Meantime the *real* movement — as distinct from all the small Socialist sects — is going on well here. We have worked hard, but it all has to be done under the nose. If we, just now, come out too much, the cry of "Marxist intrigue" would go up at once. "What fools these mortals be!" Of course a mistake was made about the Hague meeting. The English *should* have been invited, and Paul's writing to Morris was a great mistake. With others he might be asked. Alone he is worse than nothing. His army is one that would have put even Falstaff to the blush. He himself blushes at it. Morris is personally liked, but you would not get a half-dozen workmen to take him seriously.

Champion is evidently quite gone over to the Tories.[3] He tried to get a small party of Socialists to back him. Edward very nearly walked into the spider's parlour. I kept away carefully. It was all an election dodge. But if the official Socialists seem in a bad way the *real* workers are getting on. We have a hold on all the best Radical Clubs. Only last night I lectured to a capital audience, who, some three or four years ago, would either have laughed at my lecture or yelled at me. I wish we — and I wish *you* had a paper. The devil of it is that the Possibilists can put forth their lies and you have no organ in which to answer them.

As to ourselves, we're rubbing along somehow. It's jolly hard though! I often think "I'd rather be a kitten and cry mew"[4] than a woman trying to earn a living.

By the way, could you tell me approximately what about

a week or ten days would cost a girl in Paris? Alice Corthorn,[5] a friend of mine, a teacher, is anxious to spend the Easter holidays in Paris. She is a socialist (of the sentimental sort) and would *like* if it were possible to lodge with some working-class folk. Could it be done? And, *à peu près* for how much! Drop me a postcard if you can about that. Alice is a nice little body and if she goes over I hope you'll be kind to her.

Here all is much as usual. The dear old General is suffering a little with his eyes. Nym is very well, though she gets bronchitis now and again. Pumps is — Pumps.

I daren't ask you to write. But I *should* like to hear from you and about the children. They never write to me, and I long for news of them.

Our love to you and Paul,

Your affectionate sister

TUSSY

1. Thomas Mann, a member of the Amalgamated Engineers' Union and an influential force in the campaign for an eight-hour day.
2. At their April 1889 Congress the Belgians decided to send delegates to both congresses.
3. Champion had been expelled from the SDF in 1887 for accepting "Tory gold" and was now editor of the anti-Hyndman *Labour Elector*.
4. *Henry IV*, Part I, Act III, scene i (Hotspur).
5. Alice Corthorn (1859–1935) was also a friend of the Radfords and Olive Schreiner. A governess, she later worked in India as a doctor and researcher, then set up in general practice in Kensington, where by 1914 her patients included suffragettes and the local poor.

71. Eleanor to Laura

65, Chancery Lane, W.C.
8 April 1889[1]

My dear Laura,

I send you a disgraceful Paris article from the *Star*.[2] Massingham was, we are certain, met by Adolphe Smith, and has been held captive all the time of his stay in Paris. Of course this does not excuse Massingham, whose *duty* it was to hear and see both sides. Meantime what we propose is this. Bax (who is keeping fairly straight in this matter) and we went to the *Star* today. Massingham not yet back. He returns, however (they believe) by tomorrow. We shall see him and *try* to force the insertion of a *leader* putting our side of the case. Should this fail, we insist on inserting a letter of Bernstein's, dealing, however, chiefly with the article of *May 3rd*.[3] As to the article enclosed, Bax has promised to send in a protest, but that is not enough. *Vaillant must write at once.* If possible translate the letter for him — and let it go to the *Star direct*. If *I* send it, it is only "one of the Marx family-affairs." Paul should write, as I already suggested, on general grounds, and if you could draw up a short letter signed by all the men who sign the invitation to the Congress that would be excellent. Should you do this let me have a copy (in any case let me know by postcard whenever a letter is sent the *Star*) and I'll try and get it in *somewhere*.

Entre nous, our good friend Liebknecht is responsible for the whole affair. Had we got out our invitation *at once* we should have had all the English. Now I much fear it is too late. And we must be fair. They know nothing here of the real movement, and the dissensions between you and the Possibilists they think only a replica of the Socialist League and Federation differences. The deuce of it is that the League is Anarchist, and Champion's *Labour Elector* very shady (and held, not unjustly, in great contempt by most of the working members) and we have no one else to be sure of. I *did* think Massingham quite safe, but as Bax says, he's been "nobbled." We will do our best to bring him to see the error of his ways. Edward will also see Reynolds[4] (unfortunately *his* paper is also largely influenced by the Hyndman clique), and we will have Burns[5] (who is appointed delegate to the Possibilists by the Engineers' Union) and Tom Mann thoroughly posted in the facts.

I fear we shall not do much here now. We are too late in the field. But all that can yet be done shall be. If you, meanwhile, see [that] the *Star* is bombarded with letters, let me have copies of any *important* ones. *A la guerre comme à la guerre*.[6] We must try rival papers of the *Star*, if the *Star* is quite recalcitrant.

You see, Hyndman, and Smith, and a whole lot of these fellows have nothing on earth to do but loaf about, and wait till they catch a man like Massingham, e.g. [*sic*] who is ignorant of all the real facts. We, poor devils, who have to work for our living, *can't* loaf on an off-chance of netting someone. Here we are at a great disadvantage.

We're going up to see the General this evening. Will write if anything else occurs.

With love,

Yours
TUSSY

Be *sure* and get Vaillant's letter. Bax swears he will get that in at all costs, if the *Star* does not put it in willingly.

---

1. This letter and the following one are incorrectly dated April rather than May.
2. Unsigned article, "The Workmen's Party: a chat with some practical Socialists at the Hôtel de Ville" (7 May), attacking Vaillant and the Marxists. According to Eleanor, the editor of the *Star*, Massingham, had been contaminated by contact with Adolphe Smith, a member of the SDF who had made spurious attacks on Marx.
3. Unsigned article entitled "The Paris International Congress."
4. *Reynolds Weekly*, an important radical journal founded by G. W. Reynolds.
5. John Burns, also an engineer, one of the leaders of the New Union movement.
6. Figuratively, "we must take the rough with the smooth."

Lafargue wrote a letter protesting against the Star *article, and sent it to Engels who passed it on to Eleanor.*

On 6 May Lafargue finally sent the text of the invitation to the Congress to Engels. It was chiefly Liebknecht who had caused the delay: he still hoped to arrive at a reconciliation with the Possibilists, and Engels spoke of his "mania for unity." The invitation, which appealed to the workers and socialists of Europe and America, was published in the Star *under the heading "The People's Post Box."*

72. Eleanor to Laura

65, *Chancery Lane, W.C.*
10 April [*May*] *1889*

My dear Laura,

The General has just brought Paul's letter to the *Star*, and we have to send it back for many reasons.

(1) It is *much* too long, and deals too much with generalities. What we think or don't think of the Possibilists is of no interest here. We are doing all we can to get the facts about our Congress into the press (no easy matter). Your cue is to show up the *lies* of the other side. Take up the Boulé question, the Vaillant question,[1] the misrepresentation of all of our people. But don't enter into any long account of the constitution of the Congress and so forth. *That* won't go in as a letter; and we will get it in, in another form if possible. If *you* will write about Boulé and Vaillant about himself, *that* is what we want. But please don't lose time. Then too, as I suggested, a letter signed by the signatories of the invitation would be good: but again the letter must not be too long; simply state that representing such and such bodies (Bordeaux and Troyes) you invite workers to attend the Congress, etc.

(2) The letters *must* go *direct* to the *Star*. It is no good sending through us. Send to H. W. Massingham, *Star*, Stonecutter Street, E.C. Send us copies, if need be, and always let us know when and what you've sent. We will try and get the

letters of which you send copies printed elsewhere if they don't go into the *Star*.

(3) Be sure *all* your statements are quite reliable. Don't be surprised to hear the Socialist League disclaims us. They have not (I hear) sent any official acceptance, and Paul's including them is a mistake. At best they don't count as they are Anarchist: but if they disclaim us we are doubly discredited.

It's all a damned nuisance. What makes me so angry is that but for the long delay, due to Liebknecht, we should have carried the English. Our pamphlet had had the happiest effect. But when we could not follow it up, and when I had to tell the working men who come to me that I had no definite news, and this week after week, they lost heart and faith, and then the Hyndman-Broussists, with their cut and dried arrangements, ousted us. They would have been beaten here had we been able to act at once.

Now all we can do is to get *our* Congress talked of. Send letter after letter (but the letters must be *short* and *crisp*) to the *Star*. *Some* will go in. Anyhow make Paul and Vaillant write at once. Let Paul tackle the Boulé, Vaillant his personal questions.

Today's our little Jean's birthday. How I do wish I could see him!

I'm going in for a new business — type-writing. I'm buying a machine, and as soon as I've learnt the work, which is very easy, I shall set up, and issue a prospectus! I'll send you one.

Your affectionate

TUSSY

---

1. Boulé and Vaillant, candidates for the French Workers' Party, had been accused by the Possibilists of having acted in alliance with, and accepted money from, the Boulangists. Earlier in the year France had come near to a military dictatorship due to the extraordinary popularity of General Boulanger, former Minister of War.

73. Eleanor to Laura

65, Chancery Lane, W.C.
1 June 1889

My dear Laura,
Enclosed a letter from Massingham. If you'd ever been at the
Star office you would not be surprised a letter was lost. You'd
only wonder anything ever got into the paper. I've had to
search all over Massingham's table to find an article he himself
had asked me to write, and that had then "got mislaid"! If
Okecki (*is* that the name?)[1] could again write, it shall go in
at once with an explanatory note as to delay. It is worthwhile.
I'm very sorry to give all this extra trouble, but it's not my
fault. I've been working hard for our Congress, I can tell you,
and it's no easy matter here in London.
      I don't know if Engels wrote you that last week I had
Burns, Cunninghame Graham, Mann, Banner, Davis, Bernstein
and Bonnier (W. Parnell could not come but wrote) up here to
talk over matters.* Burns *promised* (but he's a rather uncertain
quantity) to put the following suggestion (suggested by us)
before the Council of the Engineers' Trades Union, of whom he
is a delegate. He is to point out that *the International* Congress
is ours, and that therefore he be empowered to ask the other
Congress to send delegates — requesting the cooperation of our
Congress. If refused, he to resign and come to us. If only we'd
had our circular a week earlier! I've seen three or four Trades
Unionists who would all have come to us but for Liebknecht's
blundering. I'm very glad we have Keir Hardy [*sic*].[2] I took
him up to see the General last November (at the time of the
Congress here) and Engels has written him frequently since.
We then explained matters to him and Hardy, who is a splendid
fellow, has helped us immensely in Scotland. I hope he may get
money to be at the Congress. He would interest you. Till recently he worked in the mines (now he gets £80 a year as sec.
of his Union — not much for a man with a wife and four children!) and is quite self-educated. To Stepniak we wrote, and
you need not notice any letter of his saying his name should be
withdrawn. He only withdrew under the impression that signers
of the Convocation must represent Societies. I've explained that

* For brief descriptions of these, the List of Names on pages 313–28 should be
consulted.

he could sign in his individual capacity. Kropotkin and the Anarchists as well as the Lawroff people are against Stepniak, and he was afraid of getting us into trouble. He has written to Vera Zassoulitch and the other Russians for us.[3]

I've today sent off five hundred copies of the last invitation, and some hundred letters and postcards, and am dead tired — for I've also "typed" a play! One more thing. I daresay you'll have your place more than full, for the Congress week. Can you get me and Edward any room *cheap* (we're very poor!) in Le Perreux for about three to four weeks — from, say, the first to the end of July? I don't want to bother *you* — but if you could get anything I should be glad. We want to be over — and I don't want to trust to luck just now in getting rooms.

I've to see half a dozen Trades Unionists tonight about the Congress — so goodbye for the present. We've lectured at Radical Clubs steadily, and now I hope to turn our work to some account. The answer to *Justice*'s idiotic "manifesto" is splendid![4]

Our love to you both

Your

TUSSY

1. Okecki was the Treasurer of the Boulé Committee; his letter to the *Star* was a protest against the charges of the Possibilists (see page 215, note 1).
2. James Keir Hardie, a young Scottish miners' leader who later founded the Independent Labour Party (ILP). See page 244, note 2.
3. Stepniak and Zasulich (Zassoulitch) were both Russian revolutionaries exiled in London.
4. A reference to Bernstein's reply, of 25 May 1889, to "Manifesto of the SDF: Plain Truths about the International Congress of Workers in Paris in 1889."

The International Socialist Labour Congress took place in the Salle Pétrelle, Paris, from 14 to 20 July 1889, and was attended by about four hundred delegates from twenty-two countries of Europe and America.

The Possibilists' International Workers' Congress, which was held at the same time in the rue de Lancry, Paris, was less successful, attracting delegates from only fourteen countries.

The Marxist Congress contained some Anarchist and reformist elements who were strongly in favour of union with the Possibilists, and this gave rise to much heated debate. At the fourth session, a vote was taken and passed on a motion proposed by Liebknecht to unite the two congresses, but the Possibilists' demands for an examination of all candidates' credentials put amalgamation out of the question, particularly for the Germans, for whom the anti-Socialist laws made registration highly dangerous.

The following aims were agreed: an eight-hour day; international demonstrations on 1 May; prohibition of work by children; work protection for women and adolescents; rules governing day, night and holiday work; disarmament of armies, and armament of citizens. The Congress declared that peace was the first and indispensable condition of the emancipation of the workers.

Eleanor and Edward arrived in France on 6 July and stayed at Le Perreux, near the Lafargues. They took advantage of their free time before the Congress to visit the Universal Exposition in Paris. They also saw something of Jenny's children, and the two elder boys, Johnny and Edgar, returned to London with them.

During the Congress Eleanor performed the role of interpreter for the English, German and French delegates.

PART FIVE

December 1890 – January 1895

The Legacy

Most of the letters that follow are from Eleanor to Laura, relating the dramatic events taking place at Regent's Park Road. They also bear witness to an unhappy dispute over the *Nachlass* (Marx's literary heritage) which clouded Eleanor's relationship with Engels in his last years.

Through her contact with union leaders — John Burns and Tom Mann of the Amalgamated Engineers, Will Thorne of the Gasworkers, whom she taught to read and write — Eleanor was now making a significant contribution to the grass-roots work of the socialist movement. In 1889 the gasworkers had achieved an eight-hour day, and major concessions had been granted to the dockworkers after their celebrated five-week strike. These successes inspired a rapid growth in the development of the New Unions — that is, unions made up of unskilled labourers as opposed to the old "aristocratic" craft unions — in the early years of the new decade.

Eleanor was in great demand as a public speaker, so much so that she was constrained to write to the press requesting that her name not be announced in advertisements unless she had already agreed to appear. Often at only a moment's notice, she would visit strikers as far apart as Scotland and the East End, encouraging them to continue the struggle. During the eighty-five-day strike at the India Rubber Works in Silvertown, in East London, she gave many rousing speeches on the workers' behalf. She formed and became Secretary of the first women's branch of the Gasworkers' Union, and at their first Annual Conference in May 1890 was unanimously elected a member of the Executive. She also rallied support for the first May Day demonstration that had been agreed on at the Paris Congress. Aveling and Lafargue participated in the rally, which was held on 4 May 1890 in Hyde Park and attracted 250 to 300 thousand people.

In Paris, May Day 1890 was celebrated by a 100,000-strong rally in the Place de la Concorde. Though the French police were at the ready, the demonstration was peaceful. But in the provinces, socialism was making less headway. Lafargue, who had put himself up at the legislative elections at Le Cher in September 1889, was defeated; so was Longuet, who had stood at Courbevoie. However, the first number of the third series of *Le Socialiste* did appear on 21 September 1890. Paul had become Secretary of the French Workers' Party and Laura — while lacking Eleanor's fervour or restless energy — was helping out with *Le Socialiste* and translating socialist documents.

In August 1890 the Avelings spent two weeks in Norway on an Ibsen pilgrimage. On their return they plunged back into political activity and Eleanor attended both the French and German Party Congresses in October.

On 4 November Helen Demuth, loyal friend and housekeeper to both Marx and Engels, died. Engels, about to celebrate his seventieth birthday, was completely disoriented, and immediately set about finding someone who could organize his household and undertake secretarial duties. He wrote to Louise Kautsky, whom he had met several years earlier in London with her husband. Louise, now divorced from Kautsky and studying midwifery in Vienna, had maintained her connections with the German Social-Democratic Party and was encouraged by Bebel and Singer, anxious that the "post" should be held by one of their circle, to accept. Louise's arrival was not welcomed by Lizzie Burns's niece, Pumps, who was adored by Engels but was treated by the Marxes with a kind of exasperated condescension. Eleanor's response to Louise, though initially sympathetic, can be seen to change as Louise began to consolidate her position in the household and to exercise her influence on the General.

Part 5 ends with the death of Engels and Eleanor's discovery that Marx was the real father of Helen's son Freddy Demuth: Engels had loyally assumed paternity in order to avoid friction in the Marx family. It was only during Engels's final illness that Sam Moore, one of his executors, told Eleanor the truth. Feeling that she needed to hear it from Engels's own mouth Eleanor visited his deathbed, but Engels could no longer speak: he had to confirm what Moore had told her by writing it on a slate.

Aveling's philandering and his irresponsible attitude to money were already causing Eleanor great unhappiness, and there is a note of despair in many of the letters that follow. Some of Eleanor's spirit has gone, and there are poignant allusions to the importance of enduring friendships.

74. Eleanor to Laura

National Union of
Gasworkers & General Labourers
of Great Britain & Ireland
141, Barking Road, E.
19 December 1890

My dear Laura,

Don't be alarmed at this paper. I've done my "duty" in the enclosed letter to Paul. Now for the pleasure of a gossip. I wish you were here to gossip — although there are some inches deep of snow on my "leads," and the cold is beastly. I should like to *tell* you the history of the last weeks. I'm incapable of writing the Epic that alone could do justice to the facts of the case. The Saturday to Sunday after your departure I spent with the General, and we "pumped" till 2.30. I was so sleepy that I hardly remember what we pumped. I have only a general impression of valiant defiance breathed against the redoubtable Pumps. Well, that Sunday passed in comparative quiet, but Pumps retired early and the General began to quake. Then things grew more exciting. There were telegrams from Austria. Louise was coming. There were many "alarums and excursions." Finally Louise arrived. Meantime the General had screwed his courage to the sticking point and Pumps had been informed that on *my* (!!) invitation Louise was coming over, and must be properly treated — on pain of a new Testament being substituted for the old. Louise came. She was, as you may suppose, dead tired: the journey straight through from Vienna, coming on the top of weeks of hard work, is no slight affair. That very day Engels would have dragged her off to Pumps, but as (we had met Louise in the morning) I had said I would call in the afternoon, the visit was postponed till the next day. Then they called, and the first day Pumps deigned to return the visit she had champagne galore. Of course the "head of the table" question cropped up.

At first the General insisted, in spite of Louise's protests that she could not and would not "carve," on the "head of the table" being occupied by her, but at the last moment he funked, and so Pumps as usual presides. To tell you all the ups and downs would be to write a volume. But you know what it would be. Only one thing is too charming to omit. On the General's birthday Pumps, getting more drunk than usual, confided to *Louise* that she "knew she had to behave to her, or she'd get cut out of the Will!" I am sorry for Louise. Bebel and all the others have told her it is her *duty* to the Party to stop. It hardly seems fair to her. She was getting on so well at Vienna, and to sacrifice her whole career is no trivial matter — no one would ask a *man* to do that. She is still so young — only just thirty. It seems not right to shut her up, and keep her from every chance of a fuller and happier life. And you know what her life here will be. Why, our poor Nymmie couldn't get out — unless she took Pumps. *Then* it was all right. Moreover, *entre nous* I don't think it will or can last. But I can, naturally, do nothing. But I see well that it will end in unpleasantness. And in any case it is hardly fair to Louise. A stranger like Marie Döcker would make her own terms. Louise can't. Well, all one can do is to look on and wait. Meantime there has been any amount of comedy and farce — and the General is more afraid of Pumps — or is it of her eye? — than ever, and more abject. On one or two Sundays when Pumps has gone home he has sent her half the food in the house — not to mention the drinkables.

Freddy[1] has behaved admirably in all respects — and Engels's irritation against him is as unfair as it is comprehensible. We should none of us like to meet our pasts, I guess, in flesh and blood. I know I always meet Freddy with a sense of guilt and of wrong done. The life of that man! To hear him tell of it all is a misery and a shame to me.

News beyond the Pumpsiad there is little. We go our usual round — which means a good deal of "sweating" for damned little pay. Edward's *Madcap* is still running at the Comedy, and he has hopes of other things. The devil of it is hopes won't pay bills. I am doing hack translations (very bad) for a new magazine. We are both doing Drama Notes, no longer for *Time*, which departed this life in the December number, but henceforth for *Tinsley's Magazine*. I do typing, and Edward writes all sorts of things — good, bad and indifferent. We both have meetings and work of that sort in every spare hour. There's really no time to consider whether life is worth living or is a most unmitigated nuisance.

Mémé's[2] letter was delightful. Tell her so. I will write her when I send her her New Year present. Talking of New Year

I dread the coming "Festivities." It is horrible. The only good thing is that the dear old General is as jolly as a sandboy (what a sandboy is, or why he should be jolly *I* don't know) and seems to get younger and younger.

How are all the children? Do you see anything of them? I shall hope to hear from you one of these days. Meantime should anything worth telling happen here, I will let you know.

Goodbye, my dear old Laura.

Your

TUSSY

1. Demuth. At this stage Eleanor still believed that he was Engels's son.
2. Jenny Longuet.

75. Eleanor to Laura

⌈*London*⌉ *31 December 1890*

My dear Laura,

Here's another year gone, and here we are wishing one another a happy "New" one. Well, wishes do no harm, anyway. We have got over the Christmas festivity. But for some excellent fooling by Bernstein and Edward we should not have got over it so easily. Pumps, ever since she knows Louise is to stay, is spoiling for a fight, and on Christmas day being — well, being elevated — scenes seemed unavoidable. Fortunately she fell asleep, and awoke in a less bellicose mood. But we all constantly feel as if we were executing Mignon's dance,[1] and that we are about to tread upon eggs — and corns. Poor old Jollymeier could not come over. We miss him much.

In spite of your vile silence I *did* intend writing you a long letter, but I've now to go and get ready for the Pumpsian festivity (I almost wish I'd broken a leg and an arm and could not go!) and you'll have to wait, not that you've any right to a letter. Please tell Mémé that we are sending our god-daughter Eleonore (of the awful eyes) 5 francs for her New Year. But these can only be sent before 1 o'clock, so must go off tomorrow. Then I shall write Eleonore and Mémé.

Meantime goodbye, my dear, and good luck to you all in the New Year.

Your affectionate
TUSSY

Please send enclosed to old Mme. Longuet.

---

1. A reference to Goethe's *Wilhelm Meister*, in which Mignon has to perform dance steps around eggs without treading on them.

The 1891 May Day rally in Hyde Park, which again drew an enormous crowd, was largely organized by the Avelings. In a stirring speech Eleanor stressed the need to work for a legalized eight-hour day, and the importance of women's participation in the New Union movement.

In Paris thousands of unemployed workers congregated in the Place de la Concorde. At a demonstration at Fourmies, in Northern France, the police opened fire on the demonstrators: ten people were killed. Lafargue, who had been campaigning in the North with other members of the French Workers' Party, was shortly afterwards sentenced to a year's imprisonment for incitement to crime.

Meanwhile preparations were going ahead for the 1891 International Congress in Brussels, convoked by the Belgian Workers' Party. There appears to have been even more confusion than usual over the organization. Eleanor was to attend as delegate for the Gasworkers' Union, the Legal Eight Hours League, the Bloomsbury Socialist Society and the Battersea Labour League. She was also translating the Congress Reports into English and compiling the one on Great Britain and Ireland.

76. Eleanor to Laura

65, Chancery Lane, W.C.
6 July 1891

My dear Laura,

We have just seen in the *Daily News* that Paul has been sentenced to twelve months' imprisonment. But I suppose he can appeal against this iniquitous sentence. Here, of course, he could not, but in France, I fancy, it is possible. Surely if he can appeal he will get off altogether, or with a month or so at the outside. How will this affect the Congress? It would be most unfortunate if he could not be present at Brussels. The Possibilists — our London ones, at any rate — mean to kick up a row if they possibly can.

And about this Congress. I am writing just now to ask if you will translate the enclosed German report into French, for the German Party. Fischer[1] has asked me to do both the English and the French, but I'm sure I should make a mess of the latter. So will you do it? Naturally the Party pays, and Fischer leaves it to me to charge what I think fit. He also suggests the *printing* of the translations here. But if you will undertake the French you could get it done at Paris. If you will write *at once* we will send you on Fischer's letter, giving details as to the number of copies and so forth. If you are as badly in want of a more or less honestly earned penny as I am, you'll accept the work.

I haven't the heart to write about the children. It is so unspeakably disgusting.[2]

Let me hear about the Report — and then I shall at last also get a letter from you. I don't know — I've given up counting — how many you are in my debt. We are anxious, too, to know about Paul.

Love from us both,

Yours
TUSSY

1. Richard Fischer, a journalist and leading member of the German Social-Democratic Party.
2. Eight years after Jenny's death Longuet had set up house in Caen with a woman called Marie, much to the indignation of the Marxes.

77. Eleanor to Laura

65, Chancery Lane, W.C.
6 August 1891

My dear Laura,

Edward has just sent me on your postcard. It is *very* good of you to offer to do the translation. But I can save you that infliction (the report is an awful length!) for an old Communard, Magny, has kindly undertaken the work. I fear it will be pretty bad, and if there is time I'll send you the proofs — if you could give them a touch up, not altering *much* because of the cost — we should all be grateful.

I am sending you the *Report*.[1] Please don't judge it too critically. I had to write it while I was terribly worried, and not very well, and constantly interrupted. It had to be so long because we have not *one* Party here to report for — but a dozen.

I am also sending you my translation of the German report. You will see (I asked the General if he did not think I had better, and he agreed) I have just one or two explanatory footnotes. English people could not know what the *Gesinde-Ordnung*[2] is — though we have something rather analogous with regard to farm servants.

I suppose you've heard from the General. I feared when I saw Schorlemmer that the General would find his voyage anything but pleasant.[3] Schorlemmer is getting *very* old, and fearfully crotchetty and bad tempered. And, of course, the weather *has* been horrible. Moreover when all's said and done, the General is happiest with his drunken enchanter Pumps. 'Tis Prospero in love with a lower kind of Caliban; for Pumps hasn't Caliban's redeeming qualities. I still hope the old man may yet go with Moore as far, at least, as Madeira, and possibly the Canaries. I hope it because it is the sea-trips that have done the General so much good. As our poor Nymmy said, he came back from them "another man." It is not only the sea — though that is much. It is even more the getting right away from all the old surroundings. So when you write, do you also urge a sea-trip upon him. If we all do, I think we shall prevail. Poor old Paul! And yet I half envy him — to be shut up and be at peace for twelve months![4]

Yesterday Vaillant and Jacques and Greulich (all three stopping at Lessner's) were here, and were very charming — I mean the Vaillants, *père et fils*, were. *What* a muddle the Belgians are making. I shall write and tell you all about how they mismanaged things here: it may amuse our prisoner. Shall you be with him as much as before? Or will he be worse treated than then?

Let me hear from you one of these times in some other form than per postcard! Come, you *are* in letter-debt now!

Give my love to Paul. How are his many children? Has he got any little chicks just now?

Love to you too, my dear Laura, from

Your affectionate
TUSSY

1. *Report from Great Britain and Ireland.*
2. A German law defining the rights and duties of masters and servants.
3. Engels had planned a coastline tour of Britain with Schorlemmer, but bad weather forced them to stay at Ryde.
4. Paul's imprisonment had begun on 30 July.

78. Eleanor to Laura

65, Chancery Lane, W.C.
12 August 1891

My dear Laura,

One line. Fischer just writes me that we should send *to Berlin* fifty copies of the English and French translations of the German report respectively: the rest to be sent direct to Brussels. Will you see to this? I suppose Guesde will bring the copies to Brussels. I am taking ours there.

Your compatriots are muddling most splendidly![1] Vaillant, as you know, is here. From him I gather one delightful fact. *Brousse* is *most* anxious now the Congress should be "sovereign," as he fears the Allemanists will oust him![2] Vaillant has promised that the Marxists will see fair play!! Isn't it all funny? I wish I could go to Le Perreux. I should like to immensely — but we propose and our pockets dispose, and when those pockets are worse than empty *que faire?* I go to Brussels for the Gas Workers — and I must come back here from the Congress. I see no possibility of a holiday *this* year! Holidays and I seem to have parted company.

A propos the General. What I really wrote was this: that your first postcard to me came *before* you knew the General had left, and that what you wrote then, you had probably also written him. He writes me that he returns to London next Monday. He *does* love the tipsy Pumps, but for all that, distance lends enchantment even to the tipsyness, and he seems anxious to get away. He rages against Pumps — and loves her. Louise had to tell him to stop his talk against her, or she could not possibly be polite to her. "How can I be friends with her when you say she is only counting upon your death?" asked Louise. The General had no answer handy. And so things are much as they were — except that the General has to be a little more guarded in his denunciations, which *we* know mean nothing.

Your affectionate

TUSSY

1. Laura was born in Belgium.
2. Allemane, a former Possibilist, had broken with Brousse in 1890 during the Châtellerault Congress.

The Brussels Congress, which finally opened on 16 August 1891, attracted some 360 delegates, many of them women. Engels wrote that the real achievement of this Congress was the exclusion of the Anarchist contingent and the inclusion of the British Trade Unions. The next letter from Eleanor indicates how the continuing hostility of the SDF and the Possibilists undermined the aims of the Congress (Hyndman was still publishing anti-Marxist leaders in Justice) *but in the event neither Hyndman nor Brousse attended, and Allemane took over the Possibilist faction.*

During the Congress the Avelings became involved in another minor scandal to do with Aveling's reputation. Ferdinand Gilles, a disreputable German journalist who had joined the SDF and become a lackey of Hyndman's, spread calumnies about him among the delegates. After the Congress Aveling, accompanied by Louise Kautsky, went to Gilles's Islington home and was later fined 40s for assaulting him. The squabble, referred to by Eleanor as the "Gillesiade," continued in the Workman's Times, *Vorwärts and* Justice.

79. Eleanor to Laura

65, *Chancery Lane, W.C.*
25 *September 1891*

My dear Laura,

Of course you know I am writing to wish you "many happy returns" of the 26th September; and equally of course you know I am wishing the wishes could be "materialized" (oh! why didn't we become Theosophists — we might be Mahatmas by now!)[1] into something more tangible than wishes. But good wishes are all I have to give. And after all there are not so many people in the world on whom one bestows even these.

I was glad to get your letter, and Ste. Pelagie is making a splendid correspondent of Paul. The more I hear of that Saints' hotel the more I wish Constans[2] would fall in with the plan

I suggested to Guesde (my cousin-in-law, now, I suppose). It was that whenever a man is condemned to Ste. Pelagie that his friends and relations should be allowed to take *"des abonnements"*[3] for a term of not less than six weeks of his sentence. Thus Paul being condemned to twelve months I would (and I'd pay for the chance!) take say three months; Edward would do the same; you might like a retreat of six weeks, and so forth. In this way the Government could indulge in heavy sentences and even profit commercially — because *on s'abonnerait à prix fixe.*[4] And yet this ungrateful Paul is eager to be off to Lille![5] Well, good luck to him. Has he a chance at Lille, or will it only be a good propagandist campaign and a five weeks' outing? From what Delcluze[6] told and has written us I should think such a campaign would be invaluable just now at Lille, where things seem a little shaky with our friends. It would certainly pull them together.

You have seen from the *Workman's Times* and from *Vorwärts* the whole Gillesiade. At present Gilles is said to be preparing a pamphlet. Let him! The only difficulty here is that one never knows where one may be landed in a libel case, and every word of what we may say would be, in a sense, libellous. And you know what that means here in the way of money. Still I'm glad of it all, and it was the only way. As Bebel writes, 20s. per *Ohrfeige*[7] is temptingly cheap. Paul writes that Deville regrets Edward did not bring up the thing at the Congress. That was impossible. We *could* not introduce the matter into the work done there. In the *Workman's Times* of this week you will find a full and very good report of the trial — done by the Editor of the paper.[8] This man was till twenty-nine years old a mill-hand; is now anxious to get into "the" movement, of which he knows about as much as a new-born babe. But he seems honest and the paper may be useful. Theoretically it is valueless: but for mere practical news as to what is being done it is reliable. By the way, it is sent you regularly, isn't it? If it is not, let me know.

As to the Brussels Congress that was really a big success: far bigger than I ever expected it would be. And I am bound to say that Volders and his brave fellow-countrymen had managed the thing admirably.[9] Of course you heard about the row kicked up here by the S.D.F. people. Well, in our "British Section" we had the thing out, and Volders — letters in hand —

showed the Hyndmanites (1) that the only difficulties made had been made by the Possibilists; (2) that the Possibilists had not even had the courage to go straight to the Brussels folk but had put up Hyndman to complain for them; (3) that they tried hard to prevent the Marxists from being at the Congress. Wise in their generation the Brussels people saw that it was a case of no Marxists no Congress, and so pitched their Possibilists overboard.

I don't think I've written you either of a very curious and very instructive little episode at the Congress with that most repulsive person Allemane. One of the English delegates — one of the "old" Unionists, named Greenwood — a very charming old fellow, though, who went with us through thick and thin (by "us" I mean the advanced section) asked me on the last morning if I would interpret something that he *must* ask Allemane. Naturally, I could not refuse, and so I went with Greenwood to Allemane. What the Englishman said was this: "In 1889 I was at the Rue de Lancry Congress where, as you will recollect, it was decided that a report should be issued, the said report to cost 5s." — *"Parfaitement."* — "Well, I paid in advance for two reports, and from that day to this have heard no more about it." Allemane's face lighted up. "Yes," quoth he, "that is quite true. And many others paid also. I began collecting material and arranging the report when Messrs. Brousse and Gély took it out of my hands. They had at this time to my knowledge 500 francs for this report from various delegates; and for all I know may have had 5000. But Messrs. Brousse, Gély, and Vely (or some such name) stuck to the money. You must apply to them for it." I advised Greenwood to apply to Smith — but there was no opportunity in the muddle of the last sitting. But still the fact — if fact it is — is worth noting. Anyhow, Allemane admitted Greenwood and others had paid for reports never issued!

No doubt you have heard that the General has been on a round trip to Scotland and Ireland. Pumps insisted on her going and *once* having a holiday, "as she had never had one"! They have returned and Pumps is as discontented as ever. On Sunday Edward and I met Louise and the General on their return (Pumps had gone on to Manchester) and he, of course, swore hard at her (Pumps). But he is just as fascinated as ever, and however much he may upbraid, she prevails. I am cherishing a wild hope — I don't see the least chance of its fulfilment — of going over to see you some time this winter, and of taking my holiday in December. How about the *conseil de famille* and the children?[10] Where is poor little Mémé? Of course I know nothing of them all.

Goodbye, dear. Give my love to Paul. Again all good wishes to you.

From your

TUSSY

My dear Laura, I have been writing so much to your husband, and my wife (*pace* Gilles) has been writing so much to you that I shall only add my love and good wishes.

EDWARD

1. Theosophy was a religious, mystical philosophy much in vogue in the late nineteenth century. Its adherents, most famously Madame Blavatsky, aimed at a spiritual perfection which, they believed, bestowed certain occult powers.
2. Jean Antoine Constans, Minister of the Interior.
3. "subscriptions."
4. "fixed-rate subscriptions would be taken out."
5. Paul had been nominated as the Radical Deputy candidate, but as he was in prison Guesde campaigned on his behalf. He was duly elected in the second round and the government granted him temporary liberty for the duration of the parliamentary session.
6. Alfred Delcluze, founder of the Calais Workers' Party.
7. "box on the ear."
8. Joseph Burgess.
9. In articles in *Justice* (18 and 25 July, 1 August 1891) Hyndman had charged the Belgian Workers' Party, led by Volders, with inefficiency in organizing the Congress and with having broken faith by following the mandate of the Marxists instead of that of the SDF and the Possibilists: there had been an inexcusable delay in sending out invitations to the SDF and the individual trade unions. Hyndman claimed to be in favour of a united congress and regretted the "secret intrigue."
10. There had been talk of a family council to discuss the care of the Longuet children, but it never materialized.

As May Day 1892 approached, the Legal Eight Hours League, with which the Avelings were involved, suggested to the Trades Council that they join forces for this year's demonstration. The Trades Council had formed a temporary alliance with the SDF and declined; both organizations then made approaches to the Radical Clubs, which unequivocally threw in their lot with the Legal Eight Hours League. The article to which Eleanor refers below (Daily Chronicle, 11 April, entitled "The Labour Movement") printed the contents of a letter from Adolphe Smith of the SDF to Shipton, Secretary of the Trades Council. It stated that the Paris Possibilists, on hearing that there might be two separate demonstrations, had decided to send delegates to join in with the Trade Unions. Eleanor was anxious that Paul should state the French Workers' Party case. She was also deeply concerned about Aveling's health, which was steadily deteriorating.

The May Day demonstration attracted a huge crowd, and Paul came over to represent France on the international stand of the Legal Eight Hours League.

80. Eleanor to Laura

[London] 15 April 1892

My dear Laura,
You will see from the enclosed that it is really important Paul should write the letter I suggest to the *Daily Chronicle* — only do you write it for him! Believe me it is really a serious matter to us here, if we are to keep in friendly relation with the only French party worth anything. The whole thing is a little game of the Possibilists. So *please* see that Paul — if he is now with you — writes at once, and if he is away, send on the letter and back it up! As it is, it looks to our friends like a gratuitous insult and as we have worked hard to bring about a good international feeling it would be a thousand pities to let Smith and Co. spoil it all. The really advanced workers here utterly distrust the Trades Council — and it is therefore the more necessary to

explain that the French parties working with the Trades Council and the Possibilists are not the *Parti Ouvrier*.

I will write you on other matters soon. I have been very busy, and Edward is far from well. He is stopping with a friend at Brighton. He has had a very bad — and indeed still has, a very bad throat — quinsy.

I want to write to tell you the latest Pumpsiads!

With love,

Your affectionate
TUSSY

81. Eleanor to Laura

65, Chancery Lane, W.C.
30 May 1892

My dear Laura,

That is real good news you send us about the paper.[1] (Its health was duly drunk yesterday at the General's.) I can't tell you how glad we are to know you folk are at last going to have a daily organ of your own in Paris. If only we had a like prospect here! But I can assure you that your having such an organ will have a *very* considerable effect here too. More considerable, I fancy, than you in Paris can quite realize. All you wrote recently of the condition to which those miserable Possibilist skunks had reduced *la ville lumière* we know only too well to be true, for it has been turned to account with great skill by our possibilists here. The condition of Paris has been the sheet-anchor of our English Brousses and Lavys; the one thing that has kept them a-going. The English are profoundly ignorant of all foreign movements, but today the ignorance no longer takes the form of contemptuous superiority it once did, but that of a perfect and really pathetic admiration of everything done abroad. So that to play off the French Possibilists against the English Marxists was a very clever dodge on the part of that most artful dodger Hyndman. That the whole (practically) of the French provinces were Marxist didn't count. To the Englishman Paris is still France, and Paris in the hands of the Possibilists meant to them a possibilist France.

No doubt the splendid victory of the municipal elections[2] has had some effect — but — as you may have gathered from my letter to the *Pall Mall*[3] — the municipal elections have been rigorously boycotted in all our English papers. Now this sort of boycott becomes a great deal more difficult once we have an organ in Paris, and here today the workers ask nothing better than to follow the "foreign" lead. So you see we rejoice at the new paper from *our* point of view besides rejoicing at it from yours. It is very good of you to give us the English correspondence. Being in constant communication with all the different organizations we know what the movement here really is. But aren't you *very* rash to ask for my French? It is proverbially more difficult to correct than to translate. But my French be upon your head! *A propos* of correspondence I send you a copy of the *Centralblatt*.[4] The details I give there about the engineers' strike may interest you and Paul. They are a piece of "inside" history, and have not been published anywhere else. I know the facts from a delegate of the Tyneside engineers to the Executive of my Union. He complained that these facts were carefully suppressed in all papers. You see our "unskilled" men being employed as "labourers" in every trade, we get to hear all the facts about all the "skilled" trades. And very interesting some of them are!

As you know Bebel and Singer[5] have been here some two weeks, and leave on Wednesday. At first Pumps was here also (Singer, I should say, stopped at the Bernsteins) and made everyone uncomfortable. When I see you I shall have a very comic-tragic story to tell you of Bebel's *last* stay here — when he had to play Joseph to Pumps's Mrs. Potiphar.[6] Now Pumps has gone but she is "sulking" in her Ryde tent, and you know how the General suffers when the amiable tippler is obdurate. Oh! dear, it would all be very funny if it weren't very unpleasant and very sad. The General is now keeping up well, but that is due to the excitement of Bebel's presence, and Beer and Mai-Wein. But when all these festivities are over the reaction will set in — and then look out for squalls! Of poor old Jolly-meier's condition[7] I suppose the General has told you. It is infinitely sad, but we have seen it coming for a long time, and the only thing Schorlemmer's friends can now hope is that the end may be soon. It is very pitiable. The General intends going to Manchester to see him for a day or so. But Schorlemmer is, I fear, past caring for visits even from his oldest and best friend, and Engels is going chiefly for his soul's easement.

My dear old Laura, how stupid it is writing when I should so like to be speaking to you! And there is so much one can say and can't write. And I go on hoping and hoping to get to Paris, and it all seems as far off and as unlikely as ever. Well, I suppose we shall manage it some day. Next week we go to Plymouth for the Conference of our Un[ion] (mind you make Paul send us a few lines!) and then Edward goes to lecture for the Socialists of Aberdeen. I went — for the German party — to Ayrshire last week.[8] But it wasn't a holiday by any means. I left (I had to see some German miners) on the Thursday evening at 9.15; reached Cumnock about 9 A.M.; was hard at work all day, caught the 9.15 at Cumnock on the Friday evening and was back in London, considerably the worse for wear, at 8 on Saturday morning.

There I'm at the end of my paper, and so I can let you off any more of this disjointed gossip. My love to the *député-rédacteur*. Edward is at the Museum or would doubtless write also.

My love to you too, my dear Laura.

Your

TUSSY

1. *Le Socialiste* was to have become a large-format daily, but the change never took place.
2. The first round of the municipal elections (except Paris) had taken place on 1 May. The Workers' Party was to gain twenty-two councils and 600 seats, many in important places such as Roubaix, Marseilles, Montluçon, etc.
3. *Pall Mall Gazette*, 24 May 1892.
4. "Die letzten englischen Strikes," in *Sozialpolitisches Centralblatt* (no. 20, 1892), a Social-Democratic weekly published in Berlin. The Amalgamated Society of Engineers, one of the craft unions, were on strike in protest against the introduction of new machinery; they were also involved in demarcation disputes, of which Eleanor gave details.
5. August Bebel and Paul Singer, leaders of the German Social-Democratic Party and old friends of Engels and the Marxes.
6. Joseph was cast into prison after having been falsely accused by Potiphar's wife (*Genesis,* ch. 39).
7. Schorlemmer was to die of lung cancer on 27 June.
8. At the request of the German Social-Democratic Party Eleanor had visited German miners working in Cumnock who had the reputation of undercutting wages and strike-breaking.

82. Eleanor to Laura

65, Chancery Lane, W.C.
26 July 1892

My dear Laura,

It is *very* good of you to have sent 50 francs for Freddy (I know *you* can't afford it!) though when Freddy asked me to see if Paul could not bring some pressure to bear on Longuet, he never *meant you* should send anything.[1] The facts are these; Freddy's wife some time ago ran away — taking with her not only most of Freddy's own things and money, but worst of all £24 placed in his keeping by his fellow-workmen. This money belongs to a small benefit fund of theirs — and on Saturday he has to account for the money. You will understand now why this is such a bad business. Freddy wrote and I wrote again and again to Longuet. But he does not even *answer* the letters, and so Freddy begged of me to try if Paul could not in some way put the matter before the trustees. Of course I have not told all *these* facts to Longuet, as Freddy does not want anyone to know — particularly not Engels. I think we shall pull through though, because Edward hopes to get something for a little operetta[2] (don't be alarmed — he was only responsible for the words!) today or tomorrow, and with what Freddy has it will be all right. It may be that I am very "sentimental" — but I can't help feeling that Freddy has had great injustice all through his life. Is it not wonderful, when you come to look things squarely in the face, how rarely we seem to practise all the fine things we preach — to others?

My dear, what a long, long time it is since I heard from you — and now I hear you are laid up. That is very rough on you, especially with Paul away. I fear both you and Paul must have been having a lot of trouble over that paper. I hear about it now and again from the General.

We have, as you know, been in the thick of an election[3] — and very interesting it has been. But what an awful lot of nonsense Bonnier[4] has been writing. Some of the internal history of this campaign has been very funny: what could be made public at present Edward and I are sending, or rather have sent, to the *Neue Zeit.*[5] One of the funniest things though we could not mention there, but here it is for you. Champion — of all people! — wrote and offered to get Edward all the money necessary if he cared to "run" anywhere!!! Of course Edward replied that first of all he had no desire to run, and secondly that he could only take money through a Committee — should he ever stand — of his constituents, but nothing privately. Of course everyone has not been so scrupulous. Other offers, direct and indirect, were made [to] Edward from other quarters too. Of the large sums of money which Mr. Hyndman so bragged of in *Justice* nothing has come. *He* was promising the money — but gave none; not even to Taylor, who was Candidate in London.[6] That too has led to all sorts of queer results — one of them being that the S.D.F. Branch in Taylor's Constituency have called upon Hyndman to withdraw from the S.D.F. because of treachery of his conduct! This same Taylor actually wrote and begged Edward and me to go and help him — and as his programme was excellent, and as he was fighting that beast Howell, we did help him. But he failed ignominiously — and that chiefly through the S.D.F. So you will understand that there are like to be more internal rows in the happy S.D.F. family.

On Sunday Louise Kautsky left for her holiday, and tomorrow the General starts for the Isle of Wight. The beloved[7] is going to bring another monster into the world. Isn't it awful? After he has been some ten or twelve days with Pumps, the General — unless she should, indeed, talk him out of it — goes to Germany; to his own place to see his brothers; probably to Berlin and Vienna, and certainly to Switzerland. I think such a journey, seeing new faces and getting quite away, will do him a world of good. The death of our poor old Jollymeier has been a very great blow to him, as you may imagine.

You see, dear, I haven't much news either. The various meetings and our own work keeps us busy. The Glass Workers' Congress kept me at it all one week translating and keeping a verbatim report, and that report I am now copying from the shorthand on to the machine. Does Paul know Rey and Rauzier, the two French delegates? I liked them very well.

Edward was over in Dublin all last week — auditing the accounts for our Union. At the present moment he is at the Museum finishing his geology book.[8] Else he would write too. Oh! dear, I wonder when I shall see you! I really would like to more than I can say. Give my love to Paul when that wanderer returns, and receive a kiss yourself and many thanks from

Your affectionate

TUSSY

Have you read Mehring's *very* interesting articles in the
Neue Zeit on our forbears — the Westphalens? You should. But
he ought to have had more told him about Mother's father.
Naturally from Ferdinand's account he could not guess what a
delightful person he must have been.[9]

My dear, you do not say to whom the order is made out. I
thought it would probably be to me so as to save Freddy the
trouble: but they say not. Will you write and say in whose
name it is made out *exactly*. Yours

T.

1. As Freddy's true paternity was still unknown, it is not clear why Lafargue was
   expected to bring pressure upon Longuet to send him money.
2. *A Hundred Years Ago*, with music by Henry Wood, had opened at the Royalty
   Theatre on 16 July.
3. In the July 1892 elections three working men, John Burns, Havelock Wilson
   and Keir Hardie, were elected as Independent Labour candidates, and several
   others as Liberals.
4. Charles Bonnier, a journalist and member of the French Workers' Party, who
   spent most of his time in Oxford.
5. "Die Wahlen in Grossbritannien," *Neue Zeit*, no. 45, 1891–92.
6. H. R. Taylor, a member of the SDF, stood as Independent Labour candidate for
   Bethnal Green, in the East End, but polled only 106 votes against George
   Howell.
7. Pumps.
8. *An Introduction to the Study of Geology* (1893).
9. Ferdinand von Westphalen, half-brother of Mrs. Marx, was Prussian Minister
   of the Interior from 1850–58.

In the following letters Eleanor refers to her activities on behalf of the International Glass Workers' Union. In 1891 she had raised funds for the Lyons Glass Workers' strike and now asked Laura to help in seeking international support for the Yorkshire and Lancashire Glass Workers, some five thousand of whom had protested about their terms of employment. The strike fund was swelled by contributions from France and Germany, and the employers eventually capitulated in April 1893, after a sixteen-week lockout.

83. Eleanor to Laura

65, Chancery Lane, W.C.
7 February 1893

My dear Laura,

I am sending you herewith an appeal from the English Glass Workers — and I send it *you* instead of myself translating it, first because you'll do it so much better than I could, and secondly because seeing how very well our Britishers behaved to the French, this appeal should go into *all* our papers. This in itself would vastly please the Yorkshire folk. So may I ask you to *at once* translate the enclosed; to get the translation printed in the *Socialiste* and all other organs, and then forward the said translation *with the English original* to Ph. Clausse, *Chemin de Garland 47, Lyon*. The English must go to him as Clausse and Greenwood[1] both are sticklers for etiquette and insist on having all the originals along with the translations. Meantime I am writing to both these gentle men to explain what I am doing. Don't be alarmed at the length of Greenwood's epistle. I get such to translate constantly, and he is the very soul of brevity (if not of wit) compared with Clausse. Anyway I count on your help. This fight means a life and death struggle here of the whole glass-working industry. It is bound to last for months. What the end will be the Lord knows — and as Edward always says, the Lord is *so* incommunicative.

Next on my list is a letter from Keir Hardie. He writes that on the 28th there is a meeting of the Scottish Labour Party,

and that he would like letters from "Lafargue and Liebknecht."
Can the *Parti Ouvrier* send a line? If they do — let them lay
stress on the *independent* side of the movement — i.e., that we
must keep clear of all other parties, because Hardie has a *very*
strong hankering after the Conservative fleshpots — which oddly
enough he tries to mix up with the "support" of the "noncon-
formist conscience!"[2] Still a letter might be useful. Especially
as it may help the Zurich as against the bogus Congress.[3] Anyhow I've given you Hardie's message, and now do what you
darned choose, as we say in polite society.

The cold here is simply awful. You may guess how that is
adding to all the horrors of the unemployed misery. The condition of things here — and by "here" I mean the whole of Great
Britain — is terrible beyond words . . . Bebel is here for a few
days, as you may have heard from the General. Pumps (alas!)
isn't gone yet. I think she will stick on as long as she possibly
can. Yesterday I had a delightful letter from Jean. He seemed
immensely pleased with a letter he had had from you and Paul.
Poor lad! It does not need much reading between the lines to
see what he really thinks of his father nor what a miserable
position he is in. At seventeen one feels things so acutely! Edward is off this evening to Bristol. He is not at all well, so I
am sorry he has to go. But it can't be helped. He returns tomorrow night. There is a "demonstration" at Bristol in connection with the scandal of calling out the military during a perfectly legitimate and peaceful demonstration.

Goodbye, my dear Laura. Our love to you both.

Your

TUSSY

---

1. Greenwood was Secretary of the Yorkshire Glass Bottle Makers; Clausse was
   leader of the Lyons Glass Workers.
2. Keir Hardie's Independent Labour Party, forerunner of the present Labour
   Party, had been inaugurated at Bradford the previous month. Its main support came from the North, and many of the 120 delegates (with the notable
   exception of Bernard Shaw, representing the London Fabians) came from
   Yorkshire and Lancashire. Aveling was elected to the Executive. The Scottish
   Labour Party had been founded in 1888.
   Eleanor was not alone among London socialists in underestimating Keir
   Hardie's significance. Her scathing remark about non-Conformism is a refer-
   ence to Hardie's encouragement of non-sectarian religion.
3. The third International Socialist Workers' Congress was held in Zurich in
   August 1893. The "bogus congress" was proposed but abandoned by the TUC,

who eventually sent delegates to Zurich. Engels, who was on a two-month journey through Germany, Austria-Hungary and Switzerland, put in an appearance on the last day and made a triumphant closing speech.

84. Eleanor to Laura

7, Gray's Inn Square, W.C.
11 November 1893

My dear Laura,

It is literally *months* since I heard from you! What has become of you? Do throw a word at me now and then. You don't know how glad I should be to get a letter now and then, for though I am always busy I am also very lonely — and letters from you would be more than welcome. The little I hear of you is always from the General.

What an abominable business this last Anarchist exploit is![1] And just when it seemed as if we were to get on a little in France! It is maddening to think of. Of course it will damage *our* people most. I am anxiously waiting to *see* what line is generally taken. I need hardly say that the mischief reacts seriously upon us here also. If you can, send me along any papers that I could use for the *Workman's Times*.

I was *very* glad Paul got the *Vorwärts*[2] correspondence. It is not much, but it's something! How do you do about the translations? You should not trust them to Natalie[3] (she does them if sent untranslated) because she is so slow and makes such a bosh of it usually. But it is a blessing to be rid of that horrible little idiot Arndt,[4] and to have Paul sending the French news. The said Arndt had the cheek to go up to the General's the other night, when I believe — I was not there myself — he got what is called a "good dressing-down."

The General, as you no doubt gather from his letters, is wonderfully well. His trip has done him an immense amount of good, and the reaction after all the excitement was not as bad as I feared it might be. Louise has him splendidly in hand, and he is happy as a schoolboy. Pumpsia's nose is hopelessly (at present) out of joint. She came up to town — and had to stop with Charlie![5] She tried to remain at least for the Sunday, but was ruthlessly bundled off! When I remember how she treated our poor Nimmy, I can't help feeling a certain malicious pleasure in her discomfiture. It is good news — I'm glad I have some! — that the General is working at vol. III, and that a very good portion of it will be sent off to Meissner immediately after Christmas — it would not be safe to send during the holiday traffic. Christmas! Oh! Laura, those awful festivities — becoming more and more terrible as one has less and less heart for them. I wish I could run away to you. Then it would be really a holiday. I'm fearfully dull and stupid, and I would not write except that I hope by doing so to get a line from you. I've been very seedy the last few days. Indeed I feel so thoroughly ill without being ill — if you can understand that bull, that I fancy I must be enjoying a little bout of influenza. I can hardly see out of my eyes; my head and back ache like mad; I've an ulcerated throat, and I'm constantly sick. Cheerful, isn't it? I only mention this as an excuse for my extra stupidity, and in the hope my miserable condition will wring a letter from you!

Edward, I am glad to say, is a good deal better than he was. His play, as you know, failed[6] — a result I fully expected, because it was *not* a good play. He knew that too, but thought *that* might save it. He is out supping with some theatrical friends — so he can't send you any messages, and as it is nearly 1 and my fire is out, I shall say goodnight also.

Do write, my dear Laura. Give my love to Paul. *He* never writes except "on business" — and then about two lines and a half!

Your affectionate sister

TUSSY

1. Possibly a reference to a bomb explosion at the Lyceum theatre in Barcelona (7 November), which caused sixteen deaths. There were many other Anarchist incidents at this time.
2. Liebknecht had asked Lafargue to write a weekly column for *Vorwärts* and to send it translated into German, so that it could appear simultaneously in *Vorwärts* and the Hamburg *Echo*.
3. Liebknecht's wife.
4. Paul Arndt, Paris correspondent of *Vorwärts*.
5. Charles Rosher, Pump's brother-in-law.
6. A comedy, *The Frog*, which had opened at the Royalty Theatre in October.

*In November 1892 Ludwig Freyberger, a young
Viennese doctor whom Louise Kautsky had met in
Vienna the year before, arrived in London to a warm
welcome from Engels, who appreciated his professional skills. Freyberger soon became a part of the
intimate circle and in February 1894 Louise, who was
then thirty-four, and Freyberger, twenty-nine, were
married. The news was conveyed to their friends by
means of a formal card.*

*This unexpected marriage did not particularly
worry the Lafargues, who sent the couple their best
wishes, but in Eleanor, concerned about the fate of her
father's papers in the event of Engels's death, it inspired fears and suspicions that came to acquire an
obsessional, even pathological, character.*

85. Eleanor to Laura

7, Gray's Inn Square, W.C.
22 February 1894

My dear Laura,

I can understand you asking the questions you do — only I can't
answer them! I know absolutely nothing, and the whole affair
has been "wrop in mistry." As to the Freyberger match being
a foregone conclusion, I suppose it was. Only I did rather doubt.
For certain private reasons, and because I *can't* see how anyone
can stand Freyberger. It's all very well to say that all tastes are
in nature. This taste seems to me a very abnormal one.

Well, we'd all our opinions one way or the other, though
no hint was ever dropped to us, and though in public the *Du*
into which they slipped in unguarded moments — (and but for
the pretence of the "Sie," as you know the "Du" in German
means very little) — was carefully avoided. Last week I was
away in the north lecturing for a week, and Edward wrote me
that the General and Louise had gone to Eastbourne. Louise
had told me that the General meant going there to get rid of
what all politely term his "lameness," so I took no special
notice of this. Judge of my surprise when I get a card — like

the one sent you. Not another line, not another word! But it *does* seem queer to take the General a-honeymooning with them. You can imagine the delicacy of his jokes on such an occasion. You ask me how he takes it. I don't know, any more than I know what arrangements they are making. I've not seen or spoken to the General alone for many months, and whatever he may think he could hardly express his opinion before those most concerned. But you know the General is always under the thumb of the "lady of the house." When Pumps was with him, lo, she was good in his sight; now Pumps is dethroned and Louise is the queen who can do no wrong. But I *am* anxious to know what the household arrangements are to be, for frankly it will be intolerable if Freyberger permanently instals himself at Regent's Park Road. It was unpleasant enough to constantly meet him there, but to know him always there!

As to Pumps' opinion I am also in the dark. If it (i.e., the marriage, not Pumps' opinion) means — which I am well-nigh sure it does not — Louise's leaving, of course she will rejoice greatly. If it means the General's house being turned into a Freyberger *ménage* she will swear, and feel herself more aggrieved than ever.

You see now why nothing was said to Paul when he was here. Nothing was said to anyone. Isn't it all odd? Louise's saying no word to me is as strange almost as the General's silence. I say almost because she had "confided" in me before and so may have felt uncomfortable in doing so again. Has the General not written to you about it? I fancy I've rather put my foot into it because I'm such a poor hand at pretending, and I never could pretend to admire the profound sagacity and brilliant wit of the new bridegroom. Well, on the whole I'm glad Louise is married. She was too young for the rather dreary life at the General's, and no doubt Karl [Kautsky] will be delighted. I've not seen the Bernsteins, so I don't know their view of this epoch-making event.

There, my dear, I've answered your questions as far as I can, and now allow me to remark that you owe me a letter, and that I won't be put off with a mean little bit of a card. Seriously, do write now and then. You have no idea how glad I am to hear from you. We were all pleased to see Paul, and to see him looking so well. When shall we see you?

As I told you, I've recently had a week in Lancashire. I

gave eight lectures in seven days, seven of them to the S.D.F. branches which had organized my "tour," and [letter incomplete]

86. Eleanor to Laura

7, Gray's Inn Square, W.C.
2 March 1894

My dear Laura,

I know you want to hear the latest news from the *ménage* of Regent's Park Road (oh! for a Balzac to paint it!) and so here it is. Just after I had written to you I received a letter from Louise in which she told me that she had only decided upon the grand step of marriage on the very day when I left London for my lecturing tour in the north! So, of course, she could tell me nothing before. Further she informed me that she — and he — were to remain with the General!! I enclose a note received yesterday which will tell you far more eloquently than I can what the present situation is. That Freyberger should hold "at homes" at the General's is certainly coming it strong.

To complicate matters still more it would seem that the Pumpses were in London (and maybe still are for all I know) and that their advent was the signal for the flight to Eastbourne.[1] How it will all work out the Lord knows. But personally I confess that invitations to the General's from a man like Freyberger are a little queer, and, in my opinion, bode no good for the future. In this sense, that the General, after all, *is* getting old. You would realize how old more if you saw him more often, and I question much if the Freyberger influence is likely to be a good one for the Party. Anyone who has the slightest knowledge of human nature must know that this gentleman is playing his own game alone. So I say again, how it will end goodness knows. The family were to return yesterday, and as we have always been to see the General directly he came back after any absence from town I suppose we must do so now. But frankly I don't look forward to the visit. And poor Louise! She *has* dropped from the frying-pan into the fire. But then with us women it is generally a question of the frying-pan or the fire and it is hard to say which is the worse. At the best our state is parlous.

Otherwise I have no news or gossip for you. After our state visit I will report again. When are you going to write to me? By the way, thanks for the *Figaro*, with the *Journée parlementaire*. It has interested me much.

Love to Paul, and a kiss to you, my dear Laura.

Your

TUSSY

1. A letter from Louise to Eleanor suggests that the whole Rosher family had proposed to descend upon Engels and that this had precipitated his departure to Eastbourne, where he stayed, with the Freybergers, from 9 February to 1 March.

87. Eleanor to Laura

7, Gray's Inn Square, W.C.
22 March 1894

My dear Laura,
The enclosed letter is from a friend of mine,[1] a medical student, who, as you will see, wants to get six months work at Paris. She is as poor as the proverbial Church mouse — or as myself — and therefore anxious about lodgings, etc. But you will see what she wants from her letter. *I* had suggested that she should live outside Paris, but as she has to be at the Hospitals by 8, and wants to use all her time, that's no good. Will you, kindly, make some enquiries for her? She is very nervous about going into strange work in a strange land, and being a stranger certain to be "taken in" in the non-biblical sense. If you can help her and befriend her a little I shall be *very* glad.

Laura, I always thought you one of the cleverest human beings I had ever known — and you write you think Freyberger "good-natured"! I would not trust a fly to his tender mercies.

He is an adventurer pure and simple, and I am heartily sorry for Louise. I confess I am also anxious on another matter — and that is all the papers, letters, MSS. etc., which are at the General's. That I am not alone capable of the thought is shown by the fact that the Bernsteins have been here, and after some hawing and ha'ing admitted that they felt anxious "about the MSS." Should anything happen to the General, they said, F. is quite capable of getting hold of anything he can and selling it! For you must remember F. is simply an anti-Semite (though I would wager my Jewish head that he's a Jew) and has nothing to do with the movement. It is no joking matter I assure you, for you know very well that anyone living with the General can manipulate him to any extent. Sam Moore (who is over again) also seemed doubtful, and he came up here and I had a talk with him. He was (and I believe is) a trustee under the General's will, and if he were here always it would be all right, as he would immediately have all papers "sealed." But he is half his time in Africa! However he told me he would try and get an opportunity of speaking to the General (who is sure to consult him as the other trustee under the Will, Gumpert, is since dead) and of making sure about all papers. I thought I ought to let you know about this, because it is really a serious question. Mohr's MSS. etc., are things we can't be too careful about. And that F. is just an adventurer playing for what he can get, you would know also if you saw him as often as I have done. It is *very* difficult because, of course, I can't well say anything to the General (it is all very well for the Bernsteins to say I *should!*) and I must just wait and see what Sam Moore says. He stopped a day or two at the General's, is now in Derbyshire "at home," and then returns again to London, when he is to see me.

Let me know if you can help Alice Corthorn.

I kiss you, my dear Laura, and don't I wish I could really instead of on paper!

Your

TUSSY

---

1. Alice Corthorn. See page 211, note 3.

This letter was written just before the birth of Louise-Frederica, the Freybergers' only child. At the prospect of this increase in the size of his household, Engels had moved into a more spacious house in the same road (41 Regent's Park Road) in October.

Contrary to the impression given by Eleanor, Engels had lost none of his lucidity, neither was he the pathetic old man she describes here. In fact, the fate of the Marx letters and manuscripts was a matter of supreme importance to him. In April 1893, after the death of Gumpert, who was one of his executors as well as his doctor, and before embarking on his two-month Continental trip, he had drawn up a new will naming Sam Moore, Bernstein and Louise as his executors. This will specified that "all the manuscripts of a literary nature in the handwriting of my deceased friend Karl Marx and all family letters written by or addressed to him which shall be in my possession at the time of my death . . . shall be given by my executors to Eleanor Marx Aveling." He evidently did not inform Eleanor of this, judging by her agitation in the letters which follow.

88. Eleanor to Laura

7, Gray's Inn Square, W.C.
5 November 1894

My dear Laura,

I will not attempt any excuses for my silence. What with Edward's illness and absence and the *very* serious state of affairs at Regent's Park, I have really not had the heart to write. But apart from everything else I feel I must not delay any longer, as you ought to understand that things have reached a pass far beyond joking. It is impossible in a letter, or a dozen letters, to explain all the complications: but I say to you most earnestly that your presence here is *urgent*. Believe me I am not exaggerating, and I should not say what I am saying except on the best grounds. You may say how can you come over now. You must *make* a reason. There are two spare rooms in the new house; while Louise is "lying-in" the General will be left alone; it is a very good time to come and "keep him company." With *three* servants there can be no question of your being too much trouble. If this won't do, invent a reason, but trust me it is high time you came. Paul's coming would be comparatively useless — without counting that the General has been and is being very much set against Paul, whose influence would therefore be nil.[1] *You* alone have some influence left, and if you came you might prevent most serious wrong. This is not my opinion only. The Bernsteins, who are very true friends, and who know exactly what the position is, have been begging of me for weeks to write and urge you to come. Alone I can do nothing. Together we might do something. When I tell you that Freyberger, through Bax and others, is spreading all through the S.D.F. and through the S.D.F. all over London (so far as our acquaintance or political relations extend) that "the Avelings have been turned out by the General, and that *now* that things are in the hands of the Freybergers all will be different," that Louise is spreading the same report all over Germany (with personal calumnies about myself that I am ashamed to write) you will see to what a pass things have come. The Bernsteins and the Mendelsons[2] (whom the F.s hate worse than poison, I suppose because they are very friendly to us and always speak so charmingly of you and Paul) *are* practically turned out, and though I don't think the poor old General even fully realizes what he is made to do, he has come to the condition where he is a mere child in the hands of this monstrous pair. To give you but one example of the General's change to me. Last Tuesday I went to see him, and in passing asked if he had heard or seen anything of Bax. I saw he looked very confused, but supposed this was because he thought I knew that F. had dined with Bax on the Saturday. I added I should like to know what he (Bax) would say to the General of the latest attacks in *Justice.* The General said he had no news of Bax, but F. had seen him on Sat! Yet, as I have since heard, that very afternoon Bax had been invited and had had a grand luncheon at the General's and could not have left the house half an hour after [*sic*] I arrived! You will say, "why this secrecy?" If you knew all the wire-pulling of the F.'s you would understand. Bax, the greatest gossip in London, is told *I* am turned out; he in turn is asked to tell the General any lies he may have heard against us, and so it works round. This is only a *small* matter, but can you imagine the General coming to this? For a long time things have been going from bad to worse, and it is a positive pain to go to the General's. When he sees me alone — which is only for a moment, he seems glad enough — and then when the two others appear, he becomes like them, and in all but words I am told I am *de trop*. And except when they bear anyone with the General the poor old man (who so hates to be alone) is left quite to himself. The two are *always* in their own "flat" — you can imagine how depressed and miserable this is for him.

But I fancy things may come to a crisis, and on this wise. When the General returned from Eastbourne I told you we did not think him at all well — but as you know I said nothing definite as to his illness. This was because the poor old man had told me *in strict confidence* of his illness — said he *had had a stroke*, but that *no one* except the F.s and myself were to know, and said he trusted to my honour not to mention it. As I did not breathe a word of it even to you, you may be sure I did not to anyone else. But on Thursday last Ede Bernstein came to me with a postcard from Kautsky in which the latter wrote: "Do you know anything of the stroke which Adler (who had been to the Congress) says the General has had. Is it true or an invention of the F.'s." Ede thought it *was* an invention but when I found this matter which the General was so anxious to keep quiet was being talked about, and knowing the sort of things Louise is constantly writing about him, I felt in self-defence I must let him know that the painful matter *was* known, and not through me. I wrote therefore, and told him of Karl's postcard, telling him quite straight *why* I wished him to know — i.e., that should the rumour come back to him he might look for its origin anywhere but in my direction. I have not heard in reply, but have reason to know (it would be too long a story to tell you how) that he is very angry — probably with me! But I go to see him Wed. and then no doubt there'll be the devil to pay. But it was necessary to stop this matter. I have only too often let things go. I can't enter into all the miserable details — it is sickening to think of them — but the broad general fact is there. Pumps *is* got rid of, and even though the General will not treat me quite like Pumps, the result may come to the same. For despite all one owes the General, we cannot submit to everything. *You* are the one person Louise dreads, and you alone could help now. The position is too serious for remaining quite passive. If you don't want to see the F.'s *sole literary* executors you must act, and that promptly. You will remember that Bebel wrote the papers would be in the right hands.[3] I think you and I should ask to know *whose* hands. If outsiders know we should, for when all is said and done this is *our* business and no one else's. The papers — especially all the private papers — are *our* concern; they belong to us — not even to Engels.

If I could tell you everything, if you could only faintly realize how matters stand, if you could see the General looking like a child at Louise before he dares even ask a friend to come and see him, if you knew how they bully and frighten him by constantly reminding him he is too old for this and too old for that, and that when one has had the "warnings" he has had, a man must etc., etc., etc.; if you understood how they are making the old man believe his very life depends on them — and saw how utterly depressed, and lonely, and miserable he is, you would see that I am not exaggerating when I say that every delay now is a danger, and that for all sakes your presence is essential. As I have told you, the very shrewd Bernstein has long been urging me to beg you to come, and only today has been saying what folly it is of us not to defend ourselves. You cannot possibly exaggerate the gravity of the position. I can do *nothing* — at any rate nothing while I am quite alone. You could still do much. How much is best proved by Louise's hatred of you, and the fact that she has not *yet* dared to set the General against you. Think very seriously of what I have written, and be assured I should not be so foolish as to urge your coming over like this unless there were very good cause. Paul's coming without you will be quite useless, believe me, may be even worse than useless.

I wish, dear, I had better and pleasanter news to give. It is all so painful (when you hear all the petty treacheries and meannesses you will be like myself and wonder if it is not some horrible nightmare) I have put off writing in very cowardice. But you *ought* to know. I can only say to you again, with all the earnestness I can, if we — you and I — are to make a final effort it must be made soon, and your presence here is urgently needed.

My love to you, dear old Lottie.

Your

TUSSY

1. After Lafargue had presented a report to the Nantes Congress in September on the modifications to the agrarian programme proposed at the Marseilles Congress, Engels had chastised him for his opportunist tendencies.
2. Stanisław and Maria Mendelson, founders of the Polish Socialist Party.
3. See Appendix 2, p. 308.

Laura did not respond to Eleanor's frenetic cries for help. Meanwhile on 14 November 1894 Engels, who was now seventy-four, had written a letter to the two sisters telling them about his will; on the same day he drew up a supplement to the will in a document addressed to his executors. He informed Laura and Eleanor that he was bequeathing the whole of his library (including the books he had inherited from Marx) to the German Party. Laura and Eleanor would both receive three-eighths of the remainder of his assets, of which they would each keep an eighth for Jenny's children. Finally, all royalties and other payments for Marx's works were to be paid directly to them.

In another letter to Laura of 17 December, Engels described his busy life and the many projects with which he was involved. He was following the socialist movement in Europe and the U.S. by reading seven daily and twenty-two weekly papers, some in languages he was still trying to learn; he was drafting the notes and preface for the edition of letters between Lassalle and Marx; he was dealing with visitors and correspondence, and was also returning to his own work, suspended for some years in the interests of getting Marx's works published. As for volume IV of Capital *(volume III had just been published by Meissner), he told Laura that the manuscript was "very rudimentary." Kautsky had deciphered a small part of it, but had been unable to finish the work; Bernstein, who had also been trained to decipher Marx's handwriting, was only just recovering from a severe depression. Engels told Laura that he intended to ask Eleanor to resume the work.*

89. Eleanor and Aveling to Laura

7, Grays Inn Square, W.C.
22 November 1894

My dear Laura,

I have not heard from you, so I hardly know if my last letter reached you, and, of course, I do not know what you think or whether you are considering the advisability of *your* coming over. I can assure you, my dear Laura, that I in no wise *over-stated*, and that things are very serious. Indeed, there is, I fear, little doubt that all the papers, if not actually already in the possession of the Freybergers, will be soon. A *very* important fact in this connection I must call your attention to, as you have probably overlooked the thing in the *Vorwärts*. I had not noticed it until Bernstein told us about it. The matter I allude to is the statement that the *4th* volume of the *Capital* will *not* be issued. Now the General has again and again said — not merely to me and Edward, but to the Bernsteins, Mendelsons, etc. — that the *4th* vol. would give him comparatively very little trouble, it being in a far more complete state than the 3rd vol. and so on. Indeed Karl Kautsky had, when in London, copied a large portion of it! Now we are suddenly told — through a public announcement, and no *private* communication to you and myself, whom, after all, it most deeply concerns — that the data are insufficient and that Engels will not issue it. Of course we are convinced that Freyberger has persuaded the General that he is not well enough to do it; the Ms will pass into the Freybergers' hands, and *they* as literary executors will issue it later on — unless we take some steps, and that pretty soon. If I *alone* speak it will do no good. The General has been convinced that like Pumps I am only speculating on him, and am only *jealous of Louise being in his house, etc.* This could not be said of you — and were you to come over, I should suggest that you and I got the General alone (you would have to bring him here to secure that!) and that we spoke to him quite straight about the Mss., telling him that we wish and have a right to know what he has decided with regard to all Mohr's papers, and that we have *no* confidence in the Freybergers. It would be no good beating about the bush. To this it must come, and I assure you that the longer we put this off the more serious the matter becomes. They are frightening the General about his health, and they have had a bell fitted up in his bedroom so that he can, should he "suddenly need help," at once ring up Freybergers! I need hardly say that the poor old man, whenever he sees that bell, thinks himself in great danger. "Ludwig's" influence grows greater the more he persuades the General he is indispensable, and now that a baby is there the General will be still more enslaved.

No doubt the General wrote and told you of *the* event. I have not yet seen either Louise or the baby, and am not anxious to, but I have not been up to the General's for a week. Edward returned last Friday, looking very ill, and complaining of a fearful pain in his side that he had been suffering from for some ten days or a fortnight. When I looked, I found he had an enormous abscess — twice the size of my fist! I at once sent for the doctor. When he saw the thing on Saturday he said it must be opened there and then. It was no joke, I can tell you, for the abscess was a very bad one, and of course, in his already weak state, such an operation was very trying for Edward. However it seems getting on all right, although there is an immense cut, and Edward is suffering not a little from the drainage tube that is fixed in the abscess. It has been a bad and anxious week, I can tell you, and Edward is still very ill and weak, but I hope on the mend now. I don't think we shall be able to stop here, however. He will need further rest and change so soon as he can get about again. The General has written most kindly and nicely — but he says he is not allowed out as he has a cold. I know he will not be allowed to come here if the Freybergers can prevent it.

Now, once more, dear Laura, will you not consider my suggestion and come over? There are *two furnished* rooms at the General's. He can't refuse or find a pretext (not that I believe *he* would wish to do either) for putting you off. And if he *did* try to put you off it would only show the greater need for your coming. Could you not come for the 28th (his birthday)? Anyhow, if you feel as I do, that it would be an absolute wrong to allow these Mss., papers and documents (including the practically complete 4th volume!) that are not only *ours*, but that we have a very distinct duty with regard to, to fall into the utterly unscrupulous hands of the Freybergers, you will not delay, but will come at once. Be assured I should not write in this way, unless I knew the extreme seriousness of the position.

I *wish* we could see you and Paul and consult together! But there is really nothing to do, but you and me, the two who have the *right* to, to have it out with the General. As things are Paul could do nothing — and the probability is that the General would either get into a rage, or put him off with excuses.

There, my dear Laura, is all I can tell you now. It is a miserable business. The Sunday before last the General had asked me to go to dinner as usual, *but had not dared* tell Freyberger he had done so!, which will show you how little he is now master in his own house. This, by the way, has two plates on the doors bearing the name, of course, of Freyberger!

Goodnight, dear. My poor Edward has been in bed some hours (he is able to be up during the day) or he would, no doubt, send messages. My love to you and Paul.

Your affectionate,

TUSSY

P.S. What say you to Jean? I *am* glad he has passed at last![1] Look out for the *Neue Zeit* of either this or next week.[2] I have an article going for Brentano, of which I hope you will approve. If you think it would interest Paul at all I could send him the rough English copy of the Ms.

My love to you —

Friday morning

Dear Laura,

Come, *come*, COME. You have no idea of the *immediate* importance of it. The General is in this mood. He will brook no interference from *any* one but you two women, whose right to demand account of your father's papers he must admit. You have to make that demand and to declare point-blank your reason, that you do not trust the Fs. Believe me — this is the only way to save the M.S. Love to you and Paul.

EDWARD

1. Jean Longuet had just passed his baccalaureat.
2. "Wie Lujo Brentano zitiert," *Die Neue Zeit*, 13. January 1894–95, vol. 1, no. 9. The article took issue with a study of early English guilds written by Lujo Brentano, a German political economist who had been critical of Marx's economic theories.

90. Eleanor to Laura

7, Gray's Inn Square, W.C.
15 December 1894

My dear Laura,

Just a line on a matter about which I should like to hear from you *at once*. This *is* the matter. Last Sunday the General began speaking of the *copying* of Mohr's MSS.; said he had given Karl some to do, but that Karl had not gone on; that he did not know whom to take as Ede Bernstein would probably refuse on the ground of want of time. Edward and I could see quite well that this was meant as a preparation for saying he would let the F.'s do it, as they are in the house, and so forth. I said I was sure Bernstein would gladly do the work. The General did not look over-pleased, but said he would ask him. He has not said one word to Bernstein, however. We did, and Ede said, of course, he would accept, if there were no one else, but he was strongly of opinion that you and I are the proper persons to do the work. It would, moreover, be a means of getting at the MSS. What do you think? The General *may* refuse me on the ground that I am very busy and would delay the work, and he *might* urge against you that you are away, and the danger of the post. But just as Karl took the MS. to Stuttgart and Bebel brought them back, so you could manage too. You could offer to fetch the MSS. you would copy, and Bonnier, who so often goes across, could take them back. We could *both* work at it, and so, at least, establish some claim. I shall not say anything till I hear from you, so please answer as soon as possible. If you agree I will at once tell the General our offer, and you could also write direct: tell him I told you the difficulty about the copying, and that you were ready to do it, either alone, or with me. Anyhow, it's a chance!

Our love to you both. Edward is slowly getting better.

Your affectionate

TUSSY

Laura finally capitulated. However, instead of broach-
ing the subject to Engels direct, she thought it more
diplomatic to write a letter to Eleanor which could be
shown to Engels. As Eleanor was out of London lec-
turing for the SDF Aveling was entrusted with the
task, at Engels's regular Sunday dinner. The letter
below describing the outcome to the Lafargues is fairly
characteristic of Aveling's style.

Engels replied to Laura on 29 December, explain-
ing that his executors had been instructed to hand
over to Eleanor, as administrator of the will, all Marx's
handwritten manuscripts and all letters addressed to
him, except the correspondence between him and En-
gels. He was well aware, he said, that he was simply
holding these papers "in trust for you"; however, since
Eleanor seemed to have doubts about it, he would have
Sam Moore draw up a new will, in which this would
be stated "distinctly and unmistakably."[1]

In a later, more affectionate letter to Laura of 19
January,[2] *Engels admitted to having felt annoyed and*
bewildered by Eleanor's behaviour, though now that
they had cleared the air he claimed that they were "as
good friends as before."

The two letters from Eleanor which follow Ave-
ling's give all the details of this painful episode.

---

1. *Frederick Engels, Paul and Laura Lafargue: Correspondence*, III, 352–353.
2. *Ibid.*, 360–361.

91. Aveling to Laura and Paul Lafargue

7, Gray's Inn Sq. W.C.
25 December 1894

To my well-beloved Laura
and Paul, greeting! Christmas ditto.
This despatch from the seat of war. I delivered, dear Madam,

your fateful letter to Eleanor to F. Engels Esq. To₁ hath the significance "inscribed to." To₂ hath the significance "presented to . . ." First results of presentation, made at 2.40 P.M. on Sunday, before dinner and in the presence of Freyberger ♂.[1] (a) As far as copying goes, all smoothness, and yes. (b) As to the MS disposal position, also smoothness combined with the deliberate reading aloud of it to and for F. ♂, who like B'rer Rabbit laid low and said nuffin. *Then*, a quite quiet, dignified statement that, *of course*, Marx's MSS. and papers were held safe in charge for his daughters and could have no other destination. This was all clear and definite and, I take it, that when once you and Eleanor have the same emphatic assurance, there is a temporary end of the matter. But *"now, gather and surmise."*[2] Likewise, *perpend*. After dinner, we have the second results. Note, that after dinner, I outslept the General and whilst I was outsleeping there was time for Freyberger ♂ to get at him, and for F. ♀ to be brought down in tears to the same end. Anyhow, on my innocent appearance, the General said in his most military manner, "Show me that letter of Laura's again." The which I did. Then the storm broke out. There was a conspiracy — there had been conspiracies ever since he had taken the new house — he knew all about it — he knew who was in it — you had been put up to write this — we had talked it all over in Paris — you and Eleanor mistrusted him — did you want a legal assignment — much repetition of the earlier assurances of the safety of everything. All this in the spluttering vein and under the workings of a yeasty conscience, and with much marching up and down and more or less effective dodging of furniture. I said it was no good bullying me. I was only a messenger and he must have it out with you two women. I roundly denied conspiracy and our prompting you — for your action in writing was, as you know, your own. Today we all dine together, merrily. And after that, have it out. I left on Sunday night, when Freyberger ♂ came amiably in again.

My love to you both.

Your

EDWARD

---

1. Zoological signs: ♂ = male, ♀ = female.
2. Polonius in *Hamlet*, Act II, scene ii.

92. Eleanor to Laura

Christmas Day. 1894.
"Peace on earth and goodwill to Man!"

My dear Old Hottentot,

To speak the language of the *beau monde*, the fat's in the fire.
How, why, you will gather from Edward's despatch. To make
that despatch somewhat clearer, however, let me tell you that
I was away lecturing in Salford (Manchester) giving lectures
I ought to have given long before, but had to postpone as I could
not leave the invalid.

On Sat. morning we went up to 41, and found all out — not
together — for the poor old man is quite left to shift for himself.
We could not wait as I had the train to catch. When I returned
yesterday (and let me say in passing that these "propaganda"
visits — three lectures a day — are very weary work) Edward
told me of what had happened. I immediately wrote to the
General, and have taken up the tone I think we are quite justified in taking — i.e., of the offended party. *Why* should the
General — unless he has an ill conscience or is being badly inspired — take a very simple question for a sign of mistrust?
Anyway I wrote thusly. That when he spoke to me of the difficulty with Ede and Karl Kautsky in getting the copying done
I had only thought of inducing Ede to do it. That later, however,
on reflection, it had occurred to me that you, or you and I together could do it, and that I had written you accordingly. I
said I had not broached the subject to him first, because I
thought you would feel I ought to ask you first, and then tell
him your decision. I said that had I thought he could so mis-
understand your letter I should not have sent it him, and that
had I not missed him on Sat., I should have *told* him about it
all. I continue: "As to the general MSS. of Mohr, you surely
must know that Laura and I are sure *you* would deal with them
as Mohr himself would have done. But you can equally understand that we should not like the letters and papers (many of a
purely personal nature) to fall into other hands than yours or
ours . . . Edward says you seemed to believe in some deep-
laid scheme. I can quite believe you do, for I should be blind
indeed if I had not seen the efforts to set you against us, and I
can hardly wonder if you think what could never have occurred
to you had our Nymmy been with you . . . It seems impos-

sible you could *really* believe Laura and I mistrust you. Whom on earth could we trust but you? . . . After this (Xmas) is over I shall speak to you of it all, and I wish Laura could be here to speak for herself. I shall say no more now, except that if you had not been very much poisoned against us you could never have thought so meanly of Mohr's children as to think they could mistrust *you*."

There! *C'est la guerre* — but it *had* to come, and we'd better have it out. Of course what I shall say is that we do *not* trust the F.'s — and I shall tell him *my* reasons; that Louise is asking me to sign and get you to sign a paper making *her* the responsible owner of the papers for fear Pumps should get hold of them first suggested the matter, and that all we ask — surely no harm in that — is to know, *what apparently an outsider like Bebel does know*, what he has decided to do with the *Nachlass*. I shall then show him the whole Louise–Bebel–Lieb[knecht]–Singer correspondence and have *that* out too. In a word, my dear, it's war, and we've got to fight. The thing the General is made to believe is that we all are only Pumpses, speculating on him. *That* we've got to disabuse him of. We ask — what every stranger is asking — to *know* what he means to do. No more.

And now, I must "dress" my invalid's wound — which is still open — and then dress myself, and set off for a merry Xmas with our dear friends the F's. What humbug it all is! And how I wish we were with you, by ourselves and no festivities to labour through!

My love to the Nigger.[1]

Yours, dear Hottentot,

TUSSY

---

1. An allusion to Paul's mulatto origins.

93. **Eleanor to Laura**

7 Gray's Inn Square, W.C.
2 January 1895

My dear Laura,

I had meant sending you the latest war bulletins, but really I am so sick of the sorry business that I put off writing. But now that you want to hear before answering the General, here are the facts up to date.

   To begin at the beginning. On Xmas day — as an appetizer for the festive meal — the General took me off to his "droring-room" and we proceeded to our first round. He had been angry, he said, at my "want of tact" in sending him your letter. Against the letter — as from you to me — he had nothing to say, but he thought my sending it him was, etc., etc., etc. Of course I did not tell him you had told me to send the letter. I simply pointed out that my sending it was the best proof that I did not think he would be offended at it. After a certain amount of sparring — during which I told him he had not been angry until others had made him so, to which he replied indignantly "No! I only was with Louise half an hour while Edward slept!" — we came to the point — the MSS. He said these were ours and would, of course, come to us. I said if I had his assurance of that I was quite satisfied and knew you would be. I added that I *had* been uneasy as I had no confidence in the F.'s and that perfect outsiders had spoken as knowing all about his intentions while we did not. This was the main result of the Xmas day round — but I declared we must have it out, and as this was what the General wished, he came up here to lunch on Friday last. Then we had our second — and so far as the General is concerned, our final round. We then went over much of the same ground again. I told him some of the things L. has been saying and writing of us, and told him too that naturally the people to whom she had said these things would deny it; that we should ourselves have the greatest contempt for August[1] if he should round on L. The General really *knows* pretty well, but naturally *must* make the best of things. I never for a second have believed that he would or could make a stand against the "energetic" mother of the "energetic" baby. But it was *essential* he should understand that *we* know also, and that we do not consider Louise a second "himself." He again said he *would see* all papers of Mohr come to us, but said nothing of his will. Of course I said I was quite satisfied, and that for the rest, I should say nothing more about it, and so on. I think you should say too that you are satisfied as to the MSS. Of course the question of the F.'s getting hold of the papers has to be faced, but that we can say and do nothing about. My reason for showing the General Bebel's letter (he had had L's version of the Bebel–Louise *affaire*) was that he should see Bebel's cool assurance to me that you and I need not trouble about Mohr's papers as *he* knew it was all right. The General was very vexed, because he knows Bebel could only have repeated what L. told him, and I saw that his tone altered very considerably after this. However at present the upshot is that the General *will* (I hope!) take definite steps to make sure about the papers, and that he declares two such *famöse Frauenzimmer*[2] as L. and I — though I am *not* so "noble" as she is — must agree. Well, we — i.e., the noble one and I, will no doubt have a stormy interview — and then all will be peace — on the surface! . . . I *wish* you could come over soon. It would be *very* good if you could. Edward is getting along but is still weak . . . Thank Heaven the ghastly festivities are over. My dear Hottentot, I wish you and Paul all good in this year.* For myself I have one comfort. It *can't* be worse than the last one!

Love and kisses.

Your

TUSSY

* So do I.

EDWARD

1. Bebel.
2. "capital wenches."

On 26 March 1895, as promised, Engels drew up a codicil to his will clarifying the position over Eleanor's rights to her father's letters and manuscripts. Bernstein and Bebel were to inherit Engels's manuscripts, the correspondence with Marx, and Engels's own author's rights. His personal belongings were to be shared among Laura, Eleanor and Louise; Louise was also to receive all furniture and effects, as well as an option on the lease of the house. Pumps's legacy was to be £2,230.

During 1895 Engels's health deteriorated steadily. He was suffering from cancer of the oesophagus and larynx, which he took for a disease of the neck glands, but his close friends knew that he was dying. In June Laura came over to stay with him in Eastbourne, and Eleanor and Aveling joined them there at the end of the month. He died peacefully at home in London on 5 August (see Appendix 3).

Engels was cremated on 10 August and at the end of the month Eleanor, Aveling, Lessner and Bernstein took his ashes to his beloved Eastbourne and scattered them into the sea.

PART SIX

August 1895 – January 1898

The World
After Marx and Engels

T HEIR LEGACIES FROM ENGELS—approximately £5,000 each, a considerable sum in 1895 — meant that for the first time in their lives Laura and Eleanor, now 49 and 40, achieved a financial security that allowed them to buy houses of their own. True to form, Eleanor took over many of Engels's tasks, in particular arranging for the publication and translation of Marx's work, and at the same time started lecturing and writing for the SDF.

Though not, to use Eleanor's phrase, "as plentiful as blackberries," Laura's letters were more frequent in the aftermath of Engels's death: there were many business matters to deal with, such as the distribution of funds to Jenny's children, and — in spite of Engels's efforts to forestall them — endless rows and disputes over the disposal of the contents of his house. These common concerns drew the sisters somewhat closer, and Laura was shattered by Eleanor's death in 1898. She and Paul were also to commit suicide, thirteen years later.

94. Laura to Eleanor

[*Le Perreux*] *27 August 1895*

My dear Tussy,

I am personally distinctly in favour of selling the stocks and securities, because a transfer of them would involve difficulties and, possibly, disputes. Crosse[1] is in a position to know whether selling is advisable and we cannot do better than follow his advice.

I had told Louise that in any case the legacy to Pumps must be paid in money and as soon as possible. She flared up when I said so, but Moore told her authoritatively that that must be so, and happily Moore's word is *law*. I do not understand her objections, seeing that she can please herself about re-investing at once.

Angèle's[2] style has improved singularly during our absence,[3] *le style c'est l'homme, et elle est actuellement à sa troisième manière.*[4]

Goodbye, my dear Tussy,

from your LAURA

1. Arthur Willson Crosse, Engels's lawyer.
2. Presumably a servant of the Lafargues.
3. At Engels's funeral.
4. "Style makes the man, and she is now in her third manner."

At the 1895 Trades Union Congress in Cardiff Aveling represented Justice as well as several continental journals. In the autumn the Avelings undertook a lecture tour in Scotland for the SDF and the Independent Labour Party (ILP), and another series of lectures in Lancashire for the SDF alone.

95. Eleanor to Laura

Green Street Green
Orpington
4 September 1895

My dear Laura,

Sam[1] has just written to me that he has not had a reply from you to his letter of the 28th August, with regard to the "sale," but that in view of what you wrote to me, of what I think, especially in view of Crosse's very strongly expressed opinion, he has now definitely advised Crosse to "sell." Of course, we shall probably lose — you don't yet know what an English solicitor's bills are — but it will save much unpleasantness. I shall instruct Crosse, so far as I am concerned, to re-invest at once. I should say that Sam asks me to let you know his final decision in the matter.

As to the children I have written Crosse that I quite agree with you, and that I am sure the wish of the General was that all the children should share equally.

I have been up to Burnley (an old-standing engagement) to give three lectures, and as Edward is at Cardiff for the Congress, Jean spent the Saturday, Sunday and Monday at Lessner's. Of course, I made it a "business" arrangement.

Things at Cardiff are bringing about a more definite split than there has yet been between the "old" and "new" Unionists, and as Sam writes, it "looks like a grand scrimmage." Burns is playing a somewhat sorry part, and although I have always believed our General's faith in him would be justified, his present action makes one feel doubtful.[2]

When are you coming over? I should like to know *approximately*, because some months ago I undertook a lecturing tour (one week) in Scotland, and I must now settle definitely if I can keep the engagement or not.

Bonnier has written me about Carmaux,[3] but (*entre nous*) the position of the glassworkers in England is quite desperate. Glassworking, so far as England is concerned, is a dying trade, and the condition of the men is fearful. In *three years* many have only had three to nine months' work. Firm after firm is going under — and you will know what that means. I fear the day for help to others is gone.

Greetings from Johnny and me to you both, and my humble regards to Novo (especially Novo), Filon, Luna and Cie.[4]

Your

TUSSY

1. Sam Moore.
2. John Burns's attacks on Keir Hardie were having a divisive effect on the workers' movement.
3. A glassworkers' strike of great significance in the French trade union movement. The employers turned the strike to their advantage: Carmaux had a strong radical tradition and they sought to break the power of the unions and enlist government intervention. Troops were called in, union leaders arrested, and the strike became a matter of national and government debate. It lasted from August 1895 until January 1896 and ultimately led to the foundation, by Jaurès and others, of a worker-controlled glass factory at Albi in October 1896.
4. Lafargue family pets.

96. Eleanor to Laura

Green Street Green
Orpington
7 September 1895

My dear Laura,

Glory to God in the highest! I have found the Lachâtre agreement.[1] I thought it might be in a box Mohr gave me (his father's) containing a few letters and odds and ends of Lupus,[2] the Darwin and Spencer letters, etc., and to which I had added letters sent on Mohr's death. But I did not want to raise any false hopes and so said nothing till I had made a search.

I enclose a copy of the agreement. Do you think you can

deal with the matter in France, or shall we communicate with Lachâtre quite officially through Crosse? If you can manage so much the better, and then I will send you the original of the agreement. But Crosse has, like Moore, told me I must sign nothing without consultation as I am (unhappily) legally responsible, not only to you, which would be easy enough, but to *Longuet*. Moore advised me to consult Crosse on all Mohr's affairs, the French translation of the *Capital* included. But as I know what a *very* expensive luxury English solicitors are (every letter 3s. 4d!) I should be glad if you would undertake the French business. If you can and will, as I have said, I'll send you the agreement itself. Meanwhile the copy will tell you what the conditions are. I confess I don't understand them altogether.

When are you coming? Do let me know. I have so many outstanding engagements that I can't definitely settle till I hear from you.

Yours
TUSSY

Love to Paul — *and* Novo and Luna, and *kind regards* to Filon.

1. French publisher of *Capital*, translated by Joseph Roy.
2. Wilhelm Wolff, to whom Marx dedicated volume I of *Capital*.

Even before Engels's estate was settled both Eleanor and Laura started house-hunting. Laura bought the house she mentions in this letter, at 20, Grande-Rue, Draveil (Seine-et-Oise), an imposing property with about thirty rooms, gardener's quarters, outbuildings, conservatories and an orange grove. Its grounds extended to the Seine and the forest of Sénart, and contained a pleasure garden, kitchen garden, hen-house and orchard. It needed renovations, however, and the Lafargues did not move in until March 1896.

Eleanor's rather more modest house in Lewisham is described in her letter of 10 December 1895.

97. Laura to Eleanor

[Le Perreux] 23 *September 1895*

My dear Tussy,

I thank you for cheque for £24 received on the 21st.

Respecting the children's money you cannot of course invest sums of £5, 10 or 20. But there is a sum of over £100 owing to them which, together with the £24 just received from Meissner, could be invested along with the rest of their money. Later on we could open a joint account at the bank if you thought fit.

Nothing definite is settled about our voyage. Paul is obliged to go to Bordeaux before we come over to London, so that we could not, in any case, leave here before the middle of October.

I have been busy, being without a servant and spending nearly all my time in "doing" the suburbs of Paris in search of a house on sale. There is one to be sold by auction on the 25th and we are in hopes we may get it. The house is so-so and requires repairing but the garden is splendid and stretches right into the *forêt de Sénart*.

We are setting out again immediately after lunch and so I bid you goodbye, hoping to see you ere long.

Your

LAURA

*Eleanor was now attempting to sort out Marx's letters
and articles and to arrange for their publication. She
made several exciting discoveries but her task was
made unduly onerous by the terms of Engels's will,
under which she had no legal access to the correspondence between Marx and Engels.*

98. Eleanor to Laura

*36 Montgomery Street
Edinburgh
8 October 1895*

My dear Laura,

Your letter has just been sent on to me here, where — as I think
I told you — we were coming for a week to lecture for the S.D.F.
When I say "here," I mean the North, for today we go to
Dundee, and then to Glasgow. Of course the S.D.F. pays the
expenses.

I *can't* understand your letter! *What* was "preposterous"
and "ill-advised" about mine to you? Neither Bernstein nor I
could know what Paul "always meant." We only knew what he
wrote — which was that Bebel and he (Bernstein) *"feraient
bien"* to make the same demand for Mohr's letters as for those
of Engels. And if they did, of course, they become responsible
for them and not we. And even if handed over, I don't see why
they should come via Bebel. Yet if Paul's suggestion were acted
on this is what they must do! Meantime I think *we* should put
in our request *at once*. Many persons who have letters of Engels
may also have letters of Marx, and may decide to send both
along together. What I suggest writing is:

To the Editor of . . .

    Sir,

    May we appeal through your columns to all those who may have
any correspondence of Karl Marx, or any other papers of Marx to
be good enough to forward them to one of us? We are anxious to get
as complete a collection of our father's letters as possible with a view
to publication. Any letters or documents that may be sent will, of
course, be taken the utmost care of, and if the senders wish it, re-

turned as soon as they have been copied. We should carry out any instruction that the possessors and senders of the letters might give as to the omission of any passages they might desire not to have published.

Yours, etc.

L.L. (Le P[erreux], etc.)
E.M.A. ([Green] S[treet] G[reen])

This was the form adopted by Darwin's and Ernest Jones's sons, and is the best for England. Of course for Germany we need only send to the *Vorwärts* with a request that the Party Press should re-copy. As to France you know best. Let me hear what you think or if you have any suggestions to make. If you agree I will send to all the London papers and through the Press Ass[ociation] to the provincial. Unfortunately here unless you *do* send to each one the letter will only go into one or two papers. Of course I will send to America — but Schlüter and Sanial will suffice there.[1]

I heard from that unmitigated cad Freyberger this morning, saying the books had been sent[2] and that they wished us to remove our "articles" — and he was ill-bred enough to add "at our expense"! As I could not (even if I were in London) get them into our Green St. Green place, I'm having them stored until we find a house. Lord send we soon may! The searching for one is a misery!

Our love to you both, and tell Paul (though I don't know why he wants to!) that he may bully me to his heart's content. I don't mind. You don't say when you're coming. Remember our safe lease expires in November.[3] I suppose I shall have to renew it? Unless you come over and make other arrangements. The General's things are all at Motteler's.[4]

Your

TUSSY

I like Guesde's cheek! But we (though not on so splendid a scale) have our Guesdes too!

---

1. Schlüter was the editor-in-chief of the *New Yorker Volkszeitung*, and Sanial of the *Journal of the Knights of Labor.*
2. Marx and Engels's library, bequeathed to the German party.
3. In September 1895 Eleanor had rented a box at Chancery Lane Deposit for three months to house Marx's papers, hoping that Laura would come and help

her sort them. The box was eventually rented for much longer than expected
and Laura was sent packets of letters to work on in France.

4. Julius Motteler, a German friend of Engels and Bernstein, a Social Democrat
living in Tufnell Park, sometimes known as the "businessman of the German
Social-Democratic Party."

99. Eleanor to Laura

Green Street Green
Orpington
19 October 1895

My dear Laura,

The enclosed has, to my knowledge, appeared in a large number
of papers, and has, no doubt, also appeared in others I have not
seen. I have also written to Library,[1] Kautsky and Adler (they
can practically cover the German and Austro-Hungarian-Bohe-
mian press) and to America.

We are just now taken up chiefly with house-hunting, for
this place is too far from London, and not pleasant for winter
weather that is setting in with a vengeance. All the *nice* houses
are too dear, and all the cheap ones are shoddy in shoddy neigh-
bourhoods. How are you faring? Did you try to get the house
Paul said you were "after"?

We were, as you know, for a week in Scotland, and if Edward had not rather broken down in health it would have been
very pleasant. We had magnificent meetings in Edinburgh,
Dundee, Glasgow, Blantyre and Greenock. Edinburgh is assuredly, with the possible exception of Prague, the most beautiful
town I have seen (the *ville lumière* included) On our return
we saw Crosse. As you probably know from him, he has now
divided the "wine" into four parts, and as soon as he gets your
consent will see that the quarter (i.e., the children's share) is
sold. He said he had a purchaser — who, I have a shrewd suspicion, is himself. Meantime I am also writing to Brett, as I
want to know (1) what he charges for storage; (2) what he
would be prepared to pay. In any case the children's share
should be sold at once.

Mr. Percy[2] with his "life policy" is going to mulct us — i.e., "the estate" — in [*sic*] £87. The General had made himself *responsible* for this sum — *ergo* the company, unless it is paid, will sue the executors. They, of course, could in turn sue Percy — but you might as well sue the man in the moon. Meantime we have suggested to Bernstein (and to Crosse) to try a compromise. As Crosse is advancing Percy money at a very high rate, it is, however, *possible* that Crosse will not be over-anxious to effect a settlement. The *only* chance with Percy, is to *threaten* that nothing will be paid out to Pumps (or anyone else) until Moore returns. As Ede and the Duchess[3] were to see Crosse on Thursday, possibly they may have come to some arrangement, of which I have not yet heard. There seems a probability that everything will be sold out (according to Crosse) in about four weeks — so there is a chance things will be arranged by Christmas!

I am copying (the print is trying so I can't go very quickly) three copies of the *Tribune* articles, on "Germany."[4] One I will send you. It is a wonderfully interesting history of 48.*

Our love to you both. *And* my respects to the four-footed members of the family, especially M. Novo.

Your
TUSSY

* I'll send you one.

1. Liebknecht.
2. Percy Rosher, Pumps's husband, for whom Engels had been paying a life insurance policy. Rosher was demanding that the payments be continued.
3. Eduard Bernstein and Louise Freyberger.
4. A reference to eighteen articles signed by Marx which appeared in the *New York Daily Tribune* and which Eleanor prepared as a book in 1896 under the title *Revolution and Counter-Revolution in Germany*. She was unaware that these articles had in fact been drafted by Engels when Marx's command of English was still shaky. In 1897 she prepared, with Aveling's help, a volume entitled *The Eastern Question*, from a series of articles signed by Marx which had also appeared in the *Tribune*, again without realizing that some of them had been drafted by Engels.

100. Eleanor to Laura

Green Street Green
Orpington
24 October 1895

My dear Laura,

Thank Paul for his letter. I shall be very glad when we can
again write one another apart from all these stupid (and for
the most part) quite unnecessary business matters.

We saw Crosse yesterday (I dread to think what the Crosse
bill will be!) and it is, of course, quite understood that if the
"estate" pays — as to save law-costs it must — Percy's £87, the
"policy" will be held by the executors as guarantee until such
time as Percy pays up. Meantime Percy complains that his wife
is to be "coerced" into paying his debt. Crosse pointed out that
we might say *we* were being coerced into paying a debt that in
no way concerned us. Percy had made an appointment with
Crosse to settle the matter — but so far has not kept it. We heard
also that Pumps was leaving on Friday for America! If it is
true I pity poor Willy Burns[1] — the one really decent and able
member of the Burns family. A really excellent fellow. But as
he already is providing — as far as he can — for his mother, a
sister, and two brothers, besides his one brother's children and
his own wife and children, it will be pretty rough if Pumps
manages to foist Percy and her brats on him too. Of course, the
American journey may be only a lie of Percy's.

Ede Bernstein has no doubt told you of the letter from
Hermann Engels[2] and the 6000 (or so) marks in Germany, and
of the Duchess's foolish letter to Hermann. Ede fortunately
stopped her writing to Hermann Engels to "keep" the money —
a gratuitous and unwarranted insult. She told Crosse that she
wished this money retained by the Engels family because Engels
and his family were not at one on political matters! The family
might fairly resent the affront of "giving" them some £500,
when the rest goes elsewhere! Of course I told Ede I did not see
any reason for being rude to people who have behaved so admirably.

Now as to the children. Crosse advises investing *their* share
simply in Consols. This will, no doubt, bring in rather less than
we hope some of our investments will, but there is the advantage

of *perfect security* and no trouble or responsibility for us. Personally I think this is the best investment for the children, but, of course, I said I could not decide till I heard from you. So let me know. A pleasing fact is that the "estate" has to pay Crosse £57 for costs re. the taking of the General's new house. Crosse said he advised the General to drop the whole thing — but he would not. So we pay the piper to which the two thieves dance. I will send you — as soon as I get some copies — a small pamphlet of mine (written for Wurm's Encyclopedia) on the English working-class movement. They have thought it good enough to issue as a pamphlet with an Introduction by Library.[3] It is not worth anything because I had to cram the immense amount of material into a very small space. *A propos.* Did you notice in the *Vorwärts*[4] the *very* cool and unfair announcement of Singer and Bebel as to the books? They simply announced twenty-seven cases of books given by the General. I had to write to Library (on other matters — Congress, etc.) and said I was more than surprised that Bebel and Singer did not so much as mention Mohr. I said I thought it would only be decent to say that a good half of the twenty-seven cases contained the admirable library of Marx, presented to the German Party (in order that the General's wish that the libraries should remain together might be carried out) by Marx's children. The Party itself would like to know, and *should* know this. I hope you will think I did well to write this. I feel it very strongly, and moreover, before long, unless we see to this at once, it will be said that Louise graciously *gave* all the books to the Party. Though she refused to give even the bookcases!

We are still house-hunting, and from all I hear, so are you! We find that all the nice houses are either let or too dear. And the "noble residences" we go to see are more often than not in some unspeakable slum. Rents here are something fearful. If, however, we can find any really nice place, Crosse strongly advises *buying* instead of paying rent. Sometimes I feel like investing in a caravan (like Dr. Gordon Stables)[5] and living gipsy-like, anywhere.

The Duke and Duchess are "launching out" in grand style. They have, or *say* they have, spent £300 on new furniture, and speak only with contempt of what they made the poor old General buy.

I suppose you can't say yet when you are coming. I wish

you could soon, so that we could go through the papers at Chancery Lane. I believe if we "weeded" them we could get the *really* valuable things into a £1.1s. or £2.2s safe. Now — unless we do this, we shall have to take on the room and pay (I think) £8.8s. The three months expire in November. Think of this, and see if you can't manage to come. If we're settled by then, of course, it will be simple enough for we shall have one spare room. If not, we might get some rooms for the week or two you would stay.

No room for more.

Love from us both,

Your

TUSSY

If you agree with what I have written Library as to the books, I wish you would write him in the same strain.

1. Nephew of Lizzie Burns, an ardent socialist who had emigrated to America.
2. Engels's brother.
3. Library = Liebknecht. The pamphlet was written for the *Volks-Lexikon*, vol. 2, and was published in England, in Aveling's translation, as "The Working Class Movement in England" (1896).
4. 20 October 1895.
5. Dr. Gordon Stables's many works offer advice on such diverse subjects as dog-breeding and "health and happiness for wives." In his *Leaves from the Log of a Gentleman Gipsy: In Wayside Camp and Caravan* (1891) he recommended caravan travel as "the most healthful and fascinating of all modes of travel."

101. Eleanor to Laura

Green Street Green
Orpington
10 December 1895

My dear Laura,

Your letter — it is dated *Dec. 8th* and is in reply to mine of *Nov. 17th!!!* — crossed one of mine sent this morning. So I have answers to many of the questions I put you — I am glad you agree about the Int. Congress[1] because I know the dear old General wanted that, and I'm glad you have decided about

Lessner. I shall at once send him my £20. But how about the children? If you and I give £20 each why not they? Jenny would have. If you think another £20 should be sent you and Paul must write it formally to Crosse and I will endorse it. That is the only way to do it without getting into a legal mess here. Moore specially pointed this out to me. *As to Freddy I really am not sure of the sum due to him, but will get it at once. I think it was about £30.* This sum also must be paid by your and Paul's and my consent through Crosse.

Now as to our house. I've bought it — but who or what is bought and sold remains to be seen. But what we want you to do is to come and see the house yourselves. Seriously you *ought* to come over — and why not for the New Year? There will be your room ready and waiting (or indeed two rooms if you like) so if things are not all quite straight you won't mind. I ought to say that my invitation is not quite as amiable as it looks. I want Paul badly to help me with the garden! There! The cat's out of the bag. If Paul has any little affection left for me he'll come and teach us to garden.

As to our house (I am Jewishly proud of my house in Jew's Walk), voilà. Ground floor: Large room (Edward's study and general room combined); dining room (opens on back garden), kitchen, scullery, pantry, coal and wine cellars, cupboards, large entrance hall. One flight of stairs (easy), bedroom, spare bed-room (*yours*), servant's room, bathroom (large enough to be another spare room on special occasions). My *study*!!! Every-where we have electric light — which is far cheaper, as we are near the Palace,[2] than gas, though gas is laid in too, and I have a gas cooking stove and gas fires in most of the upper rooms. Finally, as to furnishing all this I ought to let you know that recently the property in Austin Friars which Edward has his share in, has gone up so much that he has been able to get a very good mortgage (without of course, losing his rights in the property) on it and he is buying all the furniture that un-luckily one can't do without. I want you to know this as it would not be fair to think *I* was paying for it all. [letter incomplete]

1. A reference to the fourth Congress of the Second International, called the Inter-national Socialist Workers' and Trade Union Congress, held in London from 27 July to 1 August 1896.
2. Crystal Palace.

102. Eleanor to Laura

The Den
Jews Walk
Sydenham, London
17 January 1896

My dear Laura,
It is good of you to remember the 16th! And you always remember it in such a princely fashion! I am getting all sorts of
of things I have long hankered after — especially the *Paston
Letters*[1] and some other historical works I've much wanted.

The French scandals are indeed wonderful out of all hoop-
ing![2] There has been less about them in the English papers than
would have been the case if these weren't so full of our own
little troubles — the Transvaal, Jameson's filibustering, the German Emperor, Venezuela.[3]

I was delighted when I saw in the *Petite République* —
which is sent me regularly — that *Bel Ami* was in for it, and I
sincerely hope Séverine will come a cropper.[4] I *can't* understand
her vogue in France. What little I have read of hers I thought
unbearable. She may be *"une plume"* — but it's one that certainly gets on my nerves.

The news that the triumvirate is to enter the *Petite République*[5] is *very* good. If we can only have a daily organ in Paris
we shall soon send all the others — I mean all the other *partis*
— to blazes. I hear that Allemane, Keir Hardie and the Dutch
(i.e., the Domela Dutch) are busy concocting mischief.[6] Do you
know anything about it?

Our respects to the four-footers. I gather that Luna has been
at it again! How is Novo? Does Paul still make him shed tears?
And our love to both of you

Your
TUSSY

Tell Paul I am anxiously awaiting hints from him as to
pigeons and the garden! The delightful Hachette (most marvellous of books) just come. Many, many thanks.

---

1. Letters of a well-to-do Norfolk family from 1422 to 1509, immensely popular
   in England ever since their first publication in five volumes between 1787 and
   1823.

2. A reference to a series of scandals that swept through France at the end of 1895, in particular the exposure of Lebaudy, the "little sugar-manufacturer," for blackmail, tax fraud and insider trading, all of which made excellent fodder for the socialists.

3. After the failure of the Jameson Raid in December 1895 President Kruger of the Transvaal received a telegram of congratulations from the German Kaiser, which the British took as an affront. In Venezuela U.S. diplomacy prevented Britain from taking possession of the Orinoco River.

4. Georges de Labruyère (Bel-Ami), a Boulangist journalist involved in the Lebaudy affair, was arrested on 13 January. Séverine, a close friend, wrote two articles accusing the army officers of misconduct.

5. Probably Guesde, Lafargue and Chauvin, who controlled the socialist journal from February to May 1897.

6. During the 1896 Congress, eight of the thirteen Dutch delegates left the hall when it was decided that socialists could offer themselves for election to Parliament. "Domela" is Domela Nieuwenhuis, leader of the Dutch Socialist Movement.

Anxious to see volume IV of Capital *published, Elea-*
nor wrote to Kautsky in Germany asking him to re-
sume his deciphering of the manuscript. Kautsky may
have concealed from Eleanor the fact that he had been
so dilatory in this work that Engels had actually asked
him — without success — to return the manuscript. At
the same time Eleanor entered into negotiations with
the publisher of Neue Zeit, Dietz. *In fact volume IV*
did not appear until several years after Eleanor's
death, between 1905–10, under the title Theories of
Surplus Value.

At the end of the following letter Eleanor refers
to Aveling's relationship with the Social Democratic
Federation. Now that Engels was dead, Hyndman
was seeking a reconciliation between the SDF, the only
"Marxist" party in Britain, and its more powerful
counterpart in Germany, the Social Democratic Party.
Bernstein suggested that it was time for the Avelings
formally to become members of the SDF. But the ex-
ecutive, including Hyndman and Bax, a friend of
Freyberger's, strongly disliked Aveling and tried to
veto it, claiming that he had been intriguing against
the proposed German connection. They even sent a
circular to the various branches of the SDF asking
them not to invite him to lecture. Aveling responded
by writing a letter to all the most famous Continental
Marxists, in which he denied the accusations and
asked for their support.

103. Eleanor to Laura

The Den
Jews Walk
Sydenham, London
5 March 1896

My dear Laura,

I can't tell you when Kautsky purposes *returning* to London, for the simple reason that he has not yet turned up at all! He had a cold, and was ill to begin with. Then other things supervened. *Now* he can't come, he says, because of getting out the *Revolution and Counter-Revolution*[1] *at once*. This is a ridiculous matter, and both Bernstein and I have written the over-anxious Karl, and we now expect him any moment. As soon as he does come I will let you know. I *do* wish you could come, one of you, if only for twenty-four hours, while K.K. is here. We *must* settle all sorts of things. Especially the main question — the publication of the 4th volume. Of course to give Karl a royalty, such as Moore and Edward get for the 1st Vol., would be simple enough. But Karl will have to do more than translate, and he will have to give all, or nearly all his time to the work. And he, meantime, must live — and can't do that on future royalties. So any publisher *must* advance so much a month or week to Karl; the expenses being afterwards set off against profits, and the general division of such profits. I have not written definitely to Meissner because (1) I did not know what the terms of agreement with him were, and did not want him to suspect this ignorance; (2) because I was informed Dietz meant to see Meissner and arrange with him to bring out the 4th Vol., and as a divided publishing would do us all harm, buy up the first three volumes. But although we gathered from the letters that Dietz was to start *at once* for Hamburg, he has not done so, and now I hear he is *"nervös"*; and has to go in for a cure. So Heaven knows when we shall settle things. I think you and I will, after all, have to do that, and I'm not sure that going to Hamburg would not be the easiest way, when all is said and done. Gine Bernstein has just returned from a visit to her mother in Berlin, and she tells me poor old Library is *very* sore at the General ignoring him so absolutely in his will. He says (openly) it is because he has not like Adler and Bebel "mitgeliebt."[2]

Next as to Edward and the S.D.F. In answer to the letter sent round generally we had such replies that Hyndman *could* not hold out. As a matter of fact he was really taken in (this time) by the Freebooters,[3] who made him believe the poor old General was *longing* to meet him — Hyndman — and that we prevented it. In the face of the excellent letters from *all* the Continental people — including (and their letters were the strongest, because written before consultation with the Freebooters) Bebel and Adler, and of course Liebknecht, the Executive of the S.D.F. on Tuesday *unanimously* withdrew their statement; everyone shook hands, and the Freebooters have thus *unwillingly* helped to bring about a very useful "reconciliation" between us and the S.D.F. For years we have (to the General's distress) been on good terms with the S.D.F. *members*. Now we are *officially* to work together. You know what such "official" friendships mean — Edward and Hyndman no more love one another than do Paul and Brousse — but it is useful for the movement, and especially for the forthcoming Congress. I mentioned the Printers because I was asked to do so — and these "side" Congresses of Trade Unions have been very useful: witness the Glass-workers, shoe-makers, etc. Liebknecht comes over for three weeks in May. On the 15th he comes. On the 16th he speaks in London (the whole tour is arranged by the "Zürich Committee" of the Congress); then he goes to Southampton, Bristol . . . [letter incomplete]

1. Eleanor had sent this to Laura to translate into French and to Kautsky to translate into German. Kautsky used it as an excuse to postpone his visit to London.
2. i.e., Liebknecht was not "enamoured" with Engels, as Adler and Bebel were.
3. The Freybergers.

The fourth Congress of the Second International opened at Queen's Hall, Langham Place, London, on 27 July 1896. A wide range of socialist organizations in Britain was represented, including the SDF, the ILP, the Fabian Society and the trade unions. Among the French delegates were Lafargue, Guesde, Jaurès and Jean Longuet, who was now twenty.

Much of the Congress was spent in rowdy debate between the Anarchist, anti-parliamentary factions which the Zurich Congress had voted to exclude, and those who believed in socialist representation in Parliament. Eleanor participated as a translator and as a delegate for the Gasworkers' Union.

104. Laura to Eleanor

Draveil, S[eine] et O[ise]
1 September 1896

My dear Tussy,
Enclosed you will find Meissner's account with my acknowledgment.

I was delighted to get so long a letter, having made up my mind to wait patiently for news of you until the end of September — and agreeably surprised by the bigness of the sum remitted.

I have had the house full of people for the last few days or I should have earlier acknowledged receipt of your letter and enclosure.

I don't know whether you are at Deal or in the Den — a *crystal Den* it must be, what with gas and electricity, that would make us villagers stare.

In a former letter I inquired whether you purposed leaving town this year, with the intention of asking you to come to Draveil and have a look at our garden while it is still all green and gold. But the first I heard of your departure was by your postcard dated from the Scilly Isles — that may be all that's wonderful, but Draveil is well too.

I fancy you must be glad to be well rid of your cosmopolitan beasts — the tame ones and the wild ones, but your girl will be finding the house dull after all the excitement of Congress time.

Edward's letter, since it provoked *le saint père* to fork out 50 frs.,[1] must have been a fine bit of literature and diplomacy. We have neither seen nor heard from any member of that unholy family for this long while. Dormoy's little girl, Jeanne, a nice child between ten and eleven, is spending her holidays with us and makes me think regretfully of poor Mémé, who will be fourteen in a week or so and who continues to live *"comme l'oiseau sur la branche."*[2] Mémé's sweetness of disposition, albeit she is not very affectionate, endears her to everybody and makes her a very loveble companion.

As to the *Devenir Social*,[3] its abstention from politics is not its fault but its misfortune. It is bound to be theoretical or nothing or it would cease to get itself printed and published by Grand and Brière and consequently lose all chance of getting bought and read.

Jeanne Dormoy is here for the whole of the holidays, so that I cannot leave Draveil; her little brother, Marx, is to join her later on.[4] Our presence during the winding up business is unnecessary, but I am wanting to see you for numberless other reasons and shall be ready and willing to vacate the Castle as soon as may be.

I have got a very bad headache which makes me feel quite unreasonably idiotic, so that with a kiss apiece I will bid you farewell.

Your LAURA

Paul is sending M.'s account together with M.S.

1. Longuet.
2. "an unsettled life," lit., "like the bird on the branch."
3. *Revue internationale d'économie, d'histoire et de philosophie* (1895–98), a Marxist journal which published articles by Marx and Engels.
4. Children of the militant socialist Jean Dormoy. Marx Dormoy later became Minister of the Interior in Léon Blum's Popular Front government, was interned by the Vichy government and killed in 1941.

105. Eleanor to Laura

The Chancery Lane Safe Deposit.
61 & 62, Chancery Lane,
London, W.C.
2 January 1897

My dear Laura,

First of all a Happy New Year and I hope it'll still be happy when it grows into an old Year.

I am writing, as you will see, from Chancery Lane, whither I have brought a mass of sorted letters — and whence I am taking a fresh lot. We are beginning now to make some headway with the letters, and this brings us to the important question of what is to be done next, and the even more important question of Mohr's letters to Engels. These are, of course, in the possession of Bebel and Bernstein — and in the keeping of the Mottelers. We have appealed to everyone who has letters of Mohr to send these to us (there has not been much response; and we must soon write *personally* to Sorge and Kugelmann who must have a very large number of letters). But the most important letters *by far* are those to Engels, and in preparing the necessary documents for a biography[1] *we* must have access to these letters. This is the more imperative that Bernstein has undertaken to write for an English publisher a "Life of Engels"; it is already being advertised — and he told me he was going to write to Bebel about the Marx-Engels letters to which *he* desires access. This he can't have without Bebel's consent. There is a double lock to the box at Motteler's; one key Ede has — the other the female Freebooter as Bebel's representative. Ede won't ask Louise to go to the Mottelers with him to get the letters and hence he is postponing Engels's life. Meantime *I* think (I have said nothing of this to Ede, as I must, of course, arrange with you first) *we* should at once write *officially* to Sorge, Kugelmann, Liebknecht, *Bebel and Bernstein* to give us either the original letters — to be returned — or copies of any letters of Marx. I need not insist upon the necessity for this: you will see how essential it is. All the same we need to talk this — and many other matters — over, and I *do* wish you would, if you were well enough, come over soon. Even if you are not well the change might be good for you. I would go to you if need were, but after all, all the *papers* are here, and to go through them together would be very useful.

In addition to all this comes the fact that in *May* I must — so Crosse and Moore say — give Johnny an a/c of the moneys due to him. Before that I should very much like to consult with you generally about the children. I have a/cs also to send to you — and a very small sum, I fear, I have not yet got it clear — to forward you. But the *Revolution* seems to be going very well. Between its publication and July some four hundred copies were sold. That does not *yet* give us much, but if the sale keeps up it will.

As to the "Eastern Question"[2] there has been no end of trouble. I tried — for Sonnenschein is *such* a thing — to get another publisher: I have tried Methuen, Macmillan, Unwin (the only *likely* ones) and failed. I will make a last effort with Longman. If he fails too, we must go to Sonnenschein. I want the work out. It is so very brilliant. But many of the newspaper extracts *must* be boiled down. Else it will make a volume or volumes *no one* will take. And much *can* be boiled down. Of course it was easier for Mohr to cut a long extract from a paper and send it along than to boil down its contents. But I'm sure that for a *book* he would have boiled down the penny-a-liner. Anyhow we've *got* to or . . . [letter incomplete]

---

1. Eleanor was planning to write a biography of Marx.
2. See p. 281, note 4. Eleanor had also prepared two other works which were published after her death, in 1899: *Story of the Life of Lord Palmerston* and *Secret Diplomatic History of the Eighteenth Century*. In 1898 she published *Value, Price and Profit* with a preface by Aveling, the text of a lecture Marx gave to the Council of the First International in 1865.

106. Eleanor to Laura

Mrs Aveling
The Den,
Jews Walk,
Sydenham,
London.
10 January 1897

My dear Laura,

It was good to get quite a long letter from you — for your letters are not as plentiful as blackberries.

A line today with regard to two matters. First as to Danielson.[1] I did not mention him because I copied all the letters he has of Mohr long ago for the General, who, I believed, returned the originals. The copies I have. Danielson has written once or twice lately (there is no good news of poor Lopatine!) and has just sent me the 3rd Vol. — in Russian. He is anxious to have, as heretofore, the proofs of the next Vol., but I've told him I fear he'll have to wait yet a while for them!

Next the Italian matters. Do you or Paul know anything at all about the would-be translator — I mean about his fitness for the terribly difficult task he wants to undertake? Can he be the same Italian who once wrote to the General, and whom the General would [have] none of because he had no guarantee as to the man's capacity? In *any case* I do not think it advisable to agree to a translation without making enquiries as to the translator. We have plenty of good Italian friends who would gladly make enquiries for us — Ferri, Turati, the Labriolas and a lot of others. I shall at once write to Italy on the subject.

I am surprised we should have heard nothing (nor have I seen it mentioned in the Italian papers, or at any rate, I've not noticed anything) about the translation of Vol. 1. It has to be remembered that the book is copyright, and that the author (or his representative) *and the publisher* can make it unpleasant for the enterprising burglars who burgle literary work. Meissner — if the Vol. is translated from German, and Sonnenschein, if it is translated from the English, could, and no doubt would, at once write to the Italian publisher — I shall make enquiries and then let Meissner or Sonnenschein know about it. I know that quite recently an unauthorized English translation of Mme.

Edgren's Italian book was stopped, and — I am not sure which — either proper arrangements were made, or another publisher got the work.

I don't know if you enclosed a microbe in your letter, but I've certainly got rheumatism — and in my right arm. But it may be this damnable damp weather. The rain it raineth every-day!

Our love to you both. How's all the live stock?

Your
TUSSY

1. Russian translator of the first three volumes of *Capital* (vol. 1 in collaboration with German Alexandrovich Lopatin [Lopatine]).

For the Avelings the year 1897 was chiefly taken up with lecture tours for the SDF and participation in its anti-colonialist campaign (despite his chauvinism, Hyndman was a vigorous opponent of the British role in India). Both wrote for the new SDF monthly, the Social Democrat, and Eleanor took up her "International Notes" in Justice again, reporting on the socialist movement throughout the world.

On 8 June, while Eleanor was acting as interpreter at the eighth Miners' International Congress, Aveling, using his non-de-plume of Alec Nelson, secretly married a twenty-two-year-old aspiring actress, Eva Frye, at Chelsea Register Office. For a time he continued to live with Eleanor, who was well aware that he was occasionally unfaithful and had no reason to suspect that this liaison was any different from the others. In August, Aveling attended the annual conference of the SDF with Eleanor and was elected a member of the executive committee.

But at the end of August he walked out, taking with him everything of value in the house and leaving a note with the address of an intermediary through whom Eleanor could contact him. Eleanor was desperate: not only was Aveling seriously ill, but he had left her in a difficult position financially—he had already spent more than half the money Engels had left her. The truth about his abrupt departure may never be known, though it is conceivable, as Bernstein surmised, that Aveling had asked her to sell one of her father's manuscripts — a request she would certainly have refused.

Eleanor turned to Freddy Demuth and begged him to find Aveling. But on 1 September Aveling returned of his own accord, and they resumed their life together. The only clue we have as to what happened on Aveling's return is in a distressed letter from Eleanor to Freddy, in which she wrote: "I am face to face with a most horrible position: utter ruin — everything, to the last penny, or utter, open disgrace." It seems likely that Eleanor had to "pay Aveling off" in some way, and that he had threatened her with *public exposure unless she did so — perhaps of his liaison with Eva Frye, perhaps of Freddy's true paternity. Aveling may even have been dipping into Party funds, and the ignominy was more than Eleanor could face. Whatever passed between them, Aveling probably extorted a sum of money from Eleanor and promised to break off with Eva.*

The Avelings spent September in Draveil with the Lafargues, but Laura and Eleanor do not appear to have discussed their personal lives: it was only to Freddy that Eleanor confided her feelings. It is interesting to note that in her letters to Freddy Eleanor seemed to regard Aveling's behaviour as a "moral disease" which was quite beyond his control.

In November, although suffering from influenza, Aveling went on a lecture tour with Eleanor in Lancashire. He returned to London with congestion of the lungs; he also had an open abscess, and was in considerable pain.

Meanwhile Eleanor was continuing her socialist activities. She was actively supporting the action of the Amalgamated Society of Engineers, one of the oldest British unions, in their demand for an eight-hour day. The employers responded with a lock-out. This battle, which lasted from July 1897 to mid-January 1898, was a direct confrontation between the unions and the employers' federation. The strikers received wide international support, mainly thanks to Eleanor's efforts, but ultimately gained few concessions.

Eleanor was also much concerned about Bernstein and his increasing tendency toward revisionism. Her old friend Liebknecht ("dear old Library") had been sentenced to four months' imprisonment under the 1897 anti-socialist law, and could do little to stay Bernstein's growing influence within the German party.

107. Eleanor to Laura

The Den,
Jews Walk,
Sydenham,
London.
8 January 1898

My dear Laura,

It is like your thoughtful kindness to send my birthday present in advance of that not over-welcome anniversary. I got your letter too late yesterday to catch our post (5 o'c). It was very welcome, for, as I hardly need tell you, illness means immense expense in every way. Doctors' visits at 5s. a time, and sometimes twice a day, are no joke.

Edward *is* better. Indeed he is working again — though I wish he wouldn't. But I did not exaggerate the danger. The day after I wrote to you the doctor told me Edward might at any moment (his temperature was up to 103 at times) "take a turn for the worse," and that I ought at once to communicate with his relations. Of course I did not, because (except perhaps his sister, now living in Devonshire) there is not a relation he would want to see at any time. I only wished *you* had been a little nearer, and during those anxious hours, I did think Draveil was terribly far from Sydenham. As I have said, Edward is better, but he is still terribly weak and terribly emaciated. He is a very skeleton — mere skin and bones. And so he is not yet out of the wood, and I am still very anxious. The slightest chill would, the doctors say, be absolutely fatal — and Edward is a most unmanageable person — I write freely because he is in bed asleep (thank goodness he *does* sleep well!) and except in letters to *me alone* you must not let him know there is still cause for anxiety. If I can I shall get him off to Hastings away from the awful fogs we are having here.

And now to get away from ourselves. I think we have done the best we could for the "children" — although *all* of them (except Mémé) seem dissatisfied. Edward says (please excuse the language) they all want their bottoms smacked. They *are* a trial to one's patience, I must admit. And Paul's shirts. The enclosed will explain why he has not received them. I should have let you know before, but in all the worry I forgot. Meantime the

Burnley ass does not say *what* the size is — so I can't order here until the Lord of the Manor will let me know the inches of his lordly neck. It is curious that one should have to get *here* the shirts that are made in the north!

I am sending you today's *Chronicle* where you will find news of the strike.[1] Our great (*entre nous* our only hope) is the re-assembling of Parliament. We can hold out, so Barnes positively assures me, easily till then (and Thorne says so too). Then the game will become even more interesting. e.g., Goschen[2] will have to explain why he does not, especially in view of the Far Eastern crisis, insist upon the carrying out of the naval contracts. The employers *cannot* claim indemnity under the "strike-clause" because the men *have never struck*. They are locked out, and the employers admit that they have no quarrel with the men in all cases except some *two or three in London*. They admit it to be a question of standing by *their class*. Since the great 1853 and 1859 strikes (even including the great Dock Strike of 1889) there has been no such movement in England. Unhappily some of our Socialists don't understand, and say it is no "Socialist" movement! The imbeciles! And *never* has there been a movement in England that was so international. The help coming from abroad is magnificent, and at every meeting the "foreign brethren" are cheered to the echo. My only fear is that Germany, which has done so grandly, may slacken now that Liebknecht is not able to publish his capital articles. The *Vorwärts* is falling more and more under Bernstein's influence, and his wet-blanket articles, that no doubt you see both in *Vorwärts* and the *Neue Zeit*, are not exactly useful at the present moment. Assuredly the critical attitude is necessary and useful. But there are times when a little enthusiasm — even if "uncritical" — is of greater value. Bernstein's position is a most unfortunate one for the movement, and one that makes *our* position very difficult. It is impossible to defend his attitude, and I am in daily fear that some one will tell Barnes and that Barnes will insist upon answering Bernstein. Barnes would be sure to get me to help him — and then I should be most awkwardly placed. Unhappily there is no one, now we have not the General, to influence Bernstein, and pull him together. And Bernstein is writing the "Life" of Engels for Fisher Unwin![3] Although he must (I should think) be using the correspondence of Engels and Mohr he has said nothing to me about it. Of course we can't prevent the *use* of the letters, but by the English law not a single letter of Mohr's can be published without *our consent*. The courts have again declared that a letter is the property of the *writer* of the letter and his heirs or executors, *not* of the person to whom the letter is written. Of course I know Bernstein would *never* misuse any letter — but it is as well that we should have the legal control over them. Now dear, goodnight. My thanks to you and a kiss, and a kiss to Paul.

Your

TUSSY

P.S. I was quite shocked yesterday when . . . going to my poulterer I saw *five* guinea-fowls hanging (dead) in a row. I thought of the faithful five,[4] and felt a brute even to buy some fish! Sorry you've had to pay on *Chronicle*. I thought that for France the same rule applied as for England *and Germany* — i.e., that any newspaper (not illustrated papers) were ½d. per paper quite irrespective of weight. It is so for *Germany*.

1. The Engineers' strike. George Barnes was Secretary of the Union.
2. Chancellor of the Exchequer.
3. Bernstein does not seem to have completed this project.
4. Probably an allusion to the Lafargues' menagerie.

Aveling was operated on at University College Hospital in February 1898 and went straight to Margate with Eleanor to convalesce. They returned to Jew's Walk on 27 March.

On 31 March, Eleanor committed suicide by taking prussic acid. She was forty-three.

Two months after Engels's death, on 16 October 1895, Eleanor had drawn up a will in which she bequeathed the rights in her father's work to Jenny's children, and the rest of her belongings to Aveling. A year later, she added a codicil which specified that her author's rights should be bequeathed to Aveling for the rest of his life and should revert to Jenny's children after his death.

When Eleanor died Aveling resigned from the SDF and went to live in Battersea with his legal wife, Eva Frye. Already gravely ill, he died on 2 August 1898, four months after Eleanor.

Eleanor's suicide raised a number of questions about Aveling (see Appendices 4 and 5).

Appendices

Appendix 1

The text of the speech given by Engels at Mrs. Marx's grave, in its original English version. It was published in a German translation in Sozialdemokrat *(8 December 1881) and in French in* L'Egalité *(11 December).*

The noble-hearted woman at whose grave we stand was born in Salzwedel in 1814. Her father, Baron W[estphalen] was soon afterwards appointed R.R. in Trier where he became intimately acquainted with the Marx family. The children of both families grew up together. By the time M[arx] went to the university, he and his future wife knew that their fates would henceforth be inseparable.

In 1843, after Marx had first publicly distinguished himself as editor of the first Rh[einische] Z[ei]t[un]g, and after the suppression of that paper by the Prussian gov[ernmen]t, the marriage took place. From that day she not only followed the fortunes, the labours, the struggles of her husband, she took an active part in them with the highest intelligence and the deepest passion.

The young couple went to Paris, into an exile, first voluntary, soon compulsory. Even in Paris the Prussian government persecuted him. With regret I have to state, that a man like A. V. Humboldt so far demeaned himself as to cooperate in inducing the government of Louis-Philippe to expel M[arx] from France. The family moved to Brussels. The revolution of February ensued. During the troubles caused by this event in Brussels, the Belgian police not only arrested Marx, they must needs throw into prison his wife too, and that without the pretence of a pretext.

The revolutionary effort of 1848 collapsed in the following

year. New exile followed, first again in Paris, then, owing to
great government interferences, in London. And this time it was
real exile with all its bitterness.

The ordinary sufferings of exiles she might have overcome,
though in consequence of these she had to lose three children,
amongst them both her boys. But that all parties governmental
as well as oppositional, feudalist, liberal and so-called democratic, combined into one vast conspiracy against her husband,
heaped upon him the vilest and most baseless calumnies; that
the whole press without exception shut him out, that he stood
helpless and defenceless before antagonists whom he and she
must utterly despise; that hurt her to the life. And that lasted
for years.

But not for ever. By and by the working class of Europe
found itself placed in political conditions which gave it at least
some elbow-room. The Internat[ional] W[or]k[in]g Men's As-
s[ociation] was formed; it drew into the struggle one civilized
country after the other, and in that struggle foremost amongst
the foremost, fought her husband. Then a time began for her
which made up for many past sufferings. She lived to see the
base slanders heaped up around her husband fly away as chaff
before the wind; she lived to hear the doctrines of her husband,
to stifle which the reactionists of all countries, feudalists as well
as so-called democrats, had spent all their efforts, she lived to
hear them proclaimed openly and victoriously in all civilized
countries and all civilized languages.

She lived to see the revolutionary movement of the prole-
tariat seize one country after another and raise its head, conscious of victory, from Russia to America. And one of her last
joys, on her deathbed, was the splendid proof of an irrepres-
sible life, in spite of all repressive laws, which the German
work[in]g class gave at the late elections.

What such a woman with such clear and critical intellect,
with such political tact, with such passionate surges of character, with such capacity for self-sacrifice, has done in the revolutionary movement, that has not been pushed forward into publicity, that is not registered in the columns of the periodical
press. That is only known to those who lived near her. But that
I know, we shall often miss her bold and prudent counsels, bold
without brag, prudent without sacrifice of honor.

Of her personal qualities I need not speak. Her friends

know them and will never forget them. If ever woman found her highest happiness in rend[er]ing others happy, that woman was she.

The place where we stand is the best proof that she lived and died in the full conviction of atheist materialism. Death had no horrors for her. She knew that one day she would have to return, body and mind, to the bosom of that nature from which she had sprung. And we, who now have laid her on her last resting-place, let us keep her memory and try to be like her.

Appendix 2

August Bebel to Eleanor*

Berlin, W., 20 September 1894
. . . Whatever you think of Freyberger, I think you do him an injustice and misjudge *him and his attitude.* You can be sure that Louise will never do or tolerate anything at all harmful to your interests or to your position regarding the Gen[eral]; on the other hand, it is completely impossible and unthinkable that he would do anything against you or L[aura].

I think that if you are the slightest bit doubtful about the arrangements the Gen[eral] is making for the future, it would be best for you to ask for information yourself, which he will give you without delay. One thing I am sure of is that the organization of the literary heritage is in hands *which you can trust completely.* Your views have obviously had an effect on Liebknecht, which I regret, but which was natural enough given the relationship between the Gen[eral] and Liebknecht, which you know as well as I.

I am not revealing any secrets to you if I add that a great part of my time during my stay in London last year was spent in going through the papers of the Gen[eral] and your father, from which I hoped to glean some material of use to the history of the Party. I found relatively little, most of it being unsuitable for publication. That all this material is now in *good* order is due entirely to Louise, who carried out this work skilfully. But for her, everything would still be in the most beautiful disorder to this day. I am writing to you at such length because I would like your relationship with Louise to be once again as it was of old.

With best wishes, Your
AUGUST

* Translated from the German by Priscilla Barlow.

Appendix 3

Louise Freyberger to Eleanor*

5 August [1895]

Dear Tussy,
The dear old General fell asleep peacefully and without suffering at 10.30 today.

I left the room to change for the night-watch, was away five minutes, and when I came back all was over.

Your

LOUISE

* Translated from the German by Priscilla Barlow.

After Eleanor's death some of her friends, who had concealed the full extent of their dislike for Aveling out of deference to her, were vociferous in their denunciation of his character and his possible collusion in her suicide. There was some talk of bringing him to trial, but there was insufficient material evidence.

Liebknecht, who was released from prison on 18 March, refused to consider that Aveling might have been in some way responsible. Bernstein, however, took a very different attitude. Making use of letters which Freddy Demuth had received from Eleanor during the months before her death, he published an article entitled "Was Eleanor Marx zum Tode trieb" ("What drove Eleanor Marx to her death") in the Neue Zeit *of 21 July 1898. It was published in English in the 30 July issue of* Justice.

Appendix 5 presents part of a letter which Bernstein sent to Laura after Eleanor's death, in which he gives rein to his suspicions and to his hatred of Aveling.

Appendix 4

Liebknecht to Laura
(in French)

9 April 1898

My dear Laura,

But these are terrible things, that people are saying about Aveling. I cannot believe it all, and I wait anxiously for news from you and Paul. In any case, it was cowardice to say that Tussy might have had a morbid tendency toward *suicide*. It *is not true*. Even a few hours before her act of despair she was thinking of work in memory of her father, as shown by her letter to *Reynolds Newspaper*.[1]

Paul is back; I know, that he knows everything.

Write to me straight away, if I can be useful to you, and how. I am ready *for anything*. And now I could go to London or some other place, if it is necessary. I will do for you all that you ask of me.

But a trial against Aveling, as *Bernstein* wishes, does not seem to me to be very reasonable.

I await your news and I am at your disposal.

All the best to you and Paul. *Grüsse* [greetings] from us all.

Your

LIBRARY

---

1. In the edition of 3 April, in the column headed "Socialism," Eleanor had requested readers possessing the May/June 1865 issues of the *Eastern Post* to lend them to her. She was preparing an edition of the address read by Marx to the IWMA Council on 20 June 1865 and the *Eastern Post* had carried reports of the Council proceedings. A full obituary of Eleanor appeared in the same edition of *Reynolds Newspaper*.

Appendix 5

Bernstein to Laura

(extracts)

April 1898

. . . Of the rogue I have lately had little information. He is, however, not yet in New Zealand but enjoys life in London. He has been seen by an acquaintance of Motteler with a woman in a fashionable restaurant feasting and joking. And there is no doubt that he lives with a woman. I don't know if I told you at the time that a rumour went [round] here that Aveling had at [sic] Tussy['s] life-time secretly contracted a *legal* marriage, and that the news of this drove Tussy into death. The matter seemed to me incredible, but there are things which otherwise inexplainable, could by it be explained. Only some weeks ago I heard the following thing, and this *not as a gossiping talk* but by a man who very reluctantly started with his tale at all and then only told it to me alone (he knew your father and Engels very well, and also Tussy).

The man has a son of very sober habits who in November last went to Newcastle. At the starting station he was introduced to Aveling who also went to the North. When the young man returned he spoke to his father with words of utter contempt about Av[eling]. Called to account for this he told his father that Aveling had a woman with him on the journey, that he told it to him [sic] (the young man) adding that *Tussy was not his legal wife!*

Now this was in November last, a few months, nay weeks since the journey to Paris, which as far as we can judge was a kind of reconciliation journey after the cruel affair of the end of August, resp[ecting] the beginning of September. Why the rogue had returned to Tussy at all we can only suspect, but for me it is sure that it was her money . . . [letter incomplete]

List of Names

ADAM, Juliette, née Lambert (1836–1936)
Influential French writer and journalist, friend of Gambetta's, whose *salon* was an important meeting-place for republicans.

ADLER, Viktor (1852–1918)
Viennese doctor. Founder of the Austrian Social-Democratic Party; editor of the *Arbeiter Zeitung*. Corresponded with Engels from 1889 to 1895; was later one of the leaders of the Second International.

ALLEMANE, Jean (1843–1935)
Typographer. Communard, deported from France; after Amnesty joined the French Workers' Party (FWP). Supported the Possibilists after 1882, broke with them in 1890. Founded the Revolutionary Socialist Workers' Party and edited *Le Parti Ouvrier*, its organ.

ALLSOP, Thomas (1795–1880)
British Chartist, friend of Marx's; supported Communard refugees.

ARNDT, Paul
Paris correspondent of *Vorwärts*, German Social Democrat.

BAKUNIN, Mikhail Alexandrovich (1814–76)
Russian Anarchist, enemy of Marxism, expelled from the International at the 1872 Hague Congress.

BANCEL, Baptiste (1822–71)
French journalist and political thinker, radical bourgeois. Exiled after *coup d'état* of 2 December 1851. From 1869, member of Legislative Body. Masonic candidate.

BANNER, Robert (1855–1910)
British bookbinder, member of the SDF, then of the Socialist League. Later joined the Fabian Society.

BASTELICA, André Augustin (1845–84)
Typographer, organized the Marseilles section of the International at the end of the Second Empire. Member of the first Marseilles commune. Flirted with Bakuninism. Fled to Switzerland after fall of Commune.

BAX, Ernest Belfort (1854–1926)
British historian, philosopher and journalist, friend of Engels. One of the first disseminators of Marxist ideas in Britain. Active member of the left wing of the SDF. Co-founder of the Socialist League (1884).

BAZAINE, Achille François (1811–88)
Ff French field-marshal, monarchist. Commanded the Third Army
Corps during the war of 1870, then the Rhine Army. Surrendered at
Metz in October 1870.

BEALES, Edmond (1803–81)
British jurist. President of the British National League for the Independence of Poland, a leader of the Emancipation Society, President
of the Reform League 1865–69.

BEBEL, August (1840–1913)
Founder, with Liebknecht, of the Eisenach Marxist Workers' Party
in 1869. One of the leading organizers of the German Social-Democratic Party. Friend of Marx and Engels.

BEESLY, Edward Spencer (1831–1915)
Professor of history at University College, London. Positivist and
member of the Reform League. Presided at the inaugural meeting of
the First International, September 1864.

BERNSTEIN, Eduard (1850–1932)
Member of the German Social-Democratic Party; editor-in-chief of
Sozialdemokrat, published first in Zurich, then in London. Friend of
Marx and Engels; became revisionist after 1898.

BESANT, Annie (1847–1933)
Worked with Charles Bradlaugh 1874–88. Member of National Secularist Society, Fabian Society and the SDF; active in unionization of
unskilled workers. Later became theosophist and went to India.

BEUST, Friedrich von (1817–99)
Engels's cousin by marriage; lived in Zurich.

BISMARCK, Prince Otto von (1815–98)
Prussian statesman and diplomat, President of Prussian Cabinet
1862–71, Chancellor of the German Empire 1871–90.

BLANC, Louis (1811–82)
French Socialist leader, historian and journalist, Republican Demo-
crat, member of the provisional government of 1848. Emigrated to
England. Elected Deputy in 1871; hostile to the Commune.

BLANQUI, Auguste (1805–81)
French socialist and revolutionary who believed in insurrection of
small militant minorities. He founded numerous secret societies and
organizations. Spent most of his life in prison.

BONNIER, Charles (1863–?)
French socialist, writer and journalist. Member of the French Workers' Party, but lived mainly in England. Active in preparations for
1889 and 1891 Congresses.

BOULANGER, Georges (1837–91)
French general, fought against the Commune. Minister of War 1886–87. Very popular in France. Elected Deputy in 1889, on a platform of constitutional reform. Indicted before the High Court by Republicans. Fled to Belgium, where he committed suicide on the grave of his mistress.

BOULÉ
Socialist and trade unionist. Candidate for the 1885 Paris elections; stood against Boulanger. One of the organizers of the 1889 Congress.

BRADLAUGH, Charles (1833–91)
British freethinker, editor of the *National Reformer*. Elected MP for Northampton 1880 but refused to swear oath on the Bible. Took seat in 1886. After the Commune, turned against Marx and the IWMA.

BRENTANO, Lujo (1844–1931)
German liberal economist and university lecturer who attacked Marx's economic theories.

BRIGHT, John (1811–89)
One of the founders of Anti-Corn Law League, advocate of Free Trade and electoral reform. Member of several Liberal Cabinets.

BROUSSE, Paul (1844–1912)
French physician, one of founders of French Workers' Party. At the 1882 Saint-Etienne Congress provoked the split in the party and became one of the leaders of the Possibilists or Broussists.

BURGESS, Joseph (1853–?)
British trade unionist. Edited the *Workman's Times* 1891–94. Co-founder of the Independent Labour Party 1893.

BURNS, John (1858–1943)
Engineer. One of the leaders of the New Union movement, helped organize the 1889 dockers' strike. Became MP in 1892 and member of Liberal Cabinet 1905–1914.

CARTER, James
Member of the Reform League, of the General Council of the IWMA and corresponding secretary for Spain.

CASSAGNAC, Paul Granier de (1843–1904)
Bonapartist, duellist, editor-in-chief of *Le Pays*. Founded *L'Autorité* in 1886 and supported Boulanger.

CATHELINEAU, Henri de (1813–1904)
Royalist. In 1870 obtained permission from the Tours delegation to form a group of volunteers in the Vendée. Became a brigadier-general and turned against the Commune.

CHAMPION, Henry Hyde (1859–1928)
> Ex-army officer, resigned his commission in protest at the war in Egypt. Became Assistant Secretary of the Democratic Foundation. Founded the *Labour Elector* in 1888. Emigrated to Australia in 1893.

CHANZY, Alfred (1823–83)
> Commander of the Second Army of the Loire in the war of 1870. Became Governor of Algeria in 1873.

CLEMENCEAU, Georges (1841–1929)
> Mayor of the 18th arrondissement in Paris at the beginning of the Commune. Radical Deputy, editor of *La Justice*. Briefly supported Boulanger. Later became Premier.

CLUSERET, Gustave (1823–1900)
> Dismissed from the French army for taking part in the campaign for Italian independence with Garibaldi (1860) and for serving in the Union Army in the American Civil War (1862). Bakuninist, member of the IWMA, took part in the uprisings in Lyons and Marseilles. Member of the Commune. Imprisoned 30 April 1871 after the fall of the fort of Ivry; acquitted 21 May.

CONNOLLY, Thomas
> Leader of the stonemasons' union in the 1860s. Delegate at the 1889 International Congress.

CRÉMIEUX, Adolphe (1796–1880)
> French lawyer and statesman, played prominent part in Revolution of 1848; responsible for 1870 law which enfranchised Jews of Algeria. Minister of Justice in the Government of National Defence.

CUNNINGHAME GRAHAM, Robert (1852–1936)
> Scottish writer, aristocrat, socialist. MP 1886–92. Delegate at the 1889 International Congress. Worked with John Burns and Keir Hardie.

CUNO, Theodor (1847–1934)
> Engineer, German Social-Democratc journalist. Helped organize the Milan branch of the IWMA. Emigrated to the U.S.A. in 1878 where he became one of the leaders of the "Knights of Labor" and was involved in the *New Yorker Volkszeitung*.

DĄBROWSKI, Jarosław (1836–71)
> Polish officer involved in the 1863 insurrection in Poland. Fled to France, took part in the Commune. On 29 April 1871 appointed Commander of the Paris right bank forces; was mortally wounded on 23 May.

DANIELSON, Nikolai Frantsevich (1844–1918)
> Economist, Russian translator of *Capital*.

DELCLUZE, Alfred (1857–1923)
> Founder of the Calais Workers' Party. Delegate at the 1889, 1891 and 1893 Congresses, later joined the Independent Socialists.

DELESCLUZE, Charles (1809–71)
Jacobin, member of secret Republican societies, Commander-in-chief of Commune after death of Dąbrowski. Killed at the barricades.

DEMUTH, Helen (Nim, Nym, Nimmie, Nymmy, Lenchen) (1823–90)
Servant and faithful friend of the Marx family; moved in with Engels after Marx's death in 1883. Mother of Marx's son Freddy.

DISRAELI, Benjamin, Earl of Beaconsfield (1804–81)
English statesman and writer, MP 1837–80, leader of the Conservative Party, Prime Minister 1868 and 1874–80.

DORMOY, Jean (1851–98)
Metalworker. Follower of Jules Guesde. Town councillor in 1888, later mayor of Montluçon.

DUPONT, Eugène (1831–82)
Musical instrument maker, member of the General Council of the IWMA, President of the 1867 Lausanne Congress, corresponding secretary for France and Belgium. Member of the Commune.

DURUY, Victor (1811–94)
French historian and minister in the Second Empire, initiator of important education reforms.

ECCARIUS, Johann Georg (1818–94)
German tailor, member of the Communist League. Emigrated to London, became Secretary of the General Council of the IWMA. Delegate at all the congresses and conferences of the IWMA until 1872. Took part in the British trade union movement.

FAVRE, Jules (1809–80)
Lawyer and French politician. Republican, opposed to the Second Empire. Minister of Foreign Affairs of the National Defence and Thiers's government. Strongly opposed to the Commune. One of the first to attack the IWMA.

FERRY, Jules François Camille (1832–93)
French lawyer and statesman, elected Deputy for Paris 1869. Member of the Government of National Defence, one of the leaders of the moderate republicans. Mayor of Paris 1870–71, suppressed Commune. Chairman of Council of Ministers 1880–81 and 1883–85. Assassinated.

FISCHER, Richard (1855–1926)
Secretary of the German Social-Democratic Party, then Deputy to the Reichstag. Contributed to the *Sozialdemokrat*.

FLOURENS, Gustave (1838–71)
French ethnographer and physiologist, one of the leaders of the Commune. Fled to England in 1870; frequented the Marx household. Returned to France after the proclamation of the Third Republic. Assassinated at Châtou 3 April 1871.

Fox, Peter (?–1869)
Journalist. One of the leaders of the British League for the Independence of Poland. Participated in the foundation of the IWMA, member of the General Council, member of the executive of the Reform League.

FRANK, A.
Paris publisher, published *The Poverty of Philosophy* in 1847. Sold his business to Vieweg in 1865.

FREILIGRATH, Ferdinand (1810–76)
German poet, old friend of Marx's contributed to *Neue Rheinische Zeitung*. Member of the Communist League. Emigrated to London in 1851.

FREYBERGER, Ludwig (1865–1934)
Austrian physician, married Louise Kautsky in 1894.

FURNIVALL, Frederick James (1825–1910)
Founded the Early English Texts Society in 1864, as well as numerous other literary societies over the next twenty years. One of the editors of the Oxford *New English Dictionary*.

GAMBETTA, Léon (1838–82)
French lawyer and Republican statesman, Minister of the Interior in the Government of National Defence, joined the Tours delegation 7 October 1870 and organized the defence of the provinces. Resigned after the surrender, President of the Chamber of Deputies 1879–81, Premier 1881–82.

GELY, André
Paris town councillor. Militant trade unionist who joined the FWP after the 1879 Marseilles Congress. Later became Possibilist. Editor of *Le Prolétaire*.

GIRARDIN, Emile de (1802–81)
Conservative Deputy under the Restoration, became Republican in 1877. Editor of *La Presse*.

GLADSTONE, William Ewart (1809–98)
Leader of the Liberal Party, Disraeli's chief political adversary. Prime Minister 1868–74, 1880–85, 1886, and 1892–94.

GLAIS-BIZOIN, Alexandre (1800–77)
French lawyer, opposed to the Empire, elected in Paris November 1869. Member of the Government of National Defence, and of the Tours delegation.

GREULICH, Hermann (1842–1925)
Leader of the Zurich section of the International 1867; one of the founders of the Swiss Social-Democratic Party and leader of its right wing.

GUESDE, Jules (pseudonym of Mathieu Basile) (1845–1922)
Founder, with Paul Lafargue, of the French Workers' Party (1879). With Lafargue, the outstanding champion of Marxism in France. Became Deputy for Roubaix in 1893.

GUMPERT, Eduard (?–1893)
German physician, Manchester friend of Marx and Engels.

HARDIE, James Keir (1856–1915)
Miner and militant Scottish trade unionist. Founder and leader of the Independent Labour Party (1893) and editor of its journal *The Labour Leader*. Elected MP for West Ham South in 1892.

HELMHOLTZ, Hermann von (1821–94)
Famous German physicist, anatomist and physiologist.

HIRSCH, Carl (1841–1900)
German Social-Democratic journalist. Emigrated to Paris in 1874, was expelled, and moved first to Belgium, then, in 1879, to London, where he frequented the Marx house. Moved back to Paris in 1880.

HOWELL, George (1833–1910)
Builder, member of the TUC parliamentary committee. Member of the International from 1864–71, and of the Reform League 1865–69. MP 1885–95.

HUGHES, Thomas (1823–96)
Author of *Tom Brown's School Days* and other books. Christian Socialist, member of the steering committee of the *Workman's Advocate*, MP 1865–74.

HUMBERT, Alphonse (1846–after 1922)
French politician and Blanquist contributor to *Le Père Duchêne*. Exiled after Commune, amnestied in 1879. Municipal Councillor (1886), Deputy (1893).

HYNDMAN, Henry Mayers (1842–1921)
One of the first proponents of Marxism in England but hostile to the Marx-Engels faction. Founded the Democratic Federation in 1881, which became, in 1884, the Social Democratic Federation. Editor of its organ *Justice*.

JACLARD, Charles Victor (1843–1903)
Member of the International to 1868. Fought in the Commune, fled to Switzerland and Russia. Returned to France after amnesty.

JACQUES, Edouard (1828–1900)
French schoolteacher, moderate Republican. Member of Paris town council in 1871, elected Deputy against Boulanger in 1889.

JOHANNARD, Jules (1843–92)
Member of the General Council of the International from 1868–69 and 1871–72. Fought in the Commune and emigrated to England. Took part in the 1872 Hague Congress where he voted for the exclusion of Bakunin.

JOLLYMEIER: *see* Schorlemmer

JONES, Ernest (1819–69)
British Chartist, contributor to the *Northern Star*, supporter and friend of Marx's.

JOYNES, James (1853–93)
British schoolteacher and journalist, leading member of SDF. Founder of *To-Day*, contributor to *Justice* and *Commonweal*.

JUNG, Hermann (1830–93)
German watchmaker, emigrated to London after the 1848 Revolution. Member of the General Council of the International. Marx supporter until 1871, then joined the reformist wing of the trade union movement.

KAUB, Karl
German worker. Member of the General Council of the International. Emigrated to London, then to Paris in 1865.

KAUTSKY, Karl (1854–1938)
Austrian socialist, friend of Engels. Lived in London 1885–90. Published *Die Neue Zeit*, organ of the Social-Democratic Party, in Vienna; later developed opportunist tendencies. Contributed to the dissemination of Marxism.

KAUTSKY, Louise, née STRASSER, later FREYBERGER (1860–1950)
First wife of Karl Kautsky, who divorced her in 1889. Married Freyberger in 1894. Became Engels's secretary and housekeeper.

KELLER, Charles (1843–1913)
French socialist, member of the International. Translated part of vol. 1 of *Capital*. Took part in the Commune and later fled to Switzerland.

KOVALEVSKY (Kowalewski), Maxim Maximovich (1851–1916)
Russian sociologist, historian, jurist, ethnographer. Author of a number of works on the origins of the family and property.

KROPOTKIN, Prince Peter Alexeevich (1842–1921)
Russian geographer and Anarchist who, after his arrest in Russia, escaped to England and then Switzerland. Member of the Jurassian Federation. Returned to Russia after the 1917 Revolution.

KUGELMANN, Ludwig (1828–1902)
German physician, friend of Marx and Engels. Took part in the 1848 Revolution. Active member of the International in Hanover; delegate at the 1867 Congress in Lausanne and 1872 in Geneva. Had important correspondence with Marx between 1862 and 1872.

LABRIOLA, Antonio (1843–1904)
Italian publicist and philosopher. One of the first proponents of Marxism in Italy. Delegate at the 1893 Congress. Corresponded with Engels.

LASSALLE, Ferdinand (1825–64)
One of the founders of German socialism. Took part in the 1848 Revolution. Corresponded with Marx until 1862. Originated opportunist trend in German working-class movement. Killed in a duel.

LAURIER, Clément (1832–78)
French lawyer and political activist close to Gambetta. General Director of the Ministry of the Interior.

LAVROV, Peter Lavrovich (1823–1900)
Russian socialist and sociologist, member of the International. Fled to Geneva in 1870 to escape deportation; moved to Paris in 1877, where he worked as a journalist.

LAVY, Aimé (1850–1898)
Possibilist; Paris Deputy 1890–98.

LE DORÉ, Constant Eugène (1840–81)
Clerk at the port of Brest. Founded the Brest section of the International September 1869. In October 1870 was sentenced to two years' imprisonment for an attempted takeover of the town hall in Brest but was reprieved.

LE LUBEZ, Victor (1834–?)
French socialist. Emigrated to London. Founder member of the International and of its General Council 1864–66, when he was excluded from the Geneva Congress, accused of slander and intrigue.

LESSNER, Friedrich (1825–1910)
German tailor, friend and companion of Marx and Engels. Member of the Communist League. Emigrated to London in 1856. Member of the General Council of the International.

LIEBKNECHT, Wilhelm (Library) (1826–1900)
With Bebel, co-founder of German Social-Democratic Party. Fled to Switzerland in 1849, then to London. Returned to Germany in 1862; published *Volksstaat* and *Vorwärts*. Deputy to the Reichstag 1879–92. Close friend of Marx and Engels.

LISSAGARAY, Hippolyte Prosper Olivier (1838–1901)
Writer and journalist. Took part in the Commune, then fled to London. After the Amnesty returned to France and founded *La Bataille*. Anti-Boulangist. His *Histoire de la Commune de 1871*, which remains one of the most important accounts, was translated into English by Eleanor Marx.

LOPATIN, German Alexandrovich (1845–1918)
Russian revolutionary, friend of Marx and Engels. Member of the General Council of the International. Translated a large part of vol. 1 of *Capital* into Russian.

MAC-MAHON, Patrice de (1808–93)
French socialist, member of the International and of the Commune. 1870. Commander of the Versaillist army during the Commune, President of the Republic from 1873–89.

MALON, Benoît (1841–93)

French socialist, member of the International and of the Commune. After the Amnesty joined the Workers' Party. In 1880–81 joined Brousse in opposing the Marxists and for a time was a leading Possibilist. Founded *La Revue Socialiste* in 1885.

MANN, Thomas (1856–1941)

Metalworker. Member of the left wing of the SDF, then of the ILP, from 1893. One of the founders of New Unionism, and organizer of strike action. Joined the British Communist Party after World War I.

MASSARD, Emile (1857–1932)

French socialist journalist, member of the French Workers' Party, on the editorial staff of *Citoyen*. Left the party towards the end of the 1880s, later supported Boulanger.

MASSINGHAM, Henry (1860–1924)

Liberal editor of the *Star* (1890), *Labour World* (1891) and the *Daily Chronicle*.

MEHRING, Franz (1846–1919)

Important German historian and publicist, author of a history of German social democracy and a biography of Marx.

MEISSNER, Otto Karl (1819–1902)

Hamburg publisher of *Capital* and *The 18th Brumaire* as well as works by Engels.

MENDELSON, Stanislaw (1857–1913)

One of the founders of the Polish Socialist party. Delegate at the 1888 and 1891 International Congresses.

MESA, José (1840–1904)

Member of the International. One of the first proponents of Marxism in Spain, friend of Paul Lafargue's, one of the founders of the Spanish Workers' Party. Translated several of Marx's and Engels's works into Spanish, including *The Poverty of Philosophy*.

MILLIÈRE, Jean-Baptiste (1817–71)

French lawyer, journalist, administrator of *La Marseillaise*. Took part in the defence of Paris during the war of 1870. Elected Deputy to the Seine at the National Assembly, voted to carry on the war. Upheld the Commune at the Versailles Assembly, but did not take part in the fighting. Arrested on the orders of General de Cissey, shot 26 May 1871.

MINK, Paule (1840–1901)

French journalist and speaker of Polish origin. Supporter of the Commune, she escaped to Switzerland where she came under Bakunin's influence. After the Amnesty gave socialist propaganda tours in France.

MOILIN, Jules Antoine (1832–71)
French socialist, physician and journalist. Took part in the Commune and was shot by the Versaillists. One of Paul Lafargue's professors of medicine.

MOORE, Sam (1830–1912)
English lawyer; friend of Engels, and executor of his will. Co-translator of *The Communist Manifesto* and *Capital* into English. Member of the First International.

MORRIS, William (1834–96)
Poet, writer, artist and socialist. Member of the SDF until 1884. Founded the Socialist League, but left it in 1890 when it fell under Anarchist influence. Co-editor of *Commonweal*.

MOST, Johann (1846–1906)
Bookbinder; German Social-Democratic journalist, later Anarchist. Member of the Reichstag from 1874–78, editor of the *Berliner Freie Presse*. Expelled from Berlin in 1878, emigrated to London, where he edited *Freiheit* from 1879. Expelled from the German party in 1880; emigrated to the U.S.A. where he continued his Anarchist propaganda.

MOTTELER, Julius (1838–1907)
German Social-Democrat. Edited *Sozialdemokrat* from Switzerland and organized its undercover distribution in Germany. Expelled in 1888, moved to London, where he lived till 1901.

MURRAY, James
Former chartist, member of the IWMA and the Democratic Federation, supporter of the Commune.

MURRAY, Sir James Augustus Henry (1837–1915)
With Furnivall, one of the editors of the Oxford *New English Dictionary*.

NIEUWENHUIS, Ferdinand Domela (1846–1919)
One of the founders of the Dutch Socialist party; opposed Liebknecht; later became Anarchist.

NOIR, Victor (1848–70)
French Republican journalist, contributor to *La Marseillaise*. Assassinated 10 January 1870 by Prince Pierre Bonaparte.

ODGER, George (1820–77)
Shoemaker, one of the founders of the London Trades Council. Member of the British National League for the Independence of Poland. Took part in the inaugural session of the International; member of its General Council 1864–71. Member of the executive of the Reform League. In 1871 spoke out against the Commune and the General Council's statement. Left the General Council, which had condemned his attitude.

OKECKI, Alexandre
French socialist, manager of the weekly *L'Autonomie*, treasurer of Boulé's electoral committee. Delegate at the 1891 Congress.

OLLIVIER, Emile (1825–1913)
Republican. Liberal Minister under the Second Empire. President of the Council from January to August, 1870.

PAEPE, César de (1842–90)
Typographer, member of the IWMA, one of the founders of the Belgian Workers' Party.

PALIKAO, Charles Cousin-Montauban, Comte de Palikao (1796–1878)
French general, Prime Minister and Minister of War when the Republic was proclaimed in September 1870.

PARNELL, William
Carpenter, militant unionist. Secretary of the Labour Electoral Association. Delegate at the 1891 Congress.

PELLETAN, Pierre Eugène (1813–84)
Journalist and Republican. Member of the Legislative Body and of the National Defence Government, 1871.

PIETRI, Joseph-Marie (1820–1902)
Prefect of Police under Napoleon III. Brutally suppressed Republican demonstrations, especially during the funeral of Victor Noir.

PRIM Y PRATS, Juan (1814–70)
Spanish general, Minister of War in the provisional government of 1868. Crushed Republican uprisings.

PROUDHON, Pierre Joseph (1809–65)
French socialist theoretician, regarded as father of Anarchism. Advocated "mutualism" and rejected the class struggle. Marx attacked his ideas in *The Poverty of Philosophy*.

PRUDHOMME (1843–?)
Member of the Bordeaux section of the International. Appointed corresponding secretary by the General Council April 1866. Moved to London 1872.

QUELCH, Harry (1858–1913)
British wallpaper packer, and one of the leaders of the New Unionism and the socialist left wing. Editor-in-chief of *Justice*. Fought against opportunism in the British movement. Delegate at the 1891 and 1893 Congresses.

RADFORD, Ernest (?–1919)
Barrister, friend of the Marx family, to which he was introduced by Dollie Maitland (friend of Eleanor's), whom he later married.

RANC, Arthur (1831–1908)
Head of local security with Gambetta at Bordeaux; member of the Commune. Fled to Belgium; on his return to France, became moderate radical.

RANVIER, Gabriel (1828–79)
Blanquist. Took part in the Commune, emigrated to England, member of the General Council of the International until the 1872 Hague Congress.

RASPAIL, François (1794–1878)
French chemist and politician, who wrote annual encyclopedias on self-medication 1846–64. Took part in the 1830 and 1848 Revolutions but joined the Republican bourgeois opposition before the war of 1870; frequently imprisoned.

ROBIN, Paul (1837–1912)
French schoolteacher, Bakuninist, member of the General Council of the International 1870–71.

ROCHEFORT, Henri (1830–1913)
French polemicist, writer, political activist. Founded *La Lanterne* under the Empire, then *La Marseillaise*. Member of the Government of National Defence. Attacked Versaillists during Commune, but evaded deportation. Later supported Boulanger.

ROSE, Edward (1849–1904)
Actor and playwright who gave up his law training for literature. President of the Playgoers' Club, founded 1884. Drama critic of the *Sunday Times* 1894–96.

ROSSEL, Louis (1844–71)
Officer in Franco-Prussian War who later offered his services to the Commune. Chief of Staff to Cluseret, then delegate for War. Resigned after ten days, was arrested 8 June 1871 and shot by the Versaillists 28 November.

ROY, Joseph
Translator of the first volume of *Capital* into French.

SASSONOV, Nikolai (1815–62)
Liberal Russian journalist. Emigrated in the 1840s and contributed to various journals.

SCHEU, Andreas (1844–1925)
One of the first leaders of the Austrian Socialist Party. Emigrated to England. Member of the First International, one of the founders of the SDF.

SCHILY, Victor (1810–75)
German lawyer. Emigrated to France after the Baden uprising. Member of the First International.

SCHORLEMMER, Carl (Jollymeier) (1834–92)
Chemist, professor at Manchester University from 1859. Member of German Social-Democratic Party, close friend of Engels.

SERRAILLLIER, Auguste (1840–?)
French shoemaker, member of the First International and of the Commune. Sentenced to death *in absentia,* fled to London. Corresponding secretary of the International for France.

SÉVERINE, pseudonym of Caroline Rémy (1855–1929)
Journalist, friend of Jules Vallès, editor of *Le Cri du Peuple* from 1886–88.

SHAW, Robert (?–1869)
Painter. Took part in the foundation of the International, member of the General Council. Disseminated Marx's ideas in British trade union circles.

SHIPTON, George (1839–1911)
Editor of the *Labour Standard* 1881–85. Secretary of the London Trades Council 1871–96.

SIMON, Jules (1814–96)
French philosopher and statesman, opposed to the Empire. Member of the Legislative Body and Minister of Public Instruction in the government of National Defence and in Thiers's governments. Premier 1876–77. Anti-communard and anti-Boulangist.

SINGER, Paul (1844–1911)
With Bebel, one of the leaders of the German Social-Democratic Party. Deputy to the Reichstag from 1884–1911. Fought opportunism and revisionism.

SMITH, Adolphe, né Smythe-Headingly (1846–1924)
Member of the SDF, journalist, translator and interpreter at Socialist Congresses. Wrote articles attacking the Marxist faction.

SORGE, Friedrich (1828–1906)
Close friend and companion of Marx and Engels. Emigrated to the U.S.A. in 1852. Became Secretary General of the International after its transfer to New York (1872–74).

STEPNIAK, pseudonym of Sergei Mikhailovich Kravchinsky (1852–95)
Russian writer and publicist. Revolutionary, partisan of terrorism. In 1878 assassinated the chief of police at St. Petersburg. Emigrated to London in 1884.

TALANDIER (TALLANDIER), Pierre (1822–90)
French journalist. Participated in the 1848 Revolution. Emigrated to London in 1851. Member of the General Council of the IWMA. Deputy 1876–80 and 1881–85. Later, Bakuninist.

TAYLOR, H. R.
Unionist, member of the SDF, delegate at the 1891 Congress, candidate in the 1892 elections.

THIERS, Adolphe (1797–1877)
Statesman and historian who suppressed the Commune. President of the Third Republic 1871–73.

THORNE, William (1857–1946)
Member of the SDF and leader of the Gasworkers' Union.

TOLAIN, Henri (1828–97)
Engraver, Proudhonist. One of the founders of the French section of the IWMA but became Deputy in the National Assembly of 1871, supported the Versaillists during the Commune, and was expelled from the International. Opposed to the Amnesty.

TRIDON, Edmé (1841–71)
Journalist and historian, Blanquist. Participated in the 1866 Congress. On his return was arrested and sentenced to deportation for "conspiracy." Deputy at the National Assembly, voted against peace and resigned. Took part in the Commune and fled to Belgium, where he died soon afterwards.

TROCHU, Louis (1815–96)
Orléanist general. President of the Government of National Defence in 1870 and Governor of Paris. Suppressed the Commune.

TURATI, Filippo (1857–1932)
Italian lawyer and publicist, member of the Italian Workers' Party. Delegate at the 1891 Congress. One of the founders of the Italian Socialist Party in 1892.

UTIN, Nikolai Isaakovich (1845–83)
Russian revolutionary, organized the Geneva branch of the International. Adversary of Bakunin.

VACHEROT, Etienne (1809–97)
French philosopher and political activist, opposed to the Empire. Deputy at the Bordeaux Assembly. Mayor of the 5th arrondissement of Paris during the Commune. Later became monarchist.

VAILLANT, Edouard (1840–1915)
French physician. Blanquist before 1870. Took part in Commune, member of the International. Fled to England, frequented Marx's and Engels's houses. Broke with the International after the 1872 Hague congress. After the Amnesty founded the Revolutionary Central Committee in France. Deputy in 1894.

VERMERSCH, Eugène (1845–78)
Journalist on the *Figaro* under the Empire, and on *Le Cri du Peuple* during the siege of Paris. Founded *Le Père Duchêne*. Fled to London where he attacked the Communards and went insane.

VESINIER, Pierre (1823–1902)
    French journalist, member of International 1864, later member of Commune and manager of *Journal Officiel* (replacing Longuet). Fled to England and wrote attacks on the Commune there and in France.

VEUILLOT, Louis (1813–83)
    French Catholic writer, editor of *L'Univers Religieux*.

VINOY, Joseph (1800–80)
    Bonapartist General, Governor of Paris 22 January 1871, commander of the Versaillist army against the Commune.

VOLDERS, Jean (1855–1906)
    One of the founders of the Belgian Workers' Party in 1885. Editor-in-chief of *Le Peuple*.

WALPOLE, Spencer Horatio (1806–98)
    Tory statesman, Home Secretary in 1852, 1858–59 and 1866–67.

WHEELER, George
    Member of the General Council of the International, member of the executive of the Reform League.

WOLFF, Wilhelm, known as Lupus (1809–64)
    German journalist. Member of the Central Committee of the Communist League and of the editorial board of the *Neue Rheinische Zeitung*. Emigrated to London 1851. Close friend of Marx, who dedicated the first volume of *Capital* to him.

WRÓBLEWSKI, Walery (1836–1908)
    Polish émigré to France after the 1863 uprising. During the Commune commanded the troops in the Southern part of the city. Sentenced to death in his absence, fled to London, became corresponding secretary for Poland on General Council of the International. After the amnesty returned to France.

ZASULICH, Vera Ivanovna (1851–1919)
    Russian revolutionary. Translated Marx's work into Russian. Editor of *Iskra*.

Index

NOTE: *Page references set in roman type are to letters in the correspondence; italic numerals refer to editorial matter (introductory notes, footnotes, etc.).*